A LONGMAN TOPICS Reader

D0456363

Reading City Life

PATRICK BRUCH
University of Minnesota

RICHARD MARBACK
Wayne State University

PEARSON
Longman

New York   San Francisco   Boston
London   Toronto   Sydney   Tokyo   Singapore   Madrid
Mexico City   Munich   Paris   Cape Town   Hong Kong   Montreal

Publisher: Joseph Opiela
Marketing Manager: Wendy Albert
Production Manager: Eric Jorgensen
Project Coordination, Text Design, and Electronic Page Makeup:
    Sunflower Publishing Services
Cover Designer/Manager: Wendy Ann Fredericks
Cover Photo: © Jeff Greenberg/The Image Works
Manufacturing Buyer: Lucy Hebard
Printer and Binder: R. R. Donnelley & Sons Company/Harrisonburg
Cover Printer: Lehigh Press, Inc.

For permission to use copyrighted material, grateful acknowledgment is made to the copyright holders on pp. 217–218, which are hereby made part of this copyright page.

Library of Congress Cataloging-in-Publication Data

Reading city life/[edited by] Patrick Bruch, Richard Marback.
    p. cm.—(A Longman topics reader)
    ISBN 0-321-23516-9
    1. Sociology, Urban—United States. 2. Cities and towns—United States. I. Bruch, Patrick. II. Marback, Richard. II. Longman topics.

HT123.R35 2005
307.76—dc22   2004053355

Visit us at http://www.ablongman.com

ISBN 0-321-23516-9

    345678910—DOH—07060

CONTENTS

Reading *City Life* is a short anthology of readings for college writing students that focuses on something we all share no matter where we live: city life. We may not share city life in the sense of living on the same block; many Americans don't physically live in cities at all. But we share city life in the sense that we all produce and consume images and representations of cities— we all read city life all the time. Listening to hip-hop music, watching television shows and commercials, reading magazines and newspapers, keeping up with fashion, being sports fans, or just participating in conversations with friends and family, one of the topics that's always on the table is the topic of city life. *Reading City Life* examines social and cultural issues embedded in all of this communication and encourages reflective public writing.

City life is so central to our everyday communication because struggles over the meanings of cities address the most pressing challenges of our time: How should we understand the huge achievement gaps in our public schools? What is causing the increasing difference in the United States between life for the rich and life for the poor? How should we explain the recent explosion in the number of incarcerated Americans? What about new movements for equal rights to include new immigrants and to challenge corporate power? These questions matter to us because they hit us where we live, or where we choose not to live. When we talk about the places where we live or do not live, when we talk about cities—about neighborhoods, crime, suburbanization, race, or the meanings of citizenship—we are grappling with fundamental challenges to life in the United States today.

Like any language, language about cities encourages us to think in certain ways and to not think in other ways. In other words, language can be thought of as *stabilizing* and as *mobilizing*. What we say and think about cities and city life can become fixed and can fix us in places. Our talk about cities as dangerous or suburbs as safe can keep us out of cities and in suburbs, thus stabilizing the conceptual and geographic boundaries between cities and suburbs. Other things we say can encourage mobility, as when our talk about the exciting nightlife in cities

enables us to cross conceptual and geographic boundaries between city and suburb. More generally, phenomena of urban
life—such as suburban sprawl and gentrification, or arguments
over taxes and public schools—involve both the physical mobility
of people who do or do not move to the suburbs and the rhetorical mobilization and stabilization of particular interpretations
and meanings that encourage those people to act and argue as
they do, to stay where they are, or to move to somewhere else.
The readings in this book are organized to provide a rhetorical
approach to you as readers and writers who must choose between
stabilizing and mobilizing the meaning of contemporary urban
issues.

Reading City Life is divided into five chapters, each examining
the stability and mobility of a particular issue of city life. Each
chapter contains five or six essays offering a variety of perspectives on the issue and representing a variety of approaches to the
challenge of writing thoughtfully. Each essay is preceded and followed by brief apparatus designed to help you write more
thoughtfully in response to the selections and to engage actively
the stabilizing and mobilizing consequences of writing.

Special features of our book include the following:

- Twenty-two readings chosen to help students recognize diversity within and across identity groupings.
- Selections chosen to represent differing perspectives, to teach
  students to assess the public consequences of writing.
- Selections chosen to represent a broad variety of writing
  styles, including journalism, memoir, and storytelling.
- Introductions to each chapter written to explain the issues in
  the chapter and to provide context for differing views.
- Introductions to each reading written to provide author biog-
  raphies, suggest additional works by the author, and invite
  students to think about the author's approach.
- Three discussion questions following each essay focused on
  "stabilizing the text" to encourage analysis and evaluation of
  author's points and methods.
- Three discussion questions on "mobilizing the text" also following each essay to encourage students to apply ideas to
  their own thinking and writing.

PATRICK BRUCH
RICHARD MARBACK

CHAPTER 1

Cities and Neighborhoods

What do we say about our neighborhoods? What can our neighborhoods say to us? Who lives in a neighborhood and who leaves one both tell us something about the kind of place that neighborhood is. The reasons people give for staying or going, the ways they talk about either their connections and commitments or their longing for someplace better, reflect the quality of a neighborhood and the character of the people living there. What we say about our neighborhoods and how we occupy them tell us who we are, what holds us together, and what keeps us apart.

Neighborhoods differently define themselves in different urban areas throughout the United States. Many older cities—such as San Francisco, Houston, Miami, and New York City—have distinct ethnic neighborhoods where people have lived for generations. For example, people who live in San Francisco's Chinatown district are mostly immigrants from mainland China or Taiwan, or are descendents from immigrants from those countries; Miami has a sizable community of Cuban Americans; and Detroit's Arab-American community is among the largest in the United States. Urban neighborhoods can also be defined in primarily economic terms, with people of similar socioeconomic class living together in distinct neighborhoods. Often, neighborhoods grow out of both ethnic affinity and socioeconomic necessity. Whatever the specific character of a neighborhood, people create it out of such things as their shared ethnic heritage or socioeconomic status. For reasons of either necessity or comfort, they live among people with whom they share circumstance, heritage, religion, or language.

So the character of a neighborhood depends on a combination of cultural, economic, geographic, and social factors. In large urban areas, where people having diverse ethnic heritages, racial

1

identities, and economic circumstances interact every day, neighborhoods can be a source of comfort and stability. At the same time, ethnic, racial, or economic differences can cause mistrust and suspicion among people who do not live with each other in the same community. Whatever factors combine to define your neighborhood, your experiences living in and going through neighborhoods can be quite telling. Maybe you have had the experience of feeling uncomfortable as you travel through an unfamiliar part of your city. Maybe you or someone you know has preconceived notions about people from communities other than your own, notions that direct how you or they interact with others.

By reflecting on and writing about the nature of neighborhoods and our responses to them, we better understand the experience of living in an urban setting. As you read the essays in this chapter, you will be asked to consider the problems and prospects of urban communities. The readings in this chapter encourage your reflection and invite your written response because they explore questions about living in cities and forming communities and neighborhoods within larger urban settings. At one level, these are questions about what a home is and why a home matters. Comparing and contrasting people living in a camp of makeshift shelters with people moving into and out of a nearby hotel, Jim Burklo's essay, "Houselessness and Homelessness," challenges us to rethink what it means to be without a home. Judith Ortiz Cofer combines personal recollection with descriptions of home movies in her essay, "Silent Dancing," to illustrate the conflict felt by her father in his own home. In "Homeplace," bell hooks describes the anxiety she felt as a child when she left the security of her neighborhood to visit her grandmother. She recalls the attachment she felt to her grandmother's house, developing her sense of a "homeplace" as a haven of belonging and attachment in a world of anger and discrimination.

In her essay, "A Beautiful Day in the Neighborhood," Mary Kay Blakely weaves together experiences, thoughts, and reflections occasioned by her move from the suburbs of New York City to Manhattan, narrating her own fears and anxieties as she establishes her own sense of belonging and attachment to her new neighborhood and the street people she encounters there. Leonard Kriegel's essay, "Graffiti: Tunnel Notes of a New Yorker," brings to bear the appearance and perception of urban neighborhoods on feelings of fear and anxiety as well as belonging and attachment. Kriegel draws a distinction between what he considers the political graffiti of his childhood and the contemporary graffiti he sees every day in New York City. Through his distinction, Kriegel wonders about the future of a city in which all graffiti can be considered an artistic expression.

Taken together, the writers of the essays collected in this chapter have different views about community and community membership. Their differences combine to give us a greater understanding of the complex issues of identity and urban living, issues of deciding who we are, how we get along with others, and how we create boundaries among ourselves. As you read the essays in this chapter and write about urban neighborhoods, you will be asked to think about your own sense of community and its influence on your feelings of familiarity and unfamiliarity, comfort and discomfort, identity and difference. You will be asked to consider how your ideas and experiences of community and neighborhood shape your perceptions of yourself as they influence your interactions with others. Questions for you to consider as you read include: How do people define the boundary of their neighborhood or community within a larger urban area? In terms of class? Culture? Ethnicity? Geography? Race? What benefits do we derive from the boundaries we create for ourselves? When and how do those same neighborhood boundaries work against our best interests? When do those boundaries become barriers?

Houselessness and Homelessness
JIM BURKLO

As executive director of Urban Ministry of Palo Alto, Jim Burklo worked with community groups to address a range of urban issues. Now pastor of College Heights Church in San Mateo and a campus Minister at Stanford University, Burklo remains involved in community work and continues to write about urban issues. In "Houselessness and Homelessness," first published in Whole Earth Review, *Burklo describes a camp of tarp and plastic bag huts serving as a "home for the homeless" near where he lives and works. He contrasts this camp with the nearby Stanford Park Hotel, which provides lodging for people doing business with local high-tech companies. Reflecting on the lifestyles of inhabitants from both the hotel and the camp, Burklo calls our attention to hierarchies that lead most affluent people in this country to embrace a kind of homelessness in their lifestyle at the same time they disparage the homeless. As you read "Houselessness and Homelessness," pay particular attention to how Burklo uses the terms "houselessness" and "homelessness." Consider how his uses of these terms challenge us to use them differently to give expression to our own experiences.*

———————————— ✦ ————————————

A cluster of huts, all blue tarps and black plastic bags, straggles along the creek that demarcates Palo Alto and Menlo Park, California. This camp has been functioning since I came to town in 1979. It functioned as a home for the homeless during the seven years that I served as director of the Urban Ministry of Palo Alto, which offers hospitality and other services to people on the streets. I now live about a quarter of a mile from this camp, and pass it every day on my way home from my job as the minister of a church. I check in with the residents of this camp whenever I check out books at the Menlo Park Library, which offers hot and cold running water in its bathrooms and is not far down the railroad tracks from the creek.

Looming on the top of the creek bank above the camp is the Stanford Park Hotel, an expensive place for a different kind of homeless people to stay. It is a place for people to sleep and eat and use hot and cold running water while they do business with high-tech industrial corporations. The people who stay at the Stanford Park Hotel have the money and skills needed to live most anywhere, and as a result, a lot of them live nowhere. So much of their lives is spent in hotels, airport shuttles, and jet aircraft that they suffer from homelessness. They have houses somewhere, but often they lack homes anywhere. The people sleeping under the tarps and plastic bags in the creek bed below them have homes, but lack houses.

There is little romance in the houseless homeless life, as I learned in my work with people on the streets. But in a striking way, homeless people are more at home than the rest of us. According to the jet-setters who are members of my church, there isn't much romance in global nomadism, either. The people in the creek are indigenous, unlike the inter-urban wanderers who stay in the Stanford Park Hotel. The people living in the creek bed belong to a certain "home slice" of a specific geographic radius within which they have found ways to survive, within which they have synchronized themselves with the natural and social seasons. They know whom to trust and whom to avoid, where to get free food and clothes, which dumpsters contain the items they most need. People often asked me why the folks we served at Urban Ministry didn't move to Fresno or Modesto or other places where the cost of living is lower. I'd answer that homeless people, ironically, tend to be homebound. Most folks who live in houses are part of a mass culture, a world culture, that enables us to be unbolted from Palo Alto or Menlo Park, California, and twisted into place in Boston or Singapore or Atlanta or London. Our skills and our lifestyles are useful and acceptable just about anywhere, making us interchangeable parts in the world economic machine. We communicate with money, a language that most people everywhere understand well.

A few homeless people aren't indigenous—they are on the streets temporarily, as a result of a personal disaster of a transitory nature. Often, these folks adamantly refuse to be called homeless, even though they live in the bushes like the rest. They are still interchangeable nuts belonging to the world economic engine; they just happened to spin off their bolts and land in the gutter for a while, and in the meantime, they cling tenaciously to their passports as world citizens. If they stay in the gutter too long, they might become indigenous, a fate which frightens them. These people tend to be more isolated and emotionally upset than the long-term houseless people around them. They are acutely homeless, in every sense of the word, and often this suffering motivates them to rapidly return to jobs and houses again.

But few homeless people are interchangeable, portable economic units of the New World Order. Moving out of the hometown is a frightening prospect for someone so dependent on such a locally idiosyncratic web of delicate social and natural ecology. Most homeless people can't speak the global language of money. Their survival depends on intimate knowledge of a set of locally specific individuals—other homeless people, cops, storekeepers, library employees, and social service workers.

Some of the most "homeful" people I know are technically homeless. At Urban Ministry, we served a 93-year-old woman who, for a period of months, slept on a park bench at night. She'd been kicked out of the residential hotels in town because she was a pack rat and never cleaned her rooms. We had no trouble finding board and care placements for her, but she refused them, because they were in Mountain View, the next town to the south. "I live in Palo Alto," she bluntly informed us, and returned to her park bench until we persuaded the managers of the subsidized senior housing in her hometown to let her name jump the waiting list and get her a place indoors again. Practically every merchant in town knew her well, since, at her plaintive request, many of them were storing her moldy boxes in their storerooms so that neither she nor her possessions would be separated from her place of residence, which was the whole of downtown Palo Alto. Until she died, she was a town character who made a major contribution to the character of the town. Palo Alto really isn't the same without her smiling ancient face greeting people on the sidewalks.

"Indigenous" need not connote "indigence." It is not a term that necessarily indicates poverty or houselessness. It is a mistake to presume that only seniors or disabled or houseless or unemployable people are homebound. Whether poor or rich, indigenous people have characteristic relationships to specific geographic places. They belong where they are, and where they are belongs to them—or ought to belong to them. If they go elsewhere, by force or by choice, they tend to suffer physically, psychologically, and spiritually. But being indigenous doesn't have to be a crippling or marginalizing condition on home turf.

Each local place has its characters, upon whom the character of the place depends. Each place has people who have developed roles or businesses that are site-specific. Their skills and their habits are not geographically transferable. They might be able to move elsewhere and have the money to live for a while, or even for a long time. But, emotionally, they would dry up inside. Many older people with money retire and move, only to discover too late that they are indigenous to their home town. Outside of that geographic radius, life makes no sense.

In today's world economy it is not considered safe to be indigenous. Our places in the system are temporary assignments, subject to the whims of global forces. To become indigenous is to risk losing a place anywhere, including one's dwelling "unit." We're accustomed to the global economic system. We are attached to its material abundance, even as our souls groan at the loss of any real home on the planet. But to embrace the indigenous life is a bold move that has deep pleasures and rewards for self and others. There is a wonderful intimacy that results from the face-to-face, year-in and year-out relationships that can only come by acting as if you are indigenous to a local place. The great attraction, and the great revulsion, that people have toward rural life is the prospect of becoming dependent on a local culture, to the exclusion of being able to fit into the world economy ever again.

10   I became a minister in order to create and sustain indigenous societies, groups of people who belong to each other in a local

urban area over a long period of time. A lot of the volunteers who came to help us at Urban Ministry were spiritually homeless people with jobs and homes, yearning to taste the fruits of indigenous living. They were attracted to the sense of belonging to a place that exists among people who live on the streets. In fact, I noticed that volunteering with us was an excellent way for newcomers to Palo Alto to get to join the town and its people. It's ultimately impossible to know the streets without knowing the street people.

I went to work as the minister of a local church in order to serve homeless people who live in houses as well as in creek beds. I'm in a church because it is not a support group or a therapy group, made up of people who are looking for something specific from each other, for a specific period of time, before moving on to the next group. A church or temple is a place where people go for good, for keeps, for birth and life and death. I'm interested in organized religion only insofar as it creates and maintains deep and intimate relationships in a community of people who have come together to live indigenously, for good. Understandably, lots of people—particularly those who want to fit in anywhere on earth, in any nation or culture—fear the sectarian nature of most religious congregations, the proprietary language and habits that go with people who have strong links to tradition and to a local church or synagogue community. People are afraid to give up their homelessness, much as they suffer from it. People will hang tribal masks on the walls of their condos, but they are afraid of wearing the masks and doing the indigenous rituals in which they were used. And people are afraid of having a home that is so precious to them that they would have a hard time leaving it when they receive New World Orders to move elsewhere.

I'm haunted by the words of a man who attends the church I serve. He's a Ph.D. with a job in a high-tech Silicon Valley firm. He said that if he had to go to another office party where people did nothing but exchange small-talk, another gathering of people who had no intimacy and no real connection with each other, he would scream. I heard his soul crying out for a place to call home, a specific local circle of people worth taking the risk of depending upon for his spiritual survival. A place and a people that, if he left them, would render him heartsick.

One of the marks of indigenous people is the persistent presence of annoying people among them. A church is not an indigenous community unless there are a few people in it who are permanent thorns in the sides of the rest of its members. One of the marks of non-indigenous societies is that they throw out obnoxious participants, or the societies fall apart because the rest of the participants leave and join or create other groups. At the Urban Ministry, we had our share of annoying homeless people who drank coffee at our drop-in center every day. They reminded me that I belonged to a truly local community of indigenous human beings. Go to a city council meeting anywhere, and listen to the people who speak during the part of the meeting devoted to "oral communication" from citizens. Listen to the ones who go up to the mike week after week, causing consternation or irritation among the council members. Those oral communicators are indigenous people. If they weren't there at the city council meeting, you would know that your town was a stone-cold-dead suburb, a place belonging everywhere, and, thus, to nobody.

A place cannot hope to be home to anyone unless there are people in that place who are indigenous to it. People who are gears in the global clockwork yearn deeply for the sentiments that come from indigenous living, but fear that they would have to give up too much in order to live that way themselves. Avoiding eye contact, they will pass by local houseless indigenous people, and they will proceed on their way to shop for conversation pieces at the ethnic art store. As they commute from faceless condos to faceless tilt-up industrial headquarters buildings, they will listen to Garrison Keillor on the car radio as he describes the latest doings among the indigenous citizens of mythical Lake Wobegon. To create a homey atmosphere, spiritually homeless people will buy antiques from quaint locations. They will travel to charming spots for vacations and "leave their hearts" with the indigenous residents, who have the good sense to keep their own hearts where they keep their bodies—at home.

15   In my travels, I have observed that the greater the number of indigenous people in a place, the fewer houseless people there are in that place, relative to the population. In a culture of people who can live anywhere, and, thus, live nowhere in particular, you will find a subset of people who are reduced to living on the streets. In a culture of people who really live where they are, who are living in a permanent manner and are dependent on the local people around them, there is a social web that prevents all but a very few folks from having to live outdoors. The houseless homeless are our canaries. When they fall into the creek bed, the rest of us need to pay attention to what has become of our communities,

and take the risks and rewards that come from making the choice to live indigenously in them.

Stabilizing the Text

1. What meanings does Burklo give the terms "houselessness" and "homelessness"? Consider not only the definitions he provides but also the implications he suggests. In what senses are homeless people "homeless"? In what senses are homeless people not "homeless"? Who really is "homeless"?

2. According to Burklo, which would be preferable, homelessness or houselessness? Or perhaps something else? What do people give up when they become homeless? What do they give up when they become houseless? Do the people who occupy the camps and the hotel give up some of the same things? Or do they each give up different things? What might be their reasons for giving up one thing as opposed to another?

3. Burklo suggests that the plight of those he terms houseless and the attitudes and practices of those he considers the affluent homeless are intertwined. Just what are the connections among the affluent homeless and the indigent houseless? Think about how the affluent and the indigent might view each other. How do you think attitudes of houselessness among financially successful people influence their attitudes about homelessness and their perceptions of the homeless? How might attitudes of houselessness among the poor influence their attitudes toward homelessness and their perceptions of the wealthy homeless?

Mobilizing the Text

1. One of Burklo's themes is the sense of place. Through his discussion of the homeless and the houseless, Burklo draws out specific ideas about what a sense of place is, why a sense of place is important, and how a sense of place has gotten lost to us in the age of high-speed, long-distance travel. Locate passages in which Burklo's ideas about sense of place are clearest. Do his ideas about sense of place seem to you more old-fashioned or more forward thinking? Why? How do his ideas about sense of place compare and contrast with your own? What examples do you have to communicate your own sense of place?

2. Does Burklo give either the occupants of the camp or the occupants of the hotel too much or too little respect? Identify specific passages in which you find Burklo either fair or unfair in his representation of the homeless and the houseless. How might you otherwise represent each of these groups so as to be accurate and fair to both? Draw on your own experiences or perceptions of people who are transient to further elaborate your representation.

3. Compare and contrast homelessness and houselessness in a different setting, one in which many people come and go. Such settings are common in

our lives—they can include not only hotels but also hospitals, airports, train stations, and bus terminals, as well as dormitories, hospices, youth hostels, and extended-stay hotels. In applying Burklo's distinction between house-lessness and homelessness to one or several of these settings, you must consider what the distinction enables you to see and say. You must also be prepared to elaborate the distinction based on its application. Does the distinction between homelessness and houselessness give us new insight into a setting such as an airport or a hospital? Do places such as hospices confirm, expand, or contradict the distinctions between homelessness and houselessness?

Silent Dancing

JUDITH ORTIZ COFER

Judith Ortiz Cofer is Franklin Professor of English and Creative Writing at the University of Georgia. She is the author of the novel The Line of the Sun; *two books of poetry,* Terms of Survival *and* Reaching for the Mainland; *and the essay collection* Woman in Front of the Sun. *Her collection* Silent Dancing, *from which the following essay is excerpted, was awarded a PEN/Martha Albrand Citation in nonfiction. In* Silent Dancing, *Cofer recollects her childhood, telling of her experiences in both New Jersey and her place of birth, Puerto Rico. In the essay "Silent Dancing," first printed in the* Georgia Review *and later reprinted in* Silent Dancing, *Cofer examines issues of family relations, isolation, assimilation, and racism in daily life in an ethnic urban neighborhood. She makes clear the tensions created by these issues through her combination of detailed descriptions of childhood in a New Jersey barrio with descriptions of a home movie she watches with her mother. As you read Cofer's essay, think about the contributions made to the narrative by the inclusion of the home movie.*

---- ◆ ----

*W*e *have a home movie of this party. Several times my mother and I have watched it together, and I have asked questions about the silent revelers coming in and out of focus. It is grainy and of short duration, but it's a great visual aid to my memory of life at that time. And it is in color—the only complete scene in color I can recall from those years.*

We lived in Puerto Rico until my brother was born in 1954. Soon after, because of economic pressures on our growing family, my father joined the United States Navy. He was assigned to duty on a ship in Brooklyn Yard—a place of cement and steel that was to be his home base in the States until his retirement more than twenty years later. He left the Island first, alone, going to New York City and tracking down his uncle who lived with his family across the Hudson River in Paterson, New Jersey. There my father found a tiny apartment in a huge tenement that had once housed Jewish families but was just being taken over and transformed by Puerto Ricans, overflowing from New York City. In 1955 he sent for us. My mother was only twenty years old, I was not quite three, and my brother was a toddler when we arrived at *El Building*, as the place had been christened by its newest residents.

My memories of life in Paterson during those first few years are all in shades of gray. Maybe I was too young to absorb vivid colors and details, or to discriminate between the slate blue of the winter sky and the darker hues of the snow-bearing clouds, but that single color washes over the whole period. The building we lived in was gray, as were the streets, filled with slush the first few months of my life there. The coat my father had bought for me was similar in color and too big; it sat heavily on my thin frame.

I do remember the way the heater pipes banged and rattled, startling all of us out of sleep until we got so used to the sound that we automatically shut it out or raised our voices above the racket. The hiss from the valve punctuated my sleep (which has always been fitful) like a nonhuman presence in the room—a dragon sleeping at the entrance of my childhood. But the pipes were also a connection to all the other lives being lived around us. Having come from a house designed for a single family back in Puerto Rico—my mother's extended-family home—it was curious to know that strangers lived under our floor and above our heads, and that the heater pipe went through everyone's apartments. (My first spanking in Paterson came as a result of playing tunes on the pipes in my room to see if there would be an answer.) My mother was as new to this concept of beehive life as I was, but she had been given strict orders by my father to keep the doors locked, the noise down, ourselves to ourselves.

It seems that Father had learned some painful lessons about prejudice while searching for an apartment in Paterson. Not until years later did I hear how much resistance he had encountered with landlords who were panicking at the influx of Latinos 5 into a neighborhood that had been Jewish for a couple of generations. It made no difference that it was the American phenomenon of ethnic turnover which was changing the urban core of Paterson, and that the human flood could not be held back with an accusing finger.

"You Cuban?" one man had asked my father, pointing at his name tag on the Navy uniform—even though my father had the fair skin and light-brown hair of his northern Spanish background, and the name Ortiz is as common in Puerto Rico as Johnson is in the U.S.

"No," my father had answered, looking past the finger into his adversary's angry eyes. "I'm Puerto Rican."

"Same shit." And the door closed.

My father could have passed as European, but we couldn't. My brother and I both have our mother's black hair and olive skin, and so we lived in El Building and visited our great-uncle and his fair children on the next block. It was their private joke that they were the German branch of the family. Not many years later that area too would be mainly Puerto Rican. It was as if the heart of the city map were being gradually colored brown—*café con leche* brown. Our color.

10 *The movie opens with a sweep of the living room. It is "typical" immigrant Puerto Rican decor for the time: the sofa and chairs are square and hard-looking, upholstered in bright colors (blue and yellow in this instance), and covered with the transparent plastic that furniture salesmen then were so adept at convincing women to buy. The linoleum on the floor is light blue; if it had been subjected to spike heels (as it was in most places), there were dime-sized indentations all over it that cannot be seen in this movie. The room is full of people dressed up: dark suits for the men, red dresses for the women. When I have asked my mother why most of the women are in red that night, she has shrugged, "I don't remember. Just a coincidence." She doesn't have my obsession for assigning symbolism to everything.*

The three women in red sitting on the couch are my mother, my eighteen-year-old cousin, and her brother's girlfriend. The novia is just up from the Island, which is apparent in her body language. She sits up formally, her dress pulled over her knees. She is a pretty girl, but her posture makes her look insecure, lost in her full-skirted dress, which she has carefully tucked around her to make room for my gorgeous cousin, her future sister-in-law. My cousin has grown up in Paterson and is in her last year of high school. She doesn't have a trace of what Puerto Ricans call la mancha *(literally, the stain: the mark of the new immigrant—something about the posture, the voice, or the humble demeanor that makes it obvious to everyone the person has just arrived on the mainland). My cousin is wearing a tight, sequined, cocktail dress. Her brown hair has been lightened with peroxide around the bangs, and she is holding a cigarette expertly between her fingers, bringing it up to her mouth in a sensuous arc of her arm as she talks animatedly. My mother, who has come up to sit between the two women, both only a few years younger than herself, is somewhere between the poles they represent in our culture.*

It became my father's obsession to get out of the barrio, and thus we were never permitted to form bonds with the place or with the people who lived there. Yet El Building was a comfort to my mother, who never got over yearning for *la isla*. She felt surrounded by her language: the walls were thin, and voices speaking and arguing in Spanish could be heard all day. *Salsas* blasted out of radios, turned on early in the morning and left on for company. Women seemed to cook rice and beans perpetually—the strong aroma of boiling red kidney beans permeated the hallways.

Though Father preferred that we do our grocery shopping at the supermarket when he came home on weekend leaves, my mother insisted that she could cook only with products whose labels she could read. Consequently, during the week I accompanied her and my little brother to *La Bodega*—a hole-in-the-wall grocery store across the street from El Building. There we squeezed down three narrow aisles jammed with various products. Goya's and Libby's—those were the trademarks that were trusted by *her mamá*, so my mother bought many cans of Goya beans, soups, and condiments, as well as little cans of Libby's fruit juices for us. And she also bought Colgate toothpaste and Palmolive soap. (The final *e* is pronounced in both these products in Spanish, so for many years I believed that they were manufactured on the Island. I remember my surprise at first hearing a commercial on television in which Colgate rhymed with "ate.") We always lingered at La Bodega, for it was there that Mother breathed best, taking in the familiar aromas of the foods she knew from Mamá's kitchen. It was also there that she got to speak to the other women of El Building without violating outright Father's dictates against fraternizing with our neighbors.

Yet Father did his best to make our "assimilation" painless. I can still see him carrying a real Christmas tree up several flights of stairs to our apartment, leaving a trail of aromatic pine. He carried it formally, as if it were a flag in a parade. We were the only ones in El Building that I knew of who got presents on both Christmas day AND *dia de Reyes*, the day when the Three Kings brought gifts to Christ and to Hispanic children.

15   Our supreme luxury in El Building was having our own television set. It must have been a result of Father's guilt feelings over the isolation he had imposed on us, but we were among the first in the barrio to have one. My brother quickly became an avid watcher of Captain Kangaroo and Jungle Jim, while I loved all the series showing families. By the time I started first grade, I could have drawn a map of Middle America as exemplified by the lives of characters in *Father Knows Best, The Donna Reed Show, Leave It to Beaver, My Three Sons*, and (my favorite) *Bachelor Father*, where John Forsythe treated his adopted teenage daughter like a princess because he was rich and had a Chinese houseboy to do everything for him. In truth, compared to our neighbors in El Building, *we* were rich. My father's Navy check provided us with financial security and a standard of life that the factory workers envied. The only thing his money could not buy us was a place to live away from the barrio—his greatest wish, Mother's greatest fear.

In the home movie the men are shown next, sitting around a card table set up in one corner of the living room, playing dominoes. The clack of the ivory pieces was a familiar sound. I heard it in many houses on the Island and in many apartments in Paterson. In Leave It to Beaver *the Cleavers played bridge in every other episode; in my childhood, the men started every social occasion with a hotly debated round of dominoes. The women would sit around and watch, but they never participated in the games.*

Here and there you can see a small child. Children were always brought to parties and, whenever they got sleepy, were put to bed in the host's bedroom. Babysitting was a concept unrecognized by the Puerto Rican women I knew: a responsible mother did not leave her children with any stranger. And in a culture where children are not considered intrusive, there was no need to leave the children at home. We went where our mother went.

Of my preschool years I have only impressions: the sharp bite of the wind in December as we walked with our parents towards the brightly lit stores downtown; how I felt like a stuffed doll in my heavy coat, boots, and mittens; how good it was to walk into the five-and-dime and sit at the counter drinking hot chocolate. On Saturdays our whole family would walk downtown to shop at the big department stores on Broadway. Mother bought all our clothes at Penney's and Sears, and she liked to buy her dresses at the women's specialty shops like Lerner's and Diana's. At some point we'd go into Woolworth's and sit at the soda fountain to eat.

We never ran into other Latinos at these stores or when eating out, and it became clear to me only years later that the women from El Building shopped mainly in other places—stores owned by other Puerto Ricans or by Jewish merchants who had philosophically accepted our presence in the city and decided to make us their good customers, if not real neighbors and friends. These establishments were located not downtown but in the blocks around our street, and they were referred to generically as *La Tienda, El Bazar, La Bodega, La Botánica*. Everyone knew what was meant. These were the stores where your face did not turn a clerk to stone, where your money was as green as anyone else's.

One New Year's Eve we were dressed up like child models in the Sears catalogue: my brother in a miniature man's suit and bow tie, and I in black patent-leather shoes and a frilly dress with several layers of crinoline underneath. My mother wore a bright-red dress that night, I remember, and spike heels; her long black hair hung to her waist. Father, who usually wore his Navy uniform during his short visits home, had put on a dark civilian suit for the occasion: we had been invited to his uncle's house for a big celebration. Everyone was excited because my mother's brother Hernan—a bachelor who could indulge himself with luxuries—had bought a home movie camera, which he would be trying out that night.

Even the home movie cannot fill in the sensory details such a gathering left imprinted in a child's brain. The thick sweetness of women's perfumes mixing with the ever-present smells of food cooking in the kitchen: meat and plantain *pasteles*, as well as the ubiquitous rice dish made special with pigeon peas—*gandules*—and seasoned with precious *sofrito* sent up from the Island by somebody's mother or smuggled in by a recent traveler. *Sofrito* was one of the items that women hoarded, since it was hardly ever in stock at La Bodega. It was the flavor of Puerto Rico.

The men drank Palo Viejo rum, and some of the younger ones got weepy. The first time I saw a grown man cry was at a New Year's Eve party: he had been reminded of his mother by the smells in the kitchen. But what I remember most were the boiled

20

pasteles—plantain or yucca rectangles stuffed with corned beef or other meats, olives, and many other savory ingredients, all wrapped in banana leaves. Everybody had to fish one out with a fork. There was always a "trick" pastel—one without stuffing— and whoever got that one was the "New Year's Fool."

There was also the music. Long-playing albums were treated like precious china in these homes. Mexican recordings were popular, but the songs that brought tears to my mother's eyes were sung by the melancholy Daniel Santos, whose life as a drug addict was the stuff of legend. Felipe Rodriguez was a particular favorite of couples, since he sang about faithless women and brokenhearted men. There is a snatch of one lyric that has stuck in my mind like a needle on a worn groove: *De piedra ha de ser mi cama, de piedra la cabezera . . . la mujer que a mi me quiera . . . ha de quererme de veras. Ay, Ay, Ay, corazón, porque no amas. . . .* I must have heard it a thousand times since the idea of a bed made of stone, and its connection to love, first troubled me with its disturbing images.

The five-minute home movie ends with people dancing in a circle—the creative filmmaker must have set it up, so that all of them could file past him. It is both comical and sad to watch silent dancing. Since there is no justification for the absurd movements that music provides for some of us, people appear frantic, their faces embarrassingly intense. It's as if you were watching sex. Yet for years, I've had dreams in the form of this home movie. In a recurring scene, familiar faces push themselves forward into my mind's eye, plastering their features into distorted close-ups. And I'm asking them: "Who is *she*? Who is the old woman I don't recognize? Is she an aunt? Somebody's wife? Tell me who she is."

25   "See the beauty mark on her cheek as big as a hill on the lunar landscape of her face—well, that runs in the family. The women on your father's side of the family wrinkle early; it's the price they pay for that fair skin. The young girl with the green stain on her wedding dress is *La Novia*—just up from the Island. See, she lowers her eyes when she approaches the camera, as she's supposed to. Decent girls never look at you directly in the face. *Humilde,* humble, a girl should express humility in all her actions. She will make a good wife for your cousin. He should consider himself lucky to have met her only weeks after she arrived here. If he marries her quickly, she will make him a good Puerto Rican-style wife; but if he waits too long, she will be corrupted by the city— just like your cousin there."

"She means me. I do what I want. This is not some primitive Island I live on. Do they expect me to wear a black mantilla on my head and go to mass every day? Not me. I'm an American woman, and I will do as I please. I can type faster than anyone in my senior class at Central High, and I'm going to be a secretary to a lawyer when I graduate. I can pass for an American girl anywhere—I've tried it. At least for Italian, anyway—I never speak Spanish in public. I hate these parties, but I wanted the dress. I look better than any of these *humildes* here. *My* life is going to be different. I have an American boyfriend. He is older and has a car. My parents don't know it, but I sneak out of the house late at night sometimes to be with him. If I marry him, even my name will be American. I hate rice and beans—that's what makes these women fat."

"Your *prima* is pregnant by that man she's been sneaking around with. Would I lie to you? I'm your *Tiá Politíca*, your great-uncle's common-law wife—the one he abandoned on the Island to go marry your cousin's mother. I was not invited to this party, of course, but I came anyway. I came to tell you that story about your cousin that you've always wanted to hear. Do you remember the comment your mother made to a neighbor that has always haunted you. The only thing you heard was your cousin's name, and then you saw your mother pick up your doll from the couch and say: 'It was as big as this doll when they flushed it down the toilet.' This image has bothered you for years, hasn't it? You had nightmares about babies being flushed down the toilet, and you wondered why anyone would do such a horrible thing. You didn't dare ask your mother about it. She would only tell you that you had not heard her right, and yell at you for listening to adult conversations. But later, when you were old enough to know about abortions, you suspected.

"I am here to tell you that you were right. Your cousin was growing an *Americanito* in her belly when this movie was made. Soon after she put something long and pointy into her pretty self, thinking maybe she could get rid of the problem before breakfast and still make it to her first class at the high school. Well, *Niña*, her screams could be heard downtown. Your aunt, her mamá, who had been a midwife on the Island, managed to pull the little thing out. Yes, they probably flushed it down the toilet. What else could they do with it—give it a Christian burial in a little white casket with blue bows and ribbons? Nobody wanted that baby—least of all the father, a teacher at her school with a house in West Paterson that he was filling with real children, and a wife who was a natural blond.

"Girl, the scandal sent your uncle back to the bottle. And guess where your cousin ended up? Irony of ironies. She was sent to a village in Puerto Rico to live with a relative on her mother's side: a place so far away from civilization that you have to ride a mule to reach it. A real change in scenery. She found a man there—women like that cannot live without male company— but believe me, the men in Puerto Rico know how to put a saddle on a woman like her. *La Gringa*, they call her. Ha, ha, ha. *La Gringa* is what she always wanted to be. . . ."

30   The old woman's mouth becomes a cavernous black hole I fall into. And as I fall, I can feel the reverberations of her laughter. I hear the echoes of her last mocking words: *La Gringa, La Gringa!* And the conga line keeps moving silently past me. There is no music in my dream for the dancers.

When Odysseus visits Hades to see the spirit of his mother, he makes an offering of sacrificial blood, but since all the souls crave an audience with the living, he has to listen to many of them before he can ask questions. I, too, have to hear the dead and the forgotten speak in my dream. Those who are still part of my life remain silent, going around and around in their dance. The others keep pressing their faces forward to say things about the past.

My father's uncle is last in line. He is dying of alcoholism, shrunken and shriveled like a monkey, his face a mass of wrinkles and broken arteries. As he comes closer I realize that in his features I can see my whole family. If you were to stretch that rubbery flesh, you could find my father's face, and deep within *that* face—my own. I don't want to look into those eyes ringed in purple, in a few years he will retreat into silence, and take a long, long time to die. *Move back, Tío,* I tell him. *I don't want to hear what you have to say. Give the dancers room to move. Soon it will be midnight. Who is the New Year's Fool this time?*

Stabilizing the Text

1. Cofer describes the desire to live outside the barrio as her father's "greatest wish" and he mother's "greatest fear." According to Cofer, what were her father's reasons for wanting to live outside the barrio? What were her mother's reasons for not wanting to leave? In the essay, how do their respective attitudes establish their relationship to the neighborhood and their sense of community?

2. Cofer's essay is not a straightforward narrative. It moves back and forth across storytelling, reminiscence, and description of home movies. Cofer

signals her move from one element to the next through her use of different typefaces. What do you understand as the relationship among the separate formal elements of the essay? How and why do you make one coherent meaning out of the several pieces?

3. Does Cofer's essay give us greater insight into her family or greater insight into social issues of community building and ethnic identity? To what extent does our insight into her family depend on our awareness of certain social issues? To what extent does the insight into social issues we gain in Cofer's essay depend on our own awareness of family life?

Mobilizing the Text

1. Cofer suggests that her father wanted the members of his family to isolate themselves from their Latino neighbors. Cofer also provides insight into her father's encounters with racism in his experiences with the dominant culture. How do you relate these to each other? For example, do you think desire for isolation from his neighbors is a reasonable response to racism? In thinking about Cofer's father, what generalizations can you make about racial isolation and identification?

2. Like Cofer, many of us have visual depictions—including photos and movies—or textual representations—such as stories we tell—of our lives growing up. What story might your depictions and representations tell about something larger than yourself? Something like the nature of community or the consequences of racism? How much would such a story depend on the presentation of your depictions and representations? How much would the point of the story depend on the content of the depictions and representations?

3. To what extent do you think the story Cofer tells is the same story many, many other people would tell? Which people, and how many of them, would tell the story as Cofer had? The extent to which her story is uniquely hers, the extent to which it is a story unlike that which anyone else might tell, is the limit of what we might be able to get out of our reception of her experience. Where do you draw the line in your understanding of how much we can draw generalizations from Cofer's essay? Why do you draw the line there? What does this say to us about the relationship of personal experience to collective experience?

Homeplace: A Site of Resistance

BELL HOOKS

bell hooks (Gloria Watkins) lives in New York City where she is Distinguished Professor of English at City University of New York.

Hooks is widely regarded for her many books, essays, and lectures on race and gender relations in American culture. Among her many books are Ain't I A Woman: Black Women and Feminism; Outlaw Culture; Teaching to Transgress; *and most recently,* Teaching Community: A Pedagogy of Hope. *The essay reprinted here, "Homeplace: A Site of Resistance," is excerpted from hooks's fourth book,* Yearning: Race, Gender, and Cultural Politics. *In "Homeplace," hooks combines descriptions of her feelings as a young girl traveling across town to her grandmother's house with reflections upon the meaning of a "homeplace" in our lives. While reading this essay, consider what hooks means by the term "homeplace" and how the idea of a homeplace has meaning in your own life.*

◆

When I was a young girl the journey across town to my grandmother's house was one of the most intriguing experiences. Mama did not like to stay there long. She did not care for all that loud talk, the talk that was usually about the old days, the way life happened then—who married whom, how and when somebody died, but also how we lived and survived as black people, how the white folks treated us. I remember this journey not just because of the stories I would hear. It was a movement away from the segregated blackness of our community into a poor white neighborhood. I remember the fear, being scared to walk to Baba's (our grandmother's house) because we would have to pass that terrifying whiteness—those white faces on the porches staring us down with hate. Even when empty or vacant, those porches seemed to say "danger," "you do not belong here," "you are not safe."

Oh! that feeling of safety, of arrival, of homecoming when we finally reached the edges of her yard, when we could see the soot black face of our grandfather, Daddy Gus, sitting in his chair on the porch, smell his cigar, and rest on his lap. Such a contrast, that feeling of arrival, of homecoming, this sweetness and the bitterness of that journey, that constant reminder of white power and control.

I speak of this journey as leading to my grandmother's house, even though our grandfather lived there too. In our young minds houses belonged to women, were their special domain, not as property, but as places where all that truly mattered in life took place—the warmth and comfort of shelter, the feeding of our bodies, the nurturing of our souls. There we learned dignity, integrity of being; there we learned to have faith. The folks who made this life possible, who were our primary guides and teachers, were black women.

Their lives were not easy. Their lives were hard. They were black women who for the most part worked outside the home serving white folks, cleaning their houses, washing their clothes, tending their children—black women who worked in the fields or in the streets, whatever they could do to make ends meet, whatever was necessary. Then they returned to their homes to make life happen there. This tension between service outside one's home, family, and kin network, service provided to white folks which took time and energy, and the effort of black women to conserve enough of themselves to provide service (care and nurturance) within their own families and communities is one of the many factors that has historically distinguished the lot of black women in patriarchal white supremacist society from that of black men. Contemporary black struggle must honor this history of service just as it must critique the sexist definition of service as women's "natural" role.

Since sexism delegates to females the task of creating and   5
sustaining a home environment, it has been primarily the responsibility of black women to construct domestic households as spaces of care and nurturance in the face of the brutal harsh reality of racist oppression, of sexist domination. Historically, African-American people believed that the construction of a homeplace, however fragile and tenuous (the slave hut, the wooden shack), had a radical political dimension. Despite the brutal reality of racial apartheid, of domination, one's homeplace was the one site where one could freely confront the issue of humanization, where one could resist. Black women resisted by making homes where all black people could strive to be subjects, not objects, where we could be affirmed in our minds and hearts despite poverty, hardship, and deprivation, where we could restore to ourselves the dignity denied us on the outside in the public world.

This task of making homeplace was not simply a matter of black women providing service; it was about the construction of a safe place where black people could affirm one another and by so doing heal many of the wounds inflicted by racist domination. We could not learn to love or respect ourselves in the culture of white supremacy, on the outside; it was there on the inside, in that "homeplace," most often created and kept by black women, that we had the opportunity to grow and develop, to nurture our spirits. This task of making a homeplace, of making home a community of resistance, has been shared by black women globally, especially black women in white supremacist societies.

I shall never forget the sense of shared history, of common anguish, I felt when first reading about the plight of black women domestic servants in South Africa, black women laboring in white homes. Their stories evoked vivid memories of our African-American past. I remember that one of the black women giving testimony complained that after traveling in the wee hours of the morning to the white folks' house, after working there all day, giving her time and energy, she had "none left for her own." I knew this story. I had read it in the slave narratives of African-American women who, like Sojourner Truth, could say, "When I cried out with a mother's grief none but Jesus heard." I knew this story. I had grown to womanhood hearing about black women who nurtured and cared for white families when they longed to have time and energy to give to their own.

I want to remember these black women today. The act of remembrance is a conscious gesture honoring their struggle, their effort to keep something for their own. I want us to respect and understand that this effort has been and continues to be a radically subversive political gesture. For those who dominate and oppress us benefit most when we have nothing to give our own, when they have so taken from us our dignity, our humanness that we have nothing left, no "homeplace" where we can recover ourselves. I want us to remember these black women today, both past and present. Even as I speak there are black women in the midst of racial apartheid in South Africa, struggling to provide something for their own. "We . . . know how our sisters suffer" (Quoted in the petition for the repeal of the pass laws, August 9, 1956). I want us to honor them, not because they suffer but because they continue to struggle in the midst of suffering, because they continue to resist. I want to speak about the importance of homeplace in the midst of oppression and domination, of homeplace as a site of resistance and liberation struggle. Writing about "resistance," particularly resistance to the Vietnam war, Vietnamese Buddhist monk Thich Nhat Hahn says:

> . . . resistance, at root, must mean more than resistance against war. It is a resistance against all kinds of things that are like war. . . . So perhaps, resistance means opposition to being invaded, occupied, assaulted and destroyed by the system. The purpose of resistance, here, is to seek the healing of yourself in

order to be able to see clearly. . . . I think that communities of resistance should be places where people can return to themselves more easily, where the conditions are such that they can heal themselves and recover their wholeness.

Historically, black women have resisted white supremacist domination by working to establish homeplace. It does not matter that sexism assigned them this role. It is more important that they took this conventional role and expanded it to include caring for one another, for children, for black men, in ways that elevated our spirits, that kept us from despair, that taught some of us to be revolutionaries able to struggle for freedom. In his famous 1845 slave narrative, Frederick Douglass tells the story of his birth, of his enslaved black mother who was hired out a considerable distance from his place of residence. Describing their relationship, he writes:

> I never saw my mother, to know her as such more than four or five times in my life; and each of these times was very short in duration, and at night. She was hired by Mr. Stewart, who lived about twelve miles from my house. She made her journeys to see me in the night, traveling the whole distance on foot, after the performance of her day's work. She was a field hand, and a whipping is the penalty of not being in the field at sunrise. . . . I do not recollect of ever seeing my mother by the light of day. She was with me in the night. She would lie down with me and get me to sleep, but long before I waked she was gone.

After sharing this information, Douglass later says that he never enjoyed a mother's "soothing presence, her tender and watchful care" so that he received the "tidings of her death with much the same emotions I should have probably felt at the death of a stranger." Douglass surely intended to impress upon the consciousness of white readers the cruelty of that system of racial domination which separated black families, black mothers from their children. Yet he does so by devaluing black womanhood, by not even registering the quality of care that made his black mother travel those twelve miles to hold him in her arms. In the midst of a brutal racist system, which did not value black life, she valued the life of her child enough to resist that system, to come to him in the night, just to hold him.

Now I cannot agree with Douglass that he never knew a mother's care. I want to suggest that this mother, who dared to hold him in the night, gave him at birth a sense of value that provided a groundwork, however fragile, for the person he later became. If anyone doubts the power and significance of this maternal gesture, they would do well to read psychoanalyst Alice Miller's book, *The Untouched Key: Tracing Childhood Trauma in Creativity and Destructiveness*. Holding him in her arms, Douglass' mother provided, if only for a short time, a space where this black child was not the subject of dehumanizing scorn and devaluation but was the recipient of a quality of care that should have enabled the adult Douglass to look back and reflect on the political choices of this black mother who resisted slave codes, risking her life, to care for her son. I want to suggest that devaluation of the role his mother played in his life is a dangerous oversight. Though Douglass is only one example, we are currently in danger of forgetting the powerful role black women have played in constructing for us homeplaces that are the site for resistance. This forgetfulness undermines our solidarity and the future of black liberation struggle.

Douglass's work is important, for he is historically identified as sympathetic to the struggle for women's rights. All too often his critique of male domination, such as it was, did not include recognition of the particular circumstances of black women in relation to black men and families. To me one of the most important chapters in my first book, *Ain't I A Woman: Black Women and Feminism*, is one that calls attention to "Continued Devaluation of Black Womanhood." Overall devaluation of the role black women have played in constructing for us homeplaces that are the site for resistance undermines our efforts to resist racism and the colonizing mentality which promotes internalized self-hatred. Sexist thinking about the nature of domesticity has determined the way black women's experience in the home is perceived. In African-American culture there is a long tradition of "mother worship." Black autobiographies, fiction, and poetry praise the virtues of the self-sacrificing black mother. Unfortunately, though positively motivated, black mother worship extols the virtues of self-sacrifice while simultaneously implying that such a gesture is not reflective of choice and will, rather the perfect embodiment of a woman's "natural" role. The assumption then is that the black woman who works hard to be a responsible caretaker is only doing what she should be doing. Failure to recognize the realm of choice, and the remarkable re-visioning of both woman's role and the idea of "home" that black women consciously exercised in practice, obscures the political commitment to racial uplift, to eradicating racism, which was the philosophical core of dedication to community and home.

Though black women did not self-consciously articulate in 15 written discourse the theoretical principles of decolonization, this does not detract from the importance of their actions. They understood intellectually and intuitively the meaning of homeplace in the midst of an oppressive and dominating social reality, of homeplace as site of resistance and liberation struggle. I know of what I speak. I would not be writing this essay if my mother, Rosa Bell, daughter to Sarah Oldham, granddaughter to Bell Hooks, had not created homeplace in just this liberatory way, despite the contradictions of poverty and sexism.

In our family, I remember the immense anxiety we felt as children when mama would leave our house, our segregated community, to work as a maid in the homes of white folks. I believe that she sensed our fear, our concern that she might not return to us safe, that we could not find her (even though she always left phone numbers, they did not ease our worry). When she returned home after working long hours, she did not complain. She made an effort to rejoice with us that her work was done, that she was home, making it seem as though there was nothing about the experience of working as a maid in a white household, in that space of Otherness, which stripped her of dignity and personal power.

Looking back as an adult woman, I think of the effort it must have taken for her to transcend her own tiredness (and who knows what assaults or wounds to her spirit had to be put aside so that she could give something to her own). Given the contemporary notions of "good parenting" this may seem like a small gesture, yet in many postslavery black families, it was a gesture parents were often too weary, too beaten down to make. Those of us who were fortunate enough to receive such care understood its value. Politically, our young mother, Rosa Bell, did not allow the white supremacist culture of domination to completely shape and control her psyche and her familial relationships. Working to create a homeplace that affirmed our beings, our blackness, our love for one another was necessary resistance. We learned degrees of critical consciousness from her. Our lives were not without contradictions, so it is not my intent to create a romanticized portrait. Yet any attempts to critically assess the role of black women in liberation struggle must examine the way political concern about the impact of racism shaped black women's thinking, their sense of home, and their modes of parenting.

An effective means of white subjugation of black people globally has been the perpetual construction of economic and social
structures that deprive many folks of the means to make homeplace. Remembering this should enable us to understand the political value of black women's resistance in the home. It should
provide a framework where we can discuss the development of
black female political consciousness, acknowledging the political
importance of resistance effort that took place in homes. It is no
accident that the South African apartheid regime systematically
attacks and destroys black efforts to construct homeplace, however tenuous, that small private reality where black women and
men can renew their spirits and recover themselves. It is no accident that this homeplace, as fragile and as transitional as it may
be, a makeshift shed, a small bit of earth where one rests, is always subject to violation and destruction. For when a people no
longer have the space to construct homeplace, we cannot build a
meaningful community of resistance.

Throughout our history, African-Americans have recognized
the subversive value of homeplace, of having access to private
space where we do not directly encounter white racist aggression.
Whatever the shape and direction of black liberation struggle
(civil rights reform or black power movement), domestic space
has been a crucial site for organizing, for forming political solidarity. Homeplace has been a site of resistance. Its structure was
defined less by whether or not black women and men were conforming to sexist behavior norms and more by our struggle to uplift ourselves as a people, our struggle to resist racist domination
and oppression.

20   That liberatory struggle has been seriously undermined by
contemporary efforts to change that subversive homeplace into a
site of patriarchal domination of black women by black men,
where we abuse one another for not conforming to sexist norms.
This shift in perspective, where homeplace is not viewed as a political site, has had negative impact on the construction of black
female identity and political consciousness. Masses of black
women, many of whom were not formally educated, had in the
past been able to play a vital role in black liberation struggle. In
the contemporary situation, as the paradigms for domesticity in
black life mirrored white bourgeois norms (where home is con-
ceptualized as politically neutral space), black people began to
overlook and devalue the importance of black female labor in
teaching critical consciousness in domestic space. Many black
women, irrespective of class status, have responded to this crisis

of meaning by imitating leisure-class sexist notions of women's role, focusing their lives on meaningless compulsive consumerism.

Identifying this syndrome as "the crisis of black womanhood" in her essay, "Considering Feminism as a Model for Social Change," Sheila Radford-Hill points to the mid-sixties as that historical moment when the primacy of black woman's role in liberation struggle began to be questioned as a threat to black manhood and was deemed unimportant. Radford-Hill asserts:

> Without the power to influence the purpose and the direction of our collective experience, without the power to influence our culture from within, we are increasingly immobilized, unable to integrate self and role identities, unable to resist the cultural imperialism of the dominant culture which assures our continued oppression by destroying us from within. Thus, the crisis manifests itself as social dysfunction in the black community—as genocide, fratricide, homicide, and suicide. It is also manifested by the abdication of personal responsibility by black women for themselves and for each other. . . . The crisis of black womanhood is a form of cultural aggression: a form of exploitation so vicious, so insidious that it is currently destroying an entire generation of black women and their families.

This contemporary crisis of black womanhood might have been avoided had black women collectively sustained attempts to develop the latent feminism expressed by their willingness to work equally alongside black men in black liberation struggle. Contemporary equation of black liberation struggle with the subordination of black women has damaged collective black solidarity. It has served the interests of white supremacy to promote the assumption that the wounds of racist domination would be less severe were black women conforming to sexist role patterns.

We are daily witnessing the disintegration of African-American family life that is grounded in a recognition of the political value of constructing homeplace as a site of resistance; black people daily perpetuate sexist norms that threaten our survival as a people. We can no longer act as though sexism in black communities does not threaten our solidarity; any force which estranges and alienates us from one another serves the interests of racist domination.

Black women and men must create a revolutionary vision of black liberation that has a feminist dimension, one which is 25 formed in consideration of our specific needs and concerns. Drawing on past legacies, contemporary black women can begin to reconceptualize ideas of homeplace, once again considering the primacy of domesticity as a site for subversion and resistance. When we renew our concern with homeplace, we can address political issues that most affect our daily lives. Calling attention to the skills and resources of black women who may have begun to feel that they have no meaningful contribution to make, women who may or may not be formally educated but who have essential wisdom to share, who have practical experience that is the breeding ground for all useful theory, we may begin to bond with one another in ways that renew our solidarity.

When black women renew our political commitment to homeplace, we can address the needs and concerns of young black women who are groping for structures of meaning that will further their growth, young women who are struggling for self-definition. Together, black women can renew our commitment to black liberation struggle, sharing insights and awareness, sharing feminist thinking and feminist vision, building solidarity.

With this foundation, we can regain lost perspective, give life new meaning. We can make homeplace that space where we return for renewal and self-recovery, where we can heal our wounds and become whole.

Stabilizing the Text

1. hooks describes her sense of homeplace as a place where she learned "dignity, integrity of being" and "to have faith." What values does she oppose to dignity, integrity, and faith? What places does she associate with these "opposing" values? Do you agree with her opposition of values and her association of them with different places? What makes her opposition and association more or less believable?

2. According to hooks, where is a homeplace located? She seems to want it to be more than a place that serves as a home. What or who makes a home into a homeplace? Can any place where people interact with each other in certain ways become a homeplace? Identify passages in the essay in which hooks defines homeplace in terms of location—that it has to be here and not there. Identify passages in which hooks defines homeplace in terms of interactions—that it is where people do this and not that.

3. Consider the overlap between homeplace as a physical space, as a series of interactions, and as a set of attitudes and perceptions. At various points in the essay, hooks uses homeplace in each of these three ways. How do you account for this? To what extent do you think she is being inconsistent?

Deftly handing a complex concept? Or presenting a thought-provoking idea?

Mobilizing the Text

1. hooks uses the opening personal reflection to introduce larger social issues. Do you find her joining of the personal with the political to be effective? Why or why not? Are there connections between our personal experiences and social issues that we take for granted? Are there connections between the personal and the political we need to make more explicit?

2. In a sense, hooks finds a homeplace outside her home, across town at her grandmother's house. This suggests that a sense of homeplace can be gotten by going somewhere else. Where might people go today to find for themselves a homeplace? What do they have to go through to get there? In considering these questions, ask yourself whether and how finding a homeplace depends on the difficulties one must face in getting there.

3. Do you think people still value homeplace? Do we need such places anymore, especially since we can use cellphones or the Internet to create community almost anywhere? Or, has the site of homeplace simply shifted to a different place? What do you think the consequences of such a shift might be on our feelings for homeplace and on our associations with others?

A Beautiful Day in the Neighborhood

MARY KAY BLAKELY

Mary Kay Blakely is currently an associate professor in the Missouri School of Journalism, a contributing editor to Ms. Magazine, *and an active journalist. Blakely's essays have appeared in such national publications as the* New York Times, *the* Washington Post, Life, Vogue, *and* Newsday. *"A Beautiful Day in the Neighborhood" first appeared in* Mother Jones. *In the essay, Blakely describes her many thoughts and emotions when, after ten years of married life in the suburbs, she separates from her husband and moves to Manhattan to live by herself. Interspersed throughout her narrative are recollections of her brother, descriptions of her new Manhattan neighborhood and of encounters with homeless people, and reflections on politics. Weaving together her experiences, feelings, and thoughts in this essay, Blakely gives us insight into the significance she attaches to her neighborhood. While reading "A Beautiful Day in the Neighborhood," try to figure out for yourself how all the various narrative threads intertwine to weave together a larger story. Figure out just what Blakely is trying to communicate about living in Manhattan. One way to do this would be to keep in mind all that living in a neighborhood means to you.*

---------------- ✦ ----------------

Well past midnight on a steamy summer night last year, I clutched the handle next to the passenger's seat in a large U-Haul truck as it bounced through construction barricades on the Cross Bronx Expressway, listening to my cargo crash against the walls as Howard, knuckles white with tension, swung the loose steering wheel to keep us on course. Sheer guts had put him in the driver's seat. This man, from whom I've now been divorced a little longer than the decade we were married, inspired groans from our teenage sons with his contentment in the 55 mph lane on interstate highways. Ryan and Darren, the main glue between us for nearly 20 years, were following in the car behind, all of us exhausted and a little slaphappy after lifting and toting since dawn.

I was acutely aware that this was "the first day of the rest of your life"— certainly, it was destined to be the last day of life as I'd known it. A recently paroled mother/writer/suburbanite, I was about to begin a solo life in New York City; the first time in 47 years I would not have to filter every decision through the needs and expectations of other people. The irony of having my once-husband and two former dependents launch me into independence made this surreal journey somehow more provocative.

The close relationships in our postnuclear family continually baffled friends, but I wasn't surprised when Howard called from Ann Arbor and volunteered his two-week vacation to help me pack my emptying nest in Connecticut. The sturdy friendship we retrieved from our divorce was rebuilt slowly from the powerful alloy of regret and apology, an interactive chemistry that eventually produces genuine change. We'd never imagined, when we naively recited those vows to love and honor each other for life back in 1970, we would mainly be providing each other unlimited opportunities for mercy.

Mercy is the antidote for the crushing pain that invariably follows the loss of innocence, and only the numb don't need it. Most recently, Howard had to forgive the hard time I gave him with a memoir I'd just finished on 20 years of motherhood. Long familiar by now with the public compromises of an exwife who writes, he said reading the manuscript made him feel "like a jerk or a fool." When I asked him to identify the offending passages, it took three weeks before he called back. "It wasn't what you wrote that made me feel like a fool," he said quietly, utterly undefended. "It's my *life* I wish I could revise." Only in hindsight was it clear how he'd taken this fork instead of that, how decisions made in Michigan affected people he loved in Connecticut. Growing instead of shrinking from the truth, he understood we had no control, of course, over what other people would do with it.

The first review had arrived by fax that morning, shortly before I unplugged and packed the machine. I asked if the noxious label that would be appearing next to his name again and again had hurt. "Yeah," he admitted, "it got to me." He smiled ruefully, said he'd had a sudden image of us appearing together on a "Geraldo" show: "Deadbeat Dads and the Women Who Love Them." We laughed. Then we kept moving. 5

These are perilous times for anyone living outside "the traditional family," since the reigning politicians are determined to bring back the social dictatorship of the '50s. Certainly, the contemptuous labels we've had to live under—broken home, latchkey children, absentee mother, deadbeat dad—make it difficult for outsiders to recognize all the thinking and striving most postnuclear families do.

It's more than a little frightening to see how swiftly the White Guys' Movement has revived the old formula for ridding a country of its conscience during hard economic times: First, you label whole segments of the population as the Other. Then, when the suffering comes, it's possible to believe they deserve it. If any of your own relatives turn out to be among the despised populations—a gay son, maybe, a divorced sister—well, mercy is notably absent from the current roster of family values.

Since the neighborhood I was moving into was teeming with Others—accented immigrants, hyphenated Americans, single moms, low-income families—I knew that casualties from the "Contract on America" would be falling within my direct line of vision. It was already impossible to walk through the Upper West Side without encountering lifeless bodies laid out on every block, the parched bottom layer of the trickle-down economy. This reality apparently doesn't look so bad if you take it in through numbers and indexes in *The Wall Street Journal*, where investors declare a "good economy" if profits are up. There is scant coverage on the business pages and rarely any photos, of people going down. Mothers and children are so invisible in the national news, investors might not even know we are out here, laboring in the same economy. Business columnists uniformly regard the collapse of communism as "the triumph of capitalism." *Triumph?* From the passenger window, capitalism without compassion looks a lot like Calcutta.

As Howard took the exit on the Upper West Side and aimed the truck down Broadway, I looked out the window at the street people I'd driven past hundreds of times, but never as a neighbor. What did being a "good neighbor" mean in this community, where the utterly destitute and the fantastically wealthy live within blocks of each other? How would I stay in touch with reality, when the daily reality is so unreal? Do I put on an armband, own my affinity with the Others—or do I wear mental blinders, try not to know what I know? I've never been able to establish any distance from street people—I keep thinking they're my relatives. I still scan their faces for signs of my brother Frank, even though I know it's irrational since I delivered the eulogy at his funeral more than a decade ago.

10   I'm more or less resigned to my role as an easy mark for panhandlers—a readily identifiable "Sucker Man," as my son Darren would say in sticky situations, remembering a childhood toy with suction cups that glowed in the dark. I feel especially sucked in by street people with obvious symptoms of mental illness. Frank's madness used to terrify me, as it did him, and I spent years looking into his wild eyes on psychiatric wards, trying to make contact, trying to stare fear down by knowing it. If you make eye contact with panhandlers, know their stories, the buck in your pocket is already in their hands. I think of these tiny contributions as payments against my huge debt to all the strangers who were kind to Frank.

    We lost him periodically, between hospitals and jail cells and mental institutions and home—those scary times when this frail, brilliant, desperately ill young man was "out there" somewhere, totally dependent on the compassion of others. Walking through Manhattan, I still make sidewalk diagnoses of manic depression, autism, schizophrenia, paranoia . . . all being treated on the streets since political reformers in the late '60s stopped "warehousing" the mentally ill. Few voters back then understood the loathsome "warehouses" were the last stop for the most helpless, or that the alternative to inept and underfunded hospitals would be no care at all. A theater of the absurd, America's sidewalks reflect the insanity of a national health care policy that now jails the mentally ill before treating them.

Howard had acquired a new nickname that week after he'd dropped a 27-inch television a customer had brought in for repairs. "Hey, Crash!" the wise guys he worked with now greeted him, "How's it goin'?" With all my material possessions in the U-Haul, I had nothing to lose with Crash at the wheel since my alternate driver was Anthony, the Connecticut neighbor who'd shorn the roof off a delivery van when he plowed into a sign that read, "Clearance—8'." ("Sure I saw it," he later told the hospital staff. "I forgot I was in the stupid truck.") I already missed Anthony and the rest of the gang who regularly camped out around our kitchen table.

I loved that raucous household, blooming with growth and optimism. The quiet solitude after Ryan and Darren left for college felt abrupt. In truth, our quality time together was sometimes down to five minutes a day by then, and the main noise was running water. My landlady had been shocked by our water bills and asked if she should send a plumber to check for leaks. "No," I confessed, "I'm growing male adolescents here. They need a lot of showers." I offered to pay the difference, since watering teenagers was more economical and effective than therapy, and ultimately easier on the environment. The boys would emerge in elevated moods, skin flushed and wrapped in terry cloth. Every time I would come across those alarming headlines about young male violence and try to imagine what might save us, I'd think: Showers. If every kid in America had enough private time in the bathroom to get a grip, to feel just great for a moment . . . wouldn't it have to improve civilization?

I was lucky to find a "prewar" apartment. Manhattan shorthand for big rooms that haven't been subdivided into six studios with pantry kitchens and broom-closet bathrooms. Space is so precious in New York, custody suits over rent-controlled apartments are common when couples split up. After postwar prosperity devolved into today's social Darwinism, whole working-class families now read, watch television, eat, make love, fight, cry, laugh, yell, and sleep all in the same room.

Driving through Harlem a few years ago, I got lost in an urban canyon between tall, crumbling buildings. The narrow street was solidly double-parked, and I noticed every car was occupied: One man was reading by flashlight, another was having a cigarette, a pair of teenagers was car-dancing to a radio, another pair

15

was sinking slowly into the seat. Here, on the streets, people were in the only private room at home. It's no wonder tempers flare and violence erupts during steamy summers in the city. Who can take a shower in a car?

My neighborhood is "in transition," as we say, between an elegant past and present cruelties, a microcosm of the growing class divisions in America. One block west of my building uniformed doormen with epaulets safeguard well-to-do residents who are likely to be liberal, generous contributors to the soup kitchen in the nearby cathedral. One block east, crack vials litter the sidewalks where street people and drug addicts spend the night. The haves and havenots live cheek by jowl here—with remarkable civility I think, given the givens. The thief who would eventually steal my car radio did not break any car windows, and left a screwdriver behind on the seat. When the car was broken into again a week later nothing was taken. Somebody evidently just needed a room.

My suburban habit of getting close to neighbors is trickier here because they come and go—sometimes within the same day. It's hard to learn all their names without mailboxes. And the names sometimes change. The woman with the wild gray hair and bedroom slippers who growls at pedestrians on the west side of Broadway calls herself "Bad Bertha," but when she's sitting quietly on the east side, her hair tucked neatly into a bun and feet prettily aligned in ballet shoes, her name is "Irena." The exuberantly manic guy who works the street outside the Hungarian Pastry Shop calls himself "the Lord's Apostle" and sings a gospel rap that sounds like a kind of Gregorian Dixie. One rhyme made me laugh, and a laugh in Manhattan is worth a buck to me: "I love Christ, Jesus Christ/The only Man who's been here twice. . . . ."

But there was a dramatic shift in my street relationships when Howard, the boys, and I were finishing renovations on the apartment. That whole week, nobody hit on us for money. Instead, panhandlers grinned and nodded when we passed them during errands and lunch breaks, as though we were old comrades. Maybe they only solicit suburban commuters, I thought, and now recognize us as neighbors. Then I realized how we were dressed: paint-splattered T-shirts, sweaty kerchiefs, shoes covered with sawdust and Spackle. Crash's work outfit was truly special—Howard had grabbed a pair of old sweats from the Goodwill pile in Connecticut and didn't discover the cord was missing until he put them on in New York. We searched the vacant apartment for a piece of string or elastic, but all we came up with from work supplies was a roll of duct tape. Even the craziest panhandlers weren't tempted to solicit change from a guy wearing a cummerbund of silver duct tape.

If our degrees of separation could melt with a change of attire perhaps the current experiment with "casual days," when corporations relax formal dress codes on Fridays, should go even further. Maybe Mondays should be down-in-the-socks day. Princely executives could become paupers once a week and get to know the folks who are so invisible to *Wall Street Journal* readers. In their starched collars and knotted ties and pressed twill, so many of the Suits who bustle down Broadway dodging strollers and shopping carts look either uncomfortable or angry, as if everybody wants their stuff. Most everybody probably does.

But suppose they relieved themselves of this burden once a   20
week, surrendered their gaberdine armor and leather belts for a Goodwill outfit and roll of duct tape. Would they be less angry if nobody was hitting on them? If they got grins and nods on the streets, if they made eye contact and learned the names of the Others, would they be tempted to open up membership in the tight little group of "we Americans"? It's almost too poignant to imagine, but could the in-it-together camaraderie on the streets even move the white guys to share their drugs? The comprehensive health coverage for Congress and the military is costing taxpayers a bundle, but that entitlement program never appears on the Republicans' list of "financial burdens."

Party strategist William Kristol chastised GOP colleagues for compromising their economic goals after Democrats launched an aggressive campaign with the "politics of compassion" during the last presidential election. Addressing a conference on C-Span, he warned his fellow Republicans not to be sidetracked by worries about poor people next time. If the rich could become richer still, objections to ruthlessness become moot: "The politics of growth trump the politics of compassion," he declared over and over. Greed trumps mercy every time. It was late at night when I heard this game plan in my hotel room almost two years ago. I couldn't think of anyone to call, anything to do. Now Kristol is publisher of a new, right-wing magazine financed by Rupert Murdoch, and Kristol's colleagues have taken Capitol Hill. Should I have called 911?

After unloading and returning the truck, my tired crew crashed on mattresses flush with the floors and didn't get up until noon. The next day, muscles sore but freshly showered, we were in elevated moods after lunch in a local Chinese-Cuban restaurant.

"Chinese-Cuban-Americans," I said, wondering how I would keep track of the hyphens here. "Imagine fleeing the Gang of Four and landing in Castro country."

"Yeah," Howard said, "then risking your life in an open boat and washing up here just in time for the Gingrich Gang." Ryan and Darren gave each other a worried look, familiar by now with their progenitors' habit of getting worked up over politics. They hated hearing about suffering they couldn't do anything about. If we were going to saddle them with family values of mercy and justice in these mean times, they wanted to know how to fend off despair. Though we are not regular churchgoers—the religion in our postnuclear family is an interfaith amalgam of Catholic beatitudes and Lutheran heresies and Zen koans—I suggested a visit to St. John the Divine.

The largest Episcopal cathedral in North America, its towering spire of magnificent masonry now sits sullenly under rusted iron scaffolding, renovations stalled once more while fundraising efforts are applied to more immediate emergencies. Dean James Morton has the formidable task of convincing wealthy parishioners deeply committed to art and historic preservation that their first obligation, as Episcopalians, is to serve the community—in their case, ceaseless waves of troubled kids, addicted veterans, dying homosexuals, and homeless immigrants. In the turf wars between the Suits and the Others in this West Side Story, the cathedral is the parking lot where miracles happen.

25   Still beautiful despite its present humility, the stately edifice is buzzing with civilian activity. Before New York adopted a recycling program, parishioners brought their garbage to church, where the homeless turned aluminum cans into cash. Two biologists now work out of the church to restore the urban watershed in Upper Manhattan, and hold community workshops on environmental issues. The doors are open to anyone who wants in— on the Feast of St. Francis, when members bring pets to the procession honoring all God's creatures, even elephants come to St. John the Divine.

In the park next to the interfaith elementary school at the church, we stopped before an installation by sculptor Frederick Franck. A row of six steel panels are aligned on the lawn perpendicular to the path, each with a silhouette of the same human figure cut from the center, the first one slightly larger than life, the last a miniature version of the shrinking figure itself. The inscription quotes the Great Law of the Haudenosaunee, the Six Nations Iroquois Confederacy: "In all our deliberations we must

be mindful of the impact of our decisions on the seven generations to follow ours." Franck titled the sculpture *Seven
Generations*, but there are only six figures. The viewer, standing
squarely at the mouth of the tunnel, must become the seventh.
We each took turns looking through the five ghostly silhouettes,
connecting with the tiny figure at the end. Step aside from your
place in the human chain, it disappears.

How did the Iroquois chiefs come to their remarkably long
view of personal responsibility? How did they make the connection between their business decisions in Michigan and domestic
life in Connecticut? Were they all in difficult relationships? Did
they speak the hard truth, argue and apologize, let mercy change
them? Seemingly larger than life in their war paint and head-
dresses, did the chiefs declare a casual day at the Haudenosaunee
Council, light the pipe and pass it around? Did they inhale?

The architects of the Republican Party's future can't be worried about the next seven generations—William Kristol said it's
not even practical to care about most of *this* one. "You cannot in
practice have a federal guarantee that people won't starve," he
told *Harper's* during a candid forum with five other white guys,
explaining how Republicans envision the future. Some people
will have to suffer, but "that's just political reality," said author
David Frum. Obviously unaware of Dean Morton's work with
New York Episcopalians, Frum apparently doesn't think "the sort
of people who make $100,000 contributions to the Republican
Party" can get behind poor people. "Republicans are much more
afraid of angry symphonygoers than they are of people starving to
death," he said.

The main problem with running a merciless government is
that in a democracy, millions of voters have to agree to starvation.
This requires a certain "finesse," said media adviser Frank Luntz.
"I'll explain it in one sentence: I don't want to deliver bad news
from a golf course in Kennebunkport." Republicans are depending on Rush Limbaugh, the undisputed master of political spin,
to keep people dizzy and laughing about starvation plans.
Labeling people like me "compassion fascists" for trying to get
people like him interested in mercy, Limbaugh is so popular even
the *New York Times* compromised its editors when marketing executives hired him to advertise the newspaper. In the new morality of bottom-liners, it's OK to have a propagandist represent the
"newspaper of record," if it increases sales. Vice must be spun
into virtue before we can get to the Republican future, but everybody's doing their part.

30   Several years ago, Ivan Boesky spoke to students at the University of California while on tour to promote a new book. "Greed is healthy," he inspired them. "You can be greedy and still feel good about yourself." Boesky's invocation of avarice didn't stir any action from Republican crusaders fighting "a cultural war . . . for the soul of America," in which Pat Buchanan sees the enemies as "radical feminists and homosexuals." Talk about a dazzling public relations coup: The party championing morality in America has declared that charity is impractical, greed is healthy, compassion is fascist, and mercy is the responsibility of other people. If future schoolchildren have to recite a prayer written by these folks, whatever will it say? "Dear God, please give me more of everything than I'll ever need and I promise not to care about anyone else."

Though I'm not an Episcopalian, visiting St. John's always makes me wish I could pray. I envy the solace my family and friends have talking to God. My own spiritual meditations are generally addressed to my brother Frank, the euphoric madman who left abruptly at age 36, delirious with love and forgiveness as he answered God's call. I still want him to tell me: *Is* heaven better than the transient hotel where the Chicago police found his body? Sitting in the garden at St. John's, I remembered our last conversation on the lawn at Elgin State Hospital. He asked me why I loved him and I said, "Because you are a fool, and I love fools."

"But Jesus said, 'There are no fools,' " he replied, quoting a scriptural fragment from his seminarian days.

"I know," I replied. "But I think what Jesus really meant is that we are all fools," I said, paraphrasing J.D. Salinger. I told him I thought he was the king of fools. He laughed, said I must be the queen.

I don't blame God for the scrambled thinking that led to Frank's suicide. I can't even be sure there is a God. I believe my divinely crazy brother heard God say what he wanted to hear. Many mentally ill people think they are in direct touch with the Almighty. The Lord's apostle outside the pastry shop, the toothless guy at D'Agostino, even Bertha on her bad days will offer the panhandler's benediction: "God bless you," they say, whether the quarter comes or not. Republican Christians today are getting some frenzied directives as the political scene becomes ever crazier, and they too hear exactly what they want to hear: God wants everybody to get married, wants women to stay home, doesn't want gays in the military, doesn't want national health insurance.

I can't share their faith that a supreme benevolence is behind all these messages, but if the polls are correct and most Americans do think somebody's God should be directing all our lives, let's please not pick the one who's inspiring pro-lifers to get automatic weapons. Until we have a firmer grip on our common reality, maybe we could all follow the harmless god who's telling the autistic disciple on 34th Street, over and over: "Go to Macy's nine-to-five, Go to Macy's nine-to-five." We could leave the credit cards home, stay out of trouble. Just look.

It was a beautiful summer night on Broadway as we walked home from our last dinner together, grateful there were no more boxes to move. When a U-Haul truck rattled down the street, Crash laughed and asked, "Do you think they'd have less business if the company was named, 'U-Bust-Your-Ass'?" Our laughing foursome attracted looks from our neighbors, but few grinned or nodded, as if we'd become strangers again. Darren noticed too.

"This is too weird," he said. "People are staring at us because we look so *normal*. Like Mom and Pop and the two boys from Iowa." He was struck by the irony of having been labeled the weirdos in almost every neighborhood we've lived in, then arriving here—where weirdos abound—and being mistaken for regular guys.

"We should wear a sign," he said. "We're Not What You Think."

Maybe everyone should wear that sign through the next election, since there's so much confusion about the Other. As bad decisions in Washington crush good people in Harlem, even "liberal" politicians are telling us to prepare for further compromises—live a little leaner, do more charity work, tighten our belts. What can they be thinking? My neighbors are already living in cars, doing-it-yourself, holding pants up with duct tape. There is plenty of self-help and personal responsibility out here, where people watch each other's kids and take mostly working vacations, if we take them at all.

How did the white guys ever get the impression they are doing all the work? Because they are earning all the big bucks? Why are the Republicans so mad—why so furious with mothers? Do they need more Prozac? Since all the female labor sustaining them at home and at work is so invisible, so seemingly profitless, they can't seem to hold the picture that somebody's valuable work is responsible for the fact their children are alive, their Contracts are typed. The arrogance and ignorance of the current political leadership is so stupefying, you don't even want to argue with these boys—you "just want to *slap* them," as a high-ranking official recently told Molly Ivins. Maybe that's why the white guys loathe mothers so much—we remind them they have to share, take turns, grow up.

40   The next morning we loaded the roof of Howard's car so high with the boys' sports equipment, easels, and trunks, we had to make one last trip to the hardware store for longer bungee cords. It was a hectic departure as the Clampetts hit the road, and I waved from the curb as they mouthed their final goodbyes through the window. Still smiling, I stayed on the curb for a long time, sorry the party was over. Letting go rarely comes naturally to me, and I felt my worry reflexes kick in as the car turned the corner.

Almost every family value Howard and I tried to give our sons will give them nothing but trouble, if they choose to live them. As two young, educated white guys who could qualify as insiders if they got behind the Contract on the rest of us, there are bound to be days they'll feel like Sucker Man, stuck with mercy when greed is called trump. I know it's a peculiar wish for a mother, but I hope they never quite fit in with their crowd. Certainly their affinity with their dad, a truly original odd man out, was a heartening sign. I could see them all laughing for the next 750 miles. Folding my arms, I looked up at the cathedral. I wished I could pray. I remembered my religious instructor's belief that we were all fools, walking from one hallowed ground to the next. Dear God, I thought, please let us be merciful fools.

Stabilizing the Text

1. Why did Blakely title her essay "A Beautiful Day in the Neighborhood"? How does reference to the widely known phrase influence your reading of the essay? What understanding are we asked to have of the phrase "a beautiful day in the neighborhood"?

2. Blakely's essay does more than simply describe a day in her Manhattan neighborhood. She weaves her narrative of moving in with a range of other recollections. Identify passages in the essay in which she brings together, or transitions between, narratives. What do these combinations and transitions contribute to communicating her sense of a beautiful day in her neighborhood?

3. Blakely makes clear from the beginning of her essay that her move into Manhattan is her first relocation into the city after living most of her adult life in the suburbs. Identify passages in the essay in which you think Blakely's experience in the suburbs influences her responses to and representations

of her new neighborhood in Manhattan. For example, are her encounters with street people simply "naive"? How does our awareness of her perspective and perception alter, if at all, our reading of her essay?

Mobilizing the Text

1. Reflecting on conditions in her new Manhattan neighborhood, Blakely introduces discussions of such things as capitalism and the failure of the mental health care system. Does her move from specific encounters to national problems contribute to your perceptions of the national problems? Are you led to view those problems more readily or more empathetically? Or are you led to discount her association of the specific with the general?
2. How might you represent a beautiful day in your neighborhood? Juxtaposing your representations to specific passages in Blakely's essay, describe how your description of a beautiful day in your neighborhood would be similar to or different from hers. How might you account for the similarities or differences? Do they say more about your respective neighborhoods? More about your ideas about a beautiful day? Or more about how you represent things in written language?
3. In what ways do you think the problems and possibilities Blakely finds in her Manhattan neighborhood are problems and possibilities we can find in just about any urban area? Are things really so similar everywhere? Or are differences greater than might first appear? Either way, what does her account of her neighborhood tell us about the beauty in our own neighborhoods?

Graffiti: Tunnel Notes of a New Yorker

LEONARD KRIEGEL

Leonard Kriegel is an essayist and novelist who lives in New York City. His many books include Working Through: A Teacher's Journey in the Urban University; On Men and Manhood; *and* Falling into Life, *Kriegel's essay, "Graffiti: Tunnel Notes of a New Yorker," was originally published in* the American Scholar. *In this essay, Kriegel reflects on a lifetime of viewing graffiti in New York City. He provides a picture of New York City during World War II, comparing it to New York City today. Through his comparison, Kriegel raises questions about contributions graffiti makes to the quality of life in urban environments. He claims that graffiti eloquently captures the current state of affairs in urban America. As you read Kriegel's essay, decide for yourself the contributions graffiti makes to the quality of life in urban areas.*

✦

When I was eight, I loved to run with my friends through the tunnel leading into Reservoir Oval in the North Central Bronx. The Oval occupied the site of a former city reservoir dredged by the WPA and then landscaped with playgrounds, wading pools, softball fields, a quarter-mile dirt track, and some of the finest tennis courts in the city—all ringed by attractive bush- and tree-lined walks that provided a natural shield for the sexual probings of early adolescence. Nothing else that bordered our neighborhood—not the wilds of Bronx Park or the chestnut trees of Van Cortlandt Park or the small camel-humped rock hill in Mosholu Parkway down which we went belly-whopping on American Flyer sleds in winter—fed us so incontrovertible a sense that America's promise now included us as did the long green and gray sweep of Reservoir Oval.

We would run through that entrance tunnel like a pack of Hollywood Indians on the warpath, our whoops echoing off the walls until we emerged from its shadows into the lush green lawns and brick walks and playing fields. Our portion of the Bronx was an ethnically mixed stew of immigrant families and their children, many of whom had fled Manhattan's crowded Lower East Side tenements for the spacious, park-rich green borough where Jonas Bronck had followed his cow across the Harlem River three hundred years earlier. The Bronx was still the city's "new" borough in 1941. Sparsely settled until after World War I, our neighborhood contained typical New York working- and lower-middle-class families on the rise in an America emerging from the Depression.

We children had already been assimilated into the wider American world. All of us—Irish and Italian Catholic as well as Eastern European Jew—believed we could ride the dream of success to a singular destiny. We were not yet of an age where we could physically journey into that wider America the books we read and the movies we saw told us was ours for the taking. The Oval was where we played together. It was also where we sometimes fought each other over myths that grew increasingly foreign and more raggedly European with each passing day. (Not that we were unaware of our parents' cultural baggage: marriage between Italian and Irish Catholics was still considered "mixed" in 1941.)

Occasionally, I would chance the Oval alone, in search of more solitary adventure. A curious metamorphosis would envelope me at such times: the entrance tunnel seemed darker and more threatening, the shadows warning me to move cautiously past walls peppered with graffiti. Alone, I let loose no war whoops to echo through that emptiness. Instead, I picked my way carefully through that dark half-moon of enclosed space, as if the graffiti scrawled on its surface held the clue to my future. There was something menacing about words scrawled on walls. Like an archaeologist probing ruins, I might turn in terror at any moment and run back to the security of my apartment three blocks south of the Oval.

Most of the graffiti was of the "John loves Mary!" kind, no different from the scribbled notes we passed one another in the P.S. 80 school yard down the hill. But it was also on that tunnel's walls that I first read the rage and fury of those who stained the world with conspiratorial fantasies. As rage exploded like bullets, words burrowed into my consciousness. "Roosevelt Jew Bastard!" "Unite Unite/Keep America White!" "Father Coughlin Speaks Truth!" "Kill All Jews!" In the raw grasp of age-old hatreds, politics was plot and plot was history and that reality seemed as impregnable as it was inescapable.

Like adults, children learn to shape anger through the words they confront. The graffiti on that tunnel wall mobilized my rage, nurturing my need for vengeance in the midst of isolation. It wasn't simply the anti-Semitism I wanted vengeance upon; it was my own solitary passage through that entrance tunnel. As I moved through it alone, the tunnel was transformed into everything my budding sense of myself as embryonic American hated. Walking through it became an act of daring, for graffiti had converted its emptiness into a threat that could only be taken the way it was offered—a threat that was distinctly personal.

In no other part of that huge complex of fields and walks was graffiti in great evidence. Other than the occasional heart-linked initials carved into the green-painted slats of wooden benches, I remember nothing else defacing the Oval. One emerged from that tunnel and the graffiti disappeared—all of it, "John loves Mary!" as well as "Kill All Jews!" It was as if an unwritten compact had been silently agreed upon, allowing the tunnel leading to the Oval to be scrawled over (despite occasional whitewashing, the tunnel was dark and poorly lit) while the rest of that huge recreation

5

complex remained free of the presence of graffiti. Running that tunnel alone was an act of purgation, rewarded when one was safely home with the illusion (and occasionally the reality) of ethnic harmony.

Other than that tunnel, the presence of graffiti was localized to a few alleys and subway stations and public urinals in the New York I remember from the forties and fifties. Until the sixties, even chalk and paint adhered to the unwritten laws of proportion in neighborhoods like mine. Buildings had not yet been crusted over with curlicued shapes and exploding slashes, zigzagging to a visual anarchy that testified to a love of color and line overwhelmed by hatred of the idea that color and line do not dictate the needs of community. Even the anti-Semitic graffiti of that tunnel remains in my memory as less the product of hatred than an expression of the distance existing between groups struggling to claim a portion of the American past.

In an essay published in 1973, Norman Mailer labeled graffiti a "faith," a word that struck me even back then as an odd use of language when applied to what a graffiti writer does. From the perspective of that eight-year-old child moving through that tunnel entrance, graffiti was the very antithesis of faith. It embodied a poetics of rage and hatred, a syntax in which anyone could claim the right, if he possessed the will, to impose his needs on others. But rage is not faith, as even an eight-year-old knew. It is simply rage.

10   In today's New York—and in today's London and Paris and Amsterdam and Los Angeles—the spread of graffiti is as accurate a barometer of the decline of urban civility as anything else one can think of. Paradoxically, even as it spread, graffiti was hailed as one of the few successful attempts the voiceless in our nation's cities made to impose their presence on urban culture. If graffiti is now the most obvious form of visual pollution city landscapes are forced to endure (even more polluting than those paste-up false windows with flower pots that grow like urban ivy on the deserted apartment houses fronting the Major Deegan Parkway in the East Bronx), it has assumed for New Yorkers the shape and frame of this city's prospects. Where expectation is confused with coherence, those savage slashes on brick and sidewalk embody our idea of all that city life is and all that we can now expect it to be.

In books and photographic essays, graffiti is heralded as the art structuring the real urban landscape that the poor confront in their daily lives. "Graffiti makes a statement!" is the rallying cry of those who defend its presence. True enough—even if one believes that the statement graffiti makes chokes the very idea of what a city can be. One can argue that it is not what the statement says but the style the statement employs that lends graffiti its insistent singularity. But the evidence of the streets insists that graffiti is an urban statement whose ultimate end is nothing less than the destruction of urban life. Regardless of whether it is considered art or public nuisance, graffiti denies the possibility of an urban community by insisting that individual style is a more natural right than the communitarian demands of city life.

Defenders of graffiti may insist that its importance lies in the voice it gives to anger and that its triumph resides in the alternative it offers to rage. Perhaps so. But anyone who walks through the streets of today's New York understands that the price graffiti demands is an emotional exhaustion in which we find ourselves the victims of that same rage and anger supposedly given voice—*vented* is today's fashionable word—by these indiscriminate slashes of color plastered against brick and wall and doorway and telephone booth.

Contemporary graffiti is not particularly political—at least not in New York. On those few times when one spots graffiti that does seek to embrace a message, the politics seem prepubescent sloganeering. Few openly political sayings are lettered onto these buildings and walls. Even the huge graffiti-like wall mural of a small Trotskyite press that one sees driving north on West Street in lower Manhattan speaks not of politics but of a peculiar Third World clubbiness more characteristic of the early 1970s than of our time. Malcolm X, Che Guevarra—originally offered as a pantheon of Third World liberators, the faces over the years have taken on the likeness of the comicbook superheroes in whose image one suspects they were originally conceived and drawn. The future they appeal to is curiously apolitical, as if the revolution they promise lies frozen in a nineteenth-century photograph in which reality assumes the proportions of myth. One has the impression that these are icons that have been hung on the wall for good luck, like a rabbit's foot or one of those plastic Jesuses one sees hanging from the rear-view mirrors of battered old Chevys.

The single most effective political graffito I have seen over the past few years was not in New York. Last summer, as I drove through streets filled with the spacious walled-in homes and immaculate concrete driveways of a wealthy Phoenix suburb, on my way to visit Frank Lloyd Wright's Taliesin West, I came across

"Save Our Desert!" slashed in large dripping red letters across a brown sun-drenched adobe wall surrounding one of the huge sun palaces that root like cacti in the nouveau riche wilds of Goldwater County. Here was a graffito in which politics was central, a gauntlet thrown at the feet of developers for whom the Arizona desert is mere space to be acquired and used and disposed of for profit.

15   Perhaps because it is more traditional, political graffiti seems more understandable than these explosions of line and color and ectoplasmic scrawl now plastered like dried mucus against New York's brick and concrete. "Save Our Desert!" may be simplistic, but at least it expresses a desire to right a balance deemed unjust and unnecessary. Political graffiti intrudes on privacy by voicing a specific protest. This alone serves to distinguish it from the public stains New Yorkers now assume are as natural as blades of grass growing between the cracks in a sidewalk.

To deny this city's painful decline over the past three decades is to deny the obvious. One can measure that decline through the spread of graffiti. The process began with the insistence that these mindless blotches and savage strokes embodied a legitimate, if admittedly different, sense of fashion, that they could be viewed—indeed, they had to be viewed—as a "natural" expression of the new and daring.

Like everything else in this city, graffiti demands an emotional investment from those who defend it. One can only vindicate these slashes and blobs of color because their presence is so overwhelming. What choice do we have but to demand that the world recognize the "art" in these urban voices? Anything else forces us to examine the consequences of what we have allowed through the intimidating fear of not being in fashion. Even as acceptance is demanded, graffiti continues to pound against the city, having grown as mechanical and fixed as the sound of the boom boxes in the streets below our windows. We label graffiti "real," we label it "authentic," we label it "powerful." Like true pedants, we discuss the nuances of these different voices. We create graffiti martyrs from Keith Haring, dead of AIDS, and from Basquiat, dead of a drug overdose. In their deaths, we tell ourselves, our city lives. For their art is "urban." And urban counts. Urban must count. If not, why have we permitted what has been done to this city we claim to love?

If the graffiti plastered first on subway cars and then on billboard and doorway and brick truly constitutes an art form, then it is an art that seeks to rip out the root idea of what supposedly created it—the idea that a specifically urban culture exists. Defended as a creative act in which the city itself becomes the artist's canvas, the paradox of graffiti is the extent to which its existence connotes an implicit hatred of what a city is and what it can offer its citizens. At the core of graffiti's spread lurks the dangerously romantic notion that the city is a place of such overwhelming evil that it must be torn apart, savaged into its own death, its residents given a "voice" in the irrational hope that in this way its more urbane voices will be stilled. Graffiti slashes at the heart of New York, the heart of urbanity, by attacking the city's splendid nineteenth-century monuments of cast-iron architecture in the resurrected Soho neighborhood of lower Manhattan as indifferently as it attacks the playful 1930s art deco apartment house façades that once made the now-dingy Grand Concourse in the Bronx so singularly playful an example of urban aspiration.

New Yorkers stand like helpless mannequins before the onslaught. Graffiti does not, after all, destroy lives. It is not like the scourge of crack, or the horrendous spread of AIDS, or the rising tension in our neighborhoods between blacks and Jews and between blacks and Asians. Graffiti is no more than a background for the homeless who cage themselves in makeshift cardboard boxes or laundry baskets at night or the crazies who walk the streets engaged in heated dialogues with Jesus or Lenin or Mary Baker Eddy or George Steinbrenner or the dead yet still-celebrated Basquiat. Graffiti is innocent, or so we continue to tell ourselves even in the face of powerful evidence to the contrary. "No one ever died from graffiti!" a friend impatiently snaps, as I point out a deserted bank on the northwest corner of Fourteenth Street and Eighth Avenue, its once-attractive façade gouged and stabbed by slashes of black spray paint. "There are more important problems in this city."

Of course, there *are* more important problems in this city. Yet none speak more directly to the true state of affairs in this New York than the mushrooming graffiti in our streets. And nothing traces the actual state of those streets better than the insistence graffiti makes that there are neither rules nor obligations for the survival of urban hope and aspiration. The prospect of a voice for the voiceless illuminates every dark alley in the New Yorker's mind, like the reflection of one of those stars already extinguished millions and millions of light years away. But is that to be all those of us who claim to love this city are finally left with, these dead light gleanings of one false revolution after another, beneath whose costly illusions—in the name of fashion—we have bent this

20

great and wounded metropolis out of time and out of function and perhaps even out of its future?

Stabilizing the Text

1. Kriegel makes a distinction between older, traditional graffiti and contemporary graffiti. What does he claim the difference between traditional and contemporary graffiti to be? What reasons does he give for making this distinction? What impacts does the distinction have on his argument?

2. Kriegel contends that "the spread of graffiti is as accurate a barometer of the decline of urban civility as anything else one can think of." What do you think Kriegel means by the term "urban civility"? Is it something we have ever had? Is it something that is really in decline? Is urban civility something we should regret losing or not having? And if we have lost it, what has taken its place?

3. What portrait does Kriegel paint of the New York City of his childhood? What portrait does he paint of the New York City of his adulthood? According to Kriegel, what has changed between the past and the present other than the graffiti? What else do you think has changed? How might any of these changes contribute to Kriegel's reception of graffiti and his overall perception of city life?

Mobilizing the Text

1. Can you think of specific instances of graffiti that might contradict Kriegel's claim? Are there instances of graffiti that mean something more than, or something different from, what Kriegel suggests? What do these different instances of graffiti allow us to say about Kriegel's essay?

2. Graffiti artists of all kinds and every ability use the sides of buildings to communicate a message. That message provides people in the area an opportunity to join together in praising, blaming, or debating with the graffiti artist. Do you think the influence graffiti has on people creates opportunities for genuine community? When people have come together to talk about graffiti, whether they agree or disagree, has the graffiti done its job and encouraged interaction? Is this interaction what we mean by community?

3. There are certainly many different views on all the issues Kriegel addresses. How well does Kriegel account for these different views in his essay? What consequences follow from Kriegel's attention, or his lack of attention, to alternative points of view? Think of a point of view different from Kriegel's. Where in his essay might greater attention to that point of view change either his claims or his conclusions?

CHAPTER 2

Cities and Crime

C rime is a defining force in everyone's life. We keep our doors bolted, we lock our bicycles, we worry about being out alone after dark. Sitting in our homes in the evening, we often watch television programs that revolve around crime. And cities. Although individual crimes are committed in lots of places—in suburbs and rural communities, in boardrooms and government offices—cities are *represented* as though crime lurks on every urban corner, in every doorway, down every alley.

Each day, newspaper headlines and televised news reports tell of violent crimes in cities. Often these reports emphasize the most extreme crimes. They give the impression that lawless and violent people are everywhere: Families who take a wrong turn while driving in the city are gunned down by drug-dealing gang members; babies sleeping in their cribs are killed by stray bullets. Such images teach us to see criminal acts as inexplicable deviations from our collective actions and policies and the conditions they create. The mass media use language that plays on people's fear, frustration, and despair, making crime prevention and personal safety important concerns for all Americans. They encourage us to relate to crime in terms of how to punish it and how to distance it from our lives and actions. Politicians create election campaigns that manipulate people's beliefs, fears, and perceptions of crime, rather than asking us to reflect on the causes of crime. Think about the campaign rhetoric of people running for public office; they typically promise "tougher laws," "greater security," and "more police and prison cells"—all of which are designed to "get criminals off the street."

This is understandable, because in addition to being a figment of media sensationalism, crime is also a reality. You may know someone who has been the victim of a crime; you may have been the victim of a crime yourself. We live every day with the realities of crime, as well as with ideas about the nature and prevalence of crime created by advertising, news, politics, television, movies, and music. Like everyone else, you have to deal with actual crime and its prevention, mass-media-produced images of crime, and your attitudes about crime—which are generated by both real-world crime and the mass media. But we seldom take the time to connect our representations of crime with the realities of crime. We seldom think about how our talk of crime creates the conditions in which we are more or less likely to experience particular kinds of crimes as a society. It is this connection between representations and realities of crime that the essays in this section try to make sense of. They raise fundamental questions and provide opportunities to rethink our answers to important questions. How should we understand crime? How should we respond to it as a society? Is crime an expression of individual deviance, the mark of a violent society, or something in between? The ways in which we respond to these questions have important consequences for how we live our lives and act in our communities, and for the cities that result from our actions.

The first essay in this chapter, Bruce Shapiro's "One Violent Crime," combines a description of a sensational crime with an analysis of how reality can be quite different from news images of crime. Shapiro explains how his experience as a victim of a violent crime got used in a news story about a crime bill in the legislature. He describes not only how he felt seeing himself on television, but also how he felt victimized because his experience was unrelated to the bill it was used to illustrate. He concludes that "getting tough on crime" isn't the answer, for his attacker would not have been stopped by tougher crime legislation.

Representing the sources of violence from a different perspective, Daryl F. Gates reports statistics from the Los Angeles Police Department where he was chief in the early 1990s. In "Guns Aren't the Only Issue," Gates describes what he considers the root cause of violence in American cities and explains what he thinks will curb the spread of violence. As Gates explains, he does not believe it is guns that produce violence.

In "School Shootings and White Denial," Tim Wise uses the topic of school shootings to ground an analysis of how we as a society talk of crime. For Wise, this topic provides an opportunity to question our assumptions about who criminals are, what they look like, and how we should think about crime in general.

The final two essays in this chapter discuss different aspects of one of the largest crime agendas of the current generation—the war on drugs. In "The Drug War Goes Up in Smoke," Sasha Abramsky discusses the war on drugs as an approach to crime, which has proven to be a failure. Abramsky describes several alternatives to the drug war approach of criminalizing addiction and mass incarceration. In "Masked Racism: Reflections on the Prison Industrial Complex," Angela Y. Davis discusses what she sees as a too-often unrecognized aspect of policies like the war on drugs—the corporate interest in imprisonment as a source of massive profits. For Davis, citizens should reflect on who benefits from mass-media sensationalism and politicians' "get tough" rhetoric of crime, as well as who pays the costs directly, through imprisonment, and indirectly, through the impoverishment of public life.

Combined, the essays in this chapter provide opportunities to reflect on different possible answers to the questions of crime, writing, and city life. As people who will be living with and thinking about crime in some way or another for all of our lives, these authors offer us a chance to step back and reflect on what we get by writing about crime, and thus about cities, in different ways.

One Violent Crime

Bruce Shapiro

Bruce Shapiro is a contributing editor of the Nation *and co-author of* Legal Lynching: The Death Penalty and America's Future, *with Rev. Jesse Jackson and Congressman Jesse Jackson, Jr. He teaches investigative journalism at Yale University and is field director of the Dart Center for Journalism and Trauma. In "One Violent Crime," originally published in the* Nation, *Shapiro tells what happened on August 7, 1994, when he was among seven people severely wounded in a knife attack. Shapiro contrasts his own experience with media representations of his attack months later on the television evening news. As Shapiro describes it, the footage of the attack was not presented as having anything to do with the events of August 7; it was shown as a part of story on a "get tough" crime bill to extend prison sentences. As you read Shapiro's essay, consider the role that personal stories like Shapiro's can play in framing large abstract issues for readers.*

———————— ✦ ————————

Alone in my home, I am staring at the television screen and shouting. On the evening local news I have unexpectedly encountered video footage, several months old, of myself writhing on an ambulance gurney, bright green shirt open and drenched with blood, skin pale, knee raised, trying desperately and with utter futility to find relief from pain.

On the evening of August 7, 1994, I was among seven people stabbed and seriously wounded in a coffee bar a few blocks from my house. Any televised recollection of this incident would be upsetting. But the anger that has me shouting tonight is quite specific, and political, in origin: my picture is being shown on the news to illustrate why Connecticut's legislature plans to lock up more criminals for a longer time. A picture of my body, contorted and bleeding, has become a propaganda image in the crime war.

I had not planned to write about this assault. But for months now the politics of the nation have in large part been the politics of crime, from last year's federal crime bill through the fall elections through the Contract with America proposals awaiting action by the Senate. Among a welter of reactions to the attack, one feeling is clear: I am unwilling to be a silent poster child in this debate.

The physical and political truth about violence and crime lies in their specificity, so here is what happened: I had gone out for after-dinner coffee that evening with two friends and New Haven neighbors, Martin and Anna Broell Bresnick. At 9:45 we arrived at a recently opened coffeehouse on Audubon Street, a block occupied by an arts high school where Anna teaches, other community arts institutions, a few pleasant shops and upscale condos. Entering, we said hello to another friend, a former student of Anna's named Christina Koning, who the day before had started working behind the counter. We sat at a small table near the front of the café; about fifteen people were scattered around the room. Just before ten o'clock, the owner announced closing time. Martin stood up and walked a few yards to the counter for a final refill.

5   Suddenly there was chaos—as if a mortar shell had landed. I looked up, heard Martin call Anna's name, saw his arm raised and a flash of metal and people leaping away from a thin bearded man with a ponytail. Tables and chairs toppled. Without thinking I shouted to Anna, "Get down!" and pulled her to the floor, between our table and the café's outer wall. She clung to my shirt, I to her shoulders, and, crouching, we pulled each other toward the door.

What actually happened I was only able to tentatively reconstruct many weeks later. Apparently, as Martin headed toward the counter the thin bearded man, whose name we later learned was Daniel Silva, asked the time from a young man named Richard Colberg, who answered and turned to leave.

Without any warning, Silva pulled out a hunting knife with a six-inch blade and stabbed in the lower back a woman leaving with Colberg, a medical technician named Kerstin Braig. Then he stabbed Colberg, severing an artery in his thigh. Silva was a slight man, but he moved with demonic speed and force around the café's counter. He struck Martin in the thigh and in the arm he raised to protect his face. Our friend Chris Koning had in a moment's time pushed out the screen in a window and helped the wounded Kerstin Braig through it to safety. Chris was talking on the phone with the police when Silva lunged over the counter and stabbed her in the chest and abdomen. He stabbed Anna in the side as she and I pulled each other along the wall. He stabbed Emily Bernard, a graduate student who had been sitting quietly reading a book, in the abdomen as she tried to flee through the café's back door. All of this happened in about the time it has taken you to read this paragraph.

Meanwhile, I had made it out the café's front door onto the brick sidewalk with Anna, neither of us realizing yet that she was wounded. Seeing Martin through the window, I returned inside and we came out together. Somehow we separated, fleeing opposite ways down the street. I had gone no more than a few steps when I felt a hard punch in my back, followed instantly by the unforgettable sensation of skin and muscle tissue parting. Silva had stabbed me about six inches above my waist, just beneath my rib cage. (That single deep stroke cut my diaphragm and sliced my spleen in half.) Without thinking, I clapped my left hand over the wound even before the knife was out, and its blade caught my hand, leaving a slice across my palm and two fingers.

"Why are you doing this?" I cried out to Silva in the moment after feeling his knife punch in and yank out. As I fell to the street he leaned over my face; I vividly remember the knife's immense and glittering blade. He directed the point through my shirt into the flesh of my chest, beneath my left shoulder. I remember his brown beard, his clear blue-gray eyes looking directly into mine, the round globe of a street lamp like a halo above his head. Although I was just a few feet from a café full of people, and although Martin and Anna were only yards away, the street, the city, the world felt utterly empty except for me and this thin bearded stranger with clear eyes and a bowie knife. The space around us—well-lit, familiar Audubon Street, where for six years I had taken a child to music lessons—seemed literally to have expanded into a vast and dark canyon.

10   "You killed my mother," he answered. My own desperate response: "Please don't." Silva pulled the knifepoint out of my chest and disappeared. A moment later I saw him flying down the street on a battered, ungainly bicycle, back straight, vest flapping and ponytail flying.

After my assailant had gone I lay on the sidewalk, hand still over the wound on my back, screaming. Pain ran over me like an express train; it felt as though every muscle in my back were locked and contorted; breathing was excruciating. A security guard appeared across the street from me. I called out to him but he stood there frozen, or so it seemed. (A few minutes later, he would help police chase Silva down.) I shouted to Anna, who was hiding behind a car down the street. Still in shock and unaware of her own injury, she ran for help, eventually collapsing on the stairs of a nearby brownstone where a prayer group that was meeting upstairs answered her desperate ringing of the doorbell. From where I was lying, I saw a second-floor light in the condo complex across the way. A woman's head appeared in the window. "Please help me," I implored. "He's gone. Please help me." She shouted back that she had called the police, but she did not come to the street. I was suddenly aware of a blond woman—Kerstin Braig, though I did not know her name then—in a white-and-gray-plaid dress, sitting on the curb. I asked her for help. "I'm sorry, I've done all I can," she muttered. She raised her hand, like a medieval icon; it was covered with blood. So was her dress. She sank into a kind of stupor. Up the street I saw a police car's flashing blue lights, then another's, then I saw an officer with a concerned face and a crackling radio crouched beside me. I stayed conscious as the medics arrived and I was loaded into an ambulance—being filmed for television, as it turned out, though I have no memory of the crew's presence.

Being a victim is a hard idea to accept, even while lying in a hospital bed with tubes in veins, chest, penis, and abdomen. The spirit rebels against the idea of oneself as fundamentally powerless. So I didn't think much for the first few days about the meaning of being a victim; I saw no political dimension to my experience.

As I learned in more detail what had happened, I thought, in my jumbled-up, anesthetized state, about my injured friends—

although everyone survived, their wounds ranged from quite serious to critical—and about my wounds and surgery. I also thought about my assailant. A few facts about him are worth repeating. Until August 7 Daniel Silva was a self-employed junk dealer and a homeowner. He was white. He lived with his mother and several dogs. He had no arrest record. A New Haven police detective who was hospitalized across the hall from me recalled Silva as a socially marginal neighborhood character. He was not, apparently, a drug user. He had told neighbors about much violence in his family—indeed, not long before August 7 he showed one neighbor a scar on his thigh he said was from a stab wound.

A week earlier, Silva's seventy-nine-year-old mother had been hospitalized for diabetes. After a few days the hospital moved her to a new room; when Silva saw his mother's empty bed he panicked, but nurses swiftly took him to her new location. Still, something seemed to have snapped. Earlier on the day of the stabbings, police say, Silva released his beloved dogs, set fire to his house, and rode away on his bicycle as it burned. He arrived on Audubon Street with a single dog on a leash, evidently convinced his mother was dead. (She actually did die a few weeks after Silva was jailed.)

While I lay in the hospital, the big story on CNN was the Clinton   15
administration's 1994 crime bill, then being debated in Congress. Even fogged by morphine I was aware of the irony. I was flat on my back, the result of a particularly violent assault, while Congress eventually passed the anti-crime package I had editorialized against in *The Nation* just a few weeks earlier. Night after night in the hospital, unable to sleep, I watched the crime-bill debate replayed and heard Republicans and Democrats (who had sponsored the bill in the first place) fall over each other to prove who could be the toughest on crime.

The bill passed on August 21, a few days after I returned home. In early autumn I read the entire text of the crime bill—all 412 pages. What I found was perhaps obvious, yet under the circumstances compelling: not a single one of those 412 pages would have protected me or Anna or Martin or any of the others from our assailant. Not the enhanced prison terms, not the forty-four new death-penalty offenses, not the three-strikes-you're-out requirements, not the summary deportations of criminal aliens. And the new tougher-than-tough anti-crime provisions of the Contract with America, like the proposed abolition of the Fourth Amendment's search and seizure protections, offer no more practical protection.

On the other hand, the mental-health and social-welfare safety net shredded by Reaganomics and conservatives of both parties might have made a difference in the life of someone like my assailant—and thus in the life of someone like me. My assailant's growing distress in the days before August 7 was obvious to his neighbors. He had muttered darkly about relatives planning to burn down his house. A better-funded, more comprehensive safety net might just have saved me and six others from untold pain and trouble.

From my perspective—the perspective of a crime victim—the Contract with America and its conservative Democratic analogs are really blueprints for making the streets even less safe. Want to take away that socialist income subsidy called welfare? Fine. Connecticut Governor John Rowland proposes cutting off all benefits after eighteen months. So more people in New Haven and other cities will turn to the violence-breeding economy of crack, or emotionally implode from sheer desperation. Cut funding for those soft-headed social workers? Fine; let more children be beaten without the prospect of outside intervention, more Daniel Silvas carrying their own traumatic scars into violent adulthood. Get rid of the few amenities prisoners enjoy, like sports equipment, musical instruments, and the right to get college degrees, as proposed by the congressional right? Fine; we'll make sure that those inmates are released to their own neighborhoods tormented with unchanneled rage.

One thing I could not properly appreciate in the hospital was how deeply many friends, neighbors, and acquaintances were shaken by the coffeehouse stabbings, let alone strangers who took the time to write. The reaction of most was a combination of decent horrified empathy and a clear sense that their own presumption of safety was undermined.

20   But some people who didn't bother to acquaint themselves with the facts used the stabbings as a sort of Rorschach test on which they projected their own preconceptions about crime, violence, and New Haven. Some present and former Yale students, for instance, were desperate to see in my stabbing evidence of the great dangers of New Haven's inner city. One student newspaper wrote about "New Haven's image as a dangerous town fraught with violence." A student reporter from another Yale paper asked if I didn't think the attack proved New Haven needs better police protection. Given the random nature of this assault—it could as easily have happened in wealthy, suburban Greenwich, where a friend of mine was held up at an ATM at the point of an assault

rifle—it's tempting to dismiss such sentiments as typical products of an insular urban campus. But city-hating is central to today's political culture. Newt Gingrich excoriates cities as hopelessly pestilential, crime-ridden, and corrupt. Fear of urban crime and of the dark-skinned people who live in cities is the right's basic text, and defunding cities a central agenda item for the new congressional majority.

Yet in no small measure it was the institutions of an urban community that saved my life last August 7. That concerned police officer who found Kerstin Braig and me on the street was joined in a moment by enough emergency workers to handle the carnage in and around the coffeehouse, and his backups arrived quickly enough to chase down my assailant three blocks away. In minutes I was taken to Yale–New Haven Hospital, less than a mile away—built in part with the kind of public funding so hated by the right. As I was wheeled into the ER, several dozen doctors and nurses descended to handle all the wounded.

By then my abdomen had swelled from internal bleeding. Dr. Gerard Burns, a trauma surgeon, told me a few weeks later that I arrived on his operating table white as a ghost; my prospects, he said, would have been poor had I not been delivered so quickly, and to an ER with the kind of trauma team available only at a large metropolitan hospital. In other words, if my stabbing had taken place in the suburbs, I would have bled to death.

"Why didn't anyone try to stop him?" That question was even more common than the reflexive city-bashing. I can't even begin to guess the number of times I had to answer it. Each time, I repeated that Silva moved too fast, that it was simply too confusing. And each time, I found the question not just foolish but offensive.

"Why didn't anyone stop him?" To understand that question is to understand, in some measure, why crime is such a potent political issue. To begin with, the question carries not empathy but an implicit burden of blame; it really asks "Why didn't *you* stop him?" It is asked because no one likes to imagine oneself a victim. It's far easier to graft onto oneself the aggressive power of the attacker, to embrace the delusion of oneself as Arnold Schwarzenegger defeating a multitude single-handedly. *If I am tough enough and strong enough, I can take out the bad guys.*

The country is at present suffering from a huge version of this same delusion. This myth is buried deep in the political culture, nurtured in the historical tales of frontier violence and vigilantism and by the action-hero fantasies of film and television. Now, bolstered by the social Darwinists of the right, who see society as

25

an unfettered marketplace in which the strongest individuals flourish, this delusion frames the crime debate.

I also felt that the question "Why didn't anybody stop him?" implied only two choices: Rambo-like heroism or abject victim-hood. To put it another way, it suggests that the only possible responses to danger are the individual biological imperatives of fight or flight. And people don't want to think of themselves as on the side of flight. This is a notion whose political moment has arrived. In last year's debate over the crime bill, conservatives successfully portrayed themselves as those who would stand and fight; liberals were portrayed as ineffectual cowards.

"Why didn't anyone stop him?" That question and its underlying implications see both heroes and victims as lone individuals. But on the receiving end of a violent attack, the fights-or-flight dichotomy didn't apply. Nor did that radically individualized notion of survival. At the coffeehouse that night, at the moments of greatest threat, there were no Schwarzeneggers, no stand-alone heroes. (In fact, I doubt anyone could have "taken out" Silva; as with most crimes, his attack came too suddenly.) But neither were there abject victims. Instead, in the confusion and panic of life-threatening attack, *people reached out to one another*. This sounds simple, yet it suggests there is an instinct for mutual aid that poses a profound challenge to the atomized individualism of the right. Christina Koning helped the wounded Kerstin Braig to escape, and Kerstin in turn tried to bring Christina along. Anna and I, and then Martin and I, clung to each other, pulling one another toward the door. And just as Kerstin found me on the sidewalk rather than wait for help alone, so Richard and Emily, who had never met before, together sought a hiding place around the corner. Three of us even spoke with Silva either the moment before or the instant after being stabbed. My plea to Silva may or may not have been what kept him from pushing his knife all the way through my chest and into my heart; it's impossible to know what was going through his mind. But this impulse to communicate, to establish human contact across a gulf of terror and insanity, is deeper and more subtle than the simple formulation of fight or flight, courage or cowardice, would allow.

I have never been in a war, but I now think I understand a little the intense bond among war veterans who have survived awful carnage. It is not simply the common fact of survival but the way in which the presence of these others seemed to make survival itself possible. There's evidence, too, that those who try to go it alone suffer more. In her insightful study *Trauma and Recovery*, Judith

Herman, a psychiatrist, writes about rape victims, Vietnam War veterans, political prisoners, and other survivors of extreme violence. "The capacity to preserve social connection . . . ," she concludes, "even in the face of extremity, seems to protect people to some degree against the later development of post-traumatic syndromes. For example, among survivors of a disaster at sea, the men who had managed to escape by cooperating with others showed relatively little evidence of post-traumatic stress afterward." On the other hand, she reports that the "highly symptomatic" ones among those survivors were "'Rambos,' men who had plunged into impulsive, isolated action and not affiliated with others."

The political point here is that the Rambo justice system proposed by the right is rooted in that dangerous myth of the individual fighting against a hostile world. Recently that myth got another boost from several Republican-controlled state legislatures, which have made it much easier to carry concealed handguns. But the myth has nothing to do with the reality of violent crime, the ways to prevent it, or the needs of survivors. Had Silva been carrying a handgun instead of a knife on August 7, there would have been a massacre.

I do understand the rage and frustration behind the crime-victim movement, and I can see how the right has harnessed it. For weeks I thought obsessively and angrily of those minutes on Audubon Street, when first the nameless woman in the window and then the security guard refused to approach me—as if I, wounded and helpless, were the dangerous one. There was also a subtle shift in my consciousness a few days after the stabbing. Up until that point, the legal process and press attention seemed clearly centered on my injuries and experience, and those of my fellow victims. But once Silva was arraigned and the formal process of prosecution began, it became *his* case, not mine. I experienced an overnight sense of marginalization, a feeling of helplessness bordering on irrelevance.

Sometimes that got channeled into outrage, fear, and panic. After arraignment, Silva's bail was set at $700,000. That sounds high, but just 10 percent of that amount in cash, perhaps obtained through some relative with home equity, would have bought his pretrial release. I was frantic at even this remote prospect of Silva walking the streets. So were the six other victims and our families. We called the prosecutor virtually hourly to request higher bail. It was eventually raised to $800,000, partly because of our complaints and partly because an arson charge was added. Silva remains in the Hartford Community Correctional Center awaiting trial.

Near the six-month anniversary of the stabbings I called the prosecutor and learned that in December Silva's lawyer filed papers indicating that he intends to claim a "mental disease or defect" defense. If successful, it would send him to a maximum-security hospital for the criminally insane for the equivalent of the maximum criminal penalty. In February the court was still awaiting a report from Silva's psychiatrist. Then the prosecution will have him examined by its own psychiatrist. "There's a backlog." I was told; the case is not likely to come to trial until the end of 1995 at the earliest. Intellectually, I understand that Silva is securely behind bars, that the court system is overburdened, that the delay makes no difference in the long-term outcome. But emotionally, viscerally, the delay is devastating.

Another of my bursts of victim consciousness involved the press. Objectively, I know that many people who took the trouble to express their sympathy to me found out only through news stories. And sensitive reporting can for the crime victim be a kind of ratification of the seriousness of an assault, a reflection of the community's concern. One reporter for the daily *New Haven Register*, Josh Kovner, did produce level-headed and insightful stories about the Audubon Street attack. But most other reporting was exploitative, intrusive, and inaccurate. I was only a few hours out of surgery, barely able to speak, when the calls from television stations and papers started coming to my hospital room. Anna and Martin, sent home to recover, were ambushed by a Hartford TV crew as they emerged from their physician's office, and later rousted from their beds by reporters from another TV station ringing their doorbell. The *Register's* editors enraged all seven victims by printing our home addresses (a company policy, for some reason) and running spectacularly distressing full-color photos of the crime scene, complete with the coffee bar's bloody windowsill.

Such press coverage inspired in all of us a rage it is impossible to convey. In a study commissioned by the British Broadcasting Standards Council, survivors of violent crimes and disasters "told story after story of the hurt they suffered through the timing of media attention, intrusion into their privacy and harassment, through inaccuracy, distortion and distasteful detail in what was reported." This suffering is not superficial. To the victim of violent crime the press may reinforce the perception that the world is an uncomprehending and dangerous place.

The very same flawed judgments about "news value" con- 35
tribute significantly to a public conception of crime that is as completely divorced from the facts as a Schwarzenegger movie. One
study a few years ago found that reports on crime and justice constitute 22 to 28 percent of newspaper stories, "nearly three times
as much attention as the presidency or the Congress or the state of
the economy." And the most spectacular crimes—the stabbing of
seven people in an upscale New Haven coffee bar, for instance—
are likely to be the most "newsworthy" even though they are statis-
tically the least likely. "The image of crime presented in the media
is thus a reverse image of reality," writes sociologist Mark Warr in
a study commissioned by the National Academy of Sciences.

Media coverage also brings us to another crucial political
moral: the "seriousness" of crime is a matter of race and real estate. This has been pointed out before, but it can't be said too often. Seven people stabbed in a relatively affluent, mostly white
neighborhood near Yale University—this was big news on a slow
news night. It went national over the AP wires and international
over CNN's *Headline News*. It was covered by the *New York Times*,
and words of sympathy came to New Haven from as far as Prague
and Santiago. Because a graduate student and a professor were
among those wounded, the university sent representatives to the
emergency room. The morning after, New Haven Mayor John
DeStefano walked the neighborhood to reassure merchants and
office workers. For more than a month the regional press covered
every new turn in the case.

Horrendous as it was, though, no one was killed. Four weeks
later, a fifteen-year-old girl named Rashawnda Crenshaw was
driving with two friends about a mile from Audubon Street. As
the car in which she was a passenger turned a corner, she was
shot through the window and killed. Apparently her assailants
mistook her for someone else. Rashawnda Crenshaw was black,
and her shooting took place in the Hill, the New Haven neighborhood with the highest poverty rate. No Yale officials showed up at
the hospital to comfort Crenshaw's mother or cut through red
tape. The *New York Times* did not come calling; there were certainly no bulletins flashed around the world on CNN. The local
news coverage lasted just long enough for Rashawnda Crenshaw
to be buried.

Anyone trying to deal with the reality of crime, as opposed to the
fantasies peddled to win elections, needs to understand the complex suffering of those who are survivors of traumatic crimes, and
the suffering and turmoil of their families. I have impressive

physical scars: there is a broad purple line from my breastbone to the top of my pubic bone, an X-shaped cut into my side where the chest tube entered, a thick pink mark on my chest where the point of Silva's knife rested on a rib. On my back is the unevenly curving horizontal scar where Silva thrust the knife in and yanked it out, leaving what looks like a crooked smile. But the disruption of my psyche is, day in and day out, more noticeable. For weeks after leaving the hospital I awoke nightly agitated, drenched with perspiration. For two months I was unable to write; my brain simply refused to concentrate. Into any moment of mental repose would rush images from the night of August 7: or alternatively, my mind would not tune in at all. My reactions are still out of balance and disproportionate. I shut a door on my finger, not too hard, and my body is suddenly flooded with adrenaline and I nearly faint. Walking on the arm of my partner, Margaret, one evening I abruptly shove her to the side of the road; I have seen a tall, lean shadow on the block where we are headed and am alarmed out of all proportion. I get into an argument and find myself quaking with rage for an hour afterward, completely unable to restore calm. Though to all appearances normal, I feel at a long arm's remove from all the familiar sources of pleasure, comfort, and anger that shaped my daily life before August 7.

What psychologists call post-traumatic stress disorder is, among other things, a profoundly political state in which the world has gone wrong, in which you feel isolated from the broader community by the inarticulate extremity of experience. I have spent a lot of time in the past few months thinking about what the world must look like to those who have survived repeated violent attacks, whether children battered in their homes or prisoners beaten or tortured behind bars; as well as those, like rape victims, whose assaults are rarely granted public ratification.

40   The right owes much of its success to the anger of crime victims and the argument that government should do more for us. This appeal is epitomized by the rise of restitution laws—statutes requiring offenders to compensate their targets. On February 7 the House of Representatives passed, by a vote of 431 to 0, the Victim Restitution Act, a plank of the Contract with America that would supposedly send back to jail offenders who don't make good on their debts to their victims. In my own state, Governor Rowland recently proposed a restitution amendment to the state constitution.

On the surface it is hard to argue with the principle of reasonable restitution—particularly since it implies community recognition of the victim's suffering. But I wonder if these laws really will end up benefiting someone like me—or if they are just empty, vote-getting devices that exploit victims and could actually hurt our chances of getting speedy, substantive justice. H. Scott Wallace, former counsel to the Senate Judiciary Subcommittee on Juvenile Justice, writes in *Legal Times* that the much-touted Victim Restitution Act is "unlikely to put a single dollar into crime victims' pockets, would tie up the federal courts with waves of new damages actions, and would promote unconstitutional debtors' prisons."

I also worry that the rhetoric of restitution confuses—as does so much of the imprisonment-and-execution mania dominating the political landscape—the goals of justice and revenge. Revenge, after all, is just another version of the individualized, take-out-the-bad-guys myth. Judith Herman believes indulging fantasies of revenge worsens the psychic suffering of trauma survivors: "The desire for revenge . . . arises out of the victim's experience of complete help-lessness," and forever ties the victim's fate to the perpetrator's. Real recovery from the cataclysmic isolation of trauma comes only when "the survivor comes to understand the issues of principle that tran-scend her personal grievance against the perpetrator . . . [a] princi-ple of social justice that connects the fate of others to her own." The survivors and victims' families of the Long Island Rail Road mas-sacre have banded together not to urge that Colin Ferguson be exe-cuted but to work for gun control. What it all comes down to is this: What do survivors of violent crime really need? What does it mean to create a safe society? Do we need courts so overburdened by non-violent drug offenders that Daniel Silvas go untried for eighteen months, delays that leave victims and suspects alike in limbo? Do we need to throw nonviolent drug offenders into mandatory-sen-tence proximity with violent sociopaths and career criminals? Do we need the illusory bravado of a Schwarzenegger film—or the real political courage of those LIRR survivors?

If the use of my picture on television unexpectedly brought me face to face with the memory of August 7, some part of the attack is relived for me daily as I watch the gruesome, voyeuristically reported details of the stabbing deaths of two people in California, Nicole Brown Simpson and Ronald Goldman. It was relived even more vividly by the televised trial of Colin Ferguson. (One night soon after watching Ferguson on the evening news, I dreamed that I was on the witness stand and Silva, like Ferguson, was representing himself and questioning me.) Throughout the trial, as Ferguson spoke of falling asleep and having someone else fire his gun, I heard neither cowardly denial nor what his first lawyer called "black rage"; I heard Daniel Silva's calm, secure voice telling me I killed his mother. And when I hear testimony by the survivors of that massacre—on a train as comfortable and familiar to them as my neighborhood coffee bar—I feel a great and incommunicable fellowship.

But the public obsession with these trials, I am convinced, has no more to do with the real experience of crime victims than does the anti-crime posturing of politicians. I do not know what made my assailant act as he did. Nor do I think crime and violence can be reduced to simple political categories. I do know that the answers will not be found in social Darwinism and atomized individualism, in racism, in dismantling cities and increasing the destitution of the poor. To the contrary: every fragment of my experience suggests that the best protections from crime and the best aid to victims are the very social institutions most derided by the right. As crime victim and citizen, what I want is the reality of a safe community—not a politician's fantasyland of restitution and revenge. That is my testimony.

Stabilizing the Text

1. Why does Shapiro say that he is "unwilling to be a silent poster child" in the debate over crime?

2. According to Shapiro, certain politicians have effectively manipulated our opinions of crime to gain support for certain public policies. What does this mean? Does Shapiro suggest that these policies are or are not actually working to eliminate crime? What relationships among opinion, public policy, and real crime does Shapiro see? Do you believe him? What support in this essay do you find for your view of crime?

3. How does Shapiro use his experience as a crime victim to relate media coverage of crime, the politics of crime, and the situation of his attacker? What do you as a reader find effective about the connections he draws? What about them do you find ineffective? Does his claim to being a victim of a violent crime make you as a reader more or less prone to believe what he has to say?

Mobilizing the Text

1. What do you make of Shapiro's attitude toward violence and anticrime legislation? In what ways does his attitude make sense to you? What experiences with crime cause your attitudes towards crime to be similar to or different from Shapiro's?

2. What effect does Shapiro's description of his attack have on you as a reader? Do you empathize with him? In what ways is it fair or unfair of him to use his attack in this way?

3. Shapiro describes his feelings of helplessness during his attack and explains his desire to do something to stop his attacker. What popular images of heroes and crime fighters does his description invoke? How do such popular images shape our reading of stories like Shapiro's?

Guns Aren't the Only Issue
Daryl F. Gates

Daryl F. Gates was, until 1992, the chief of the Los Angeles Police Department. He was forced to resign his position amid controversy and complaints over how his officers responded to the 1992 Los Angeles riots. In "Guns Aren't the Only Issue," first published in the Police Chief *magazine while he was still chief of police in Los Angeles, Gates presents a range of statistics to argue that guns are not the only, or even the primary, weapon used by people committing violent crimes. He is making this argument in response to groups that call for tighter restrictions on handguns and firearms as a way to curb violent crime. Gates suggests that rather than restricting legal access to guns, we should focus on teaching children to resist pressure to experiment with drugs on one hand, and stiffen penalties for criminals on the other. As you read Gates's essay, pay attention to the understanding of crime that he offers. Do you think his suggestions would lead to more or to less violence?*

◆

Guns, knives, chainsaws, syringes, rope and blunt objects serve many diverse legitimate purposes. Unfortunately, they are all part of a long list of items used for a common purpose. They are tools of violence in our violence-prone population. In Los Angeles, each of those instruments has been used to commit the ultimate violence—murder. It is no surprise that the murder weapon of choice, however, is a gun.

In 1986, of 831 homicide victims in Los Angeles, 520 were murdered by suspects using a gun. Of these, 374 murderers used a handgun, 35 used a rifle, 56 used a shotgun and 55 used an unknown type of firearm. Of 2,411 forcible rapes, 277 rapists used a gun; of 30,105 robberies, 9,862 robbers used a gun; and of 33,560 aggravated assaults, 7,911 suspects used firearms. Of those

66,907 violent crimes, 28 percent were committed by criminals armed with guns.

Viewed in that light, perhaps it is understandable that in the desire to reduce violence in our society, we have focused on reducing access to the favored instrument of death more strongly than we have on the wielders of those instruments. In my view, we should not limit our primary attention to only those who are canny enough to select the best tool for their violence. Rather, we should give equal attention to the other 72 percent of violent crimes where some instrument other than a gun was unlawfully used.

Through education, prevention, swift prosecution and commensurately severe punishment, we should focus on the core of the problem—violent people. In keeping with that concept, and in concert with other criminal justice agencies and community organizations, the LAPD is developing wide-ranging programs that are designed to break the cycle of criminal violence.

5　　By way of example, I shall describe one program that has been designed to attack the criminal connection between narcotics, violence and weapons. The bonding agents of this destructive linkage include the following facts:

- The average age of first use of marijuana is 10 years.
- Marijuana is usually the *introductory* drug of abuse that leads to abuse of hard narcotics.
- Narcotics abuse is an epidemic, fueled by a multi-billion dollar narcotics industry that severely threatens the survival of our society.
- Criminals at all levels, including street gangs and organized crime, are heavily involved in narcotic trafficking.
- Major narcotic seizures are often accompanied by seizures of sophisticated firearms and other weapons that are possessed in violation of existing laws.
- Sixty-one percent of the homicides committed in Los Angeles are related to narcotics.

All of the instruments cited earlier have been used as murder weapons in narcotic-related homicides.

The department's attempt to dismantle this nexus includes vigorous enforcement of the many gun laws, but our primary focus is on the common denominator—the people who comprise or supply the illicit drug market. Our strategy is to remove the profits of the narcotic industry by arresting traffickers and abusers at all levels, interdicting their product, seizing assets of suppliers and buyers, vigorously prosecuting offenders, and curbing our society's enormous appetite for illicit drugs through prevention and education programs.

In 1986, the LAPD compiled some impressive statistics in pursuing its strategy. More than 6½ tons of cocaine, 66 pounds of heroin and over 800,000 units of PCP were seized, as were substantial quantities of most other narcotics and illicit drugs. The total street value of all narcotic seizures was $2.8 billion. In addition, over $29.7 million in cash and 2,194 guns were seized. The department made over 46,000 narcotic arrests. Despite those numbers, no claim is made that the narcotic industry has been crippled in Los Angeles. To the contrary, it is still the city's number one crime problem. However, LAPD is making its presence felt and will continue to do so until the anticipated results of these long-range educational programs are achieved.

The centerpiece of our educational programs is DARE (Drug Abuse Resistance Education), the purpose of which is to produce future generations of drug-free Americans. The program was started in 1983 as a joint effort of the LAPD and the Los Angeles Unified School District, which developed the curriculum. It is taught by uniformed police officers in every elementary and junior high school in the district. DARE gives children the skills to recognize and resist both the subtle and the overt pressures that cause them to experiment with drugs and alcohol. The program has spread to 398 communities in 31 states, to Department of Defense overseas schools and to New Zealand.

So far, the effects of the program on students, teachers, parents and the community have exceeded our expectations. Obviously, it is a long-range program. The extent of DARE's ultimate success will be measured by the decline in the demand for drugs. Without a demand, there is no profit, no market competition and no drug-related violence. Therefore, there is no application of the tools of violence, including guns. When those things happen, the nexus will have been broken.

Skeptics might say that such programs take too long, that the results are too uncertain, that commitments are too tenuous and that quick-fix solutions are better. Many of their violence reduction quick-fix solutions focus almost exclusively on guns. But I think they err through omission. Certainly, the many gun laws we now have must be strictly enforced and vigorously prosecuted. But to suggest that the violence now committed by using guns would be eliminated if guns were not lawfully available is a gross exaggeration of their causal connection with the total problem of criminal violence.

I think a far more effective approach is to increase our intolerance for any form of criminal violence, regardless of the weapon used. We must strive to eliminate our tendency to resolve social conflicts through violence. Until then, we must use to the fullest extent those tools of deterrence that are now constitutionally available. This includes capital punishment when appropriate—and it is appropriate far more frequently than it is used.

Stabilizing the Text

1. What does Gates consider the main cause of violence in America today? What are some of his suggestions for addressing this?
2. What assumptions about crime and law and order does Gates have? Pick out of the essay words, phrases, or sentences that express these assumptions. In what ways do these assumptions seem fair and in what ways do they seem unfair? Do they lay blame for crime in the appropriate place? What might be some other assumptions about crime and how would Gates's essay be different if he wrote it based on those assumptions?
3. Gates suggests that, at least for now, we should fight to end violence through "tools of deterrence," such as the death penalty. How do you evaluate this argument? Is it logical to "fight" violence? What else can we do?

Mobilizing the Text

1. What terms does Gates use to characterize the violence of criminals? What terms does he use to characterize violence used by police? What attitudes do these terms reveal regarding police and regarding criminals? In what ways do these attitudes shape his conclusions?
2. Gates supplies a wealth of statistics to support his claims that the LAPD programs are effective in combating crime. How well do his statistics support his case? How can the statistics be read as supporting the argument that the LAPD programs are not successful?
3. Whom do you imagine Gates is arguing against in this essay? Indicate specific passages that suggest whom he is opposing. Do you think these are the same people who would be reading *Police Chief*, the magazine in which this essay originally appeared? If not, why do you think he published the piece there?

School Shootings and White Denial
Tim Wise

Tim Wise is the director of the Association for White Anti-Racist Education (AWARE) in Nashville, Tennessee. He lectures widely

about the need to combat institutional racism, gender bias, and the
growing gap between rich and poor in the United States. His articles
have appeared in magazines and newspapers throughout the world.
In "School Shootings and White Denial," which first appeared on
AlterNet.org, Wise examines media and public responses to school
shootings for what those responses reveal about popular understand-
ings of crime and violence. For Wise, popular representations and
perceptions of crime are often "blinded" by racism. As you read this
essay, think about your own knowledge of how the reality of crime
compares to the truths of crime that Wise discusses and the role
played by writing in challenging or endorsing perceptions of crime.

◆

I can think of no other way to say this, so here goes: An awful lot of white folks need to pull our heads out of our collective ass. Two more children are dead and thirteen are injured, and another community is scratching its blonde scalp, utterly perplexed as to how a school shooting the likes of the one in Santee, California could happen. After all, as the Mayor of the town said on CNN: "We're a solid town, a good town, with good kids; a good church-going town; an All-American town." Well, maybe that's the problem.

I said this after Columbine and no one listened, so I'll say it again: Most whites live in a state of self-delusion. We think danger is black or brown, not to mention poor, and if we can just move far enough away from "those people," we'll be safe. If we can just find an "all-American" town, life will be better, because "things like this just don't happen here."

Well excuse me for pointing this out, but in case you hadn't noticed, "here" is about the only place these kinds of things do happen. Oh sure, there's plenty of violence in urban communities too. But mass murder, wholesale slaughter, kill-'em-all-let-God-sort-'em-out kinda' craziness seems made for those "safe" white suburbs or rural communities. Yet the FBI insists there is no "profile" of a school shooter.

Come again? White boy after white boy after white boy decides to use their classmates for target practice, and yet there is no profile? In the past two years, 32 young men have either carried out mass murder against classmates and teachers or planned to do so, only to be foiled at the last minute. Thirty of these have been white. Yet there is no profile? Imagine if these killers and would be killers had nearly all been black. Would we still hesitate to put a racial face on the perpetrators? Doubtful.

5   Indeed, if any black child, especially in the white suburbs of Littleton or Santee, were to openly discuss plans to murder fellow students, as happened at Columbine and Santana High, you can bet somebody would have turned them in and the cops would have beat a path to their door. But when whites discuss murderous intentions, our racial stereotypes of danger too often lead us to ignore it. They're just "talking" and won't really do anything, we tell ourselves. How many have to die before we rethink that nonsense? How many parents, Mayors and Sheriffs must we listen to, describing how "normal" their community is, and how they can't understand what went wrong?

I'll tell you what went wrong and it's not TV, rap music, video games or a lack of prayer in school. What went wrong is that white Americans ignored dysfunction and violence when it only seemed to affect other communities, and thereby blinded ourselves to the chaos that never remains isolated forever. That which affects the urban "ghetto" today will be coming to a Wal-Mart near you tomorrow, and was actually there all along, merely hidden by layers of privilege that allow most white folks to cover up our own pathologies.

What went wrong is that we allowed ourselves to be lulled into a false sense of security by media representations of crime and violence that portray both as the province of those who are anything but white like us. We ignore the warning signs, because in our minds, the warning signs don't live in our neighborhood, but across town, in that place where we lock our car doors on the rare occasion we have to drive there. That false sense of security—the result of race and class stereotypes—then gets people killed. And still we act amazed.

But listen up my fellow white Americans: Our children are no better, no more moral, and no more decent than anyone else. Dysfunction is all around us, whether we choose to recognize it or not, and not only in terms of school shootings.

According to the Centers for Disease Control's "Youth Risk Behavior Survey," and the *Monitoring the Future* Report from the National Institutes on Drug Abuse, it is *our* children, and not those of the urban ghetto who are most likely to use drugs.

10   White high school students are seven times more likely than blacks to have used cocaine and heroin, eight times more likely to have smoked crack, and ten times more likely to have used LSD. What's more, it is *white* youth between the ages of 12–17 who are more likely to sell drugs: one third more likely than their black counterparts; and it is *white* youth who are twice as likely to

binge drink, and nearly twice as likely as blacks to drive drunk; and *white* males are twice as likely as black males to bring a weapon to school.

Yet I would bet a valued body part that there aren't 100 white people in Santee, or most anywhere else who have ever heard a single one of the statistics above. Because the media doesn't report on white dysfunction; at least not in a fashion that leads one to recognize the dysfunction as explicitly white.

A few years ago, *U.S. News* ran a story entitled: "A Shocking look at blacks and crime." Yet never has any media outlet discussed the "shocking" whiteness of these shoot-em-ups. Indeed, every time media commentators discuss the similarities in these crimes, they mention that the shooters were boys who got picked on, but never do they seem to notice a certain highly visible melanin deficiency. Color-blind, I guess.

White-blind is more like it, as I figure these folks would spot color with a quickness were some of it to stroll into their community. Indeed, Santee's whiteness is so taken for granted by its residents that the Mayor, in that CNN interview, thought nothing of saying on the one hand that the town was 82 percent white, but that on the other hand, "this is America." Well that *isn't* America, and it especially isn't California, where whites are only half of the population. This is a town that is *removed* from America, from its own state, and yet its Mayor thinks *they* are the normal ones; so much so that when asked about racial diversity, he replied that there weren't many of different "ethni-tis-tities." Not a word. Not even close.

I'd like to think that after this one, people would wake up, take note, and rethink their stereotypes of who the dangerous ones are. But deep down, I know better. The folks hitting the snooze button on this none-too-subtle alarm are my own people after all, and I know their blindness like the back of my hand.

Stabilizing the Text

1. What is Wise's main point in this essay? Describe the tone of the essay and how it relates to that point. Identify specific words or phrases that you think contribute to establishing Wise's tone and consider how his tone would likely affect potential audiences' reactions to his main point.

2. What example does Wise use in this essay that works the very best or the very worst in your opinion? Analyze that part of the essay and explain what it is about the example that makes it so striking.

3. What purpose is served in this essay by the government crime statistics Wise cites? What point is he trying to make about popular perceptions of crime?

Mobilizing the Text

1. Consider Wise's claim that "the media doesn't report on white dysfunction." Do you agree with this claim? If not, why not? If so, how can you explain this reality? Does it or does it not apply to spheres of life other than crime? In other words, do the media ever represent whites as a group? What are the consequences for whites and others of these media representations?
2. What does Wise think lies at the root of school shootings? For him, what kinds of white denial are revealed by school shootings and popular reactions to them?
3. Does Wise seem to you to be hopeful about the future of people's perceptions of crime? What reasons does his essay present to be hopeful or not? How hopeful are you concerning these issues? Is the presence of a perspective like Wise's one reason for hope?

The Drug War Goes Up in Smoke
SASHA ABRAMSKY

Sasha Abramsky is a freelance journalist and author of Hard Time Blues: How Politics Built a Prison Nation, *in addition to articles that have appeared in the* Atlantic Monthly, New York *magazine, the* Village Voice, *and* Rolling Stone. *In "The Drug War Goes Up in Smoke," Abramsky compares major efforts to reform drug laws in individual states to federal policies that continue to press for large-scale incarceration. As you read Abramsky's essay, consider how competing understandings of drug crimes get either justified or proven to be accurate and which view you find most convincing.*

———————————— ✦ ————————————

The war on terror may be too new to declare victory or defeat. But this nation has been fighting a war on drugs for more than a quarter-century, ever since New York Governor Nelson Rockefeller mandated harsh drug sentencing in 1973—and it may be time to announce that this is one war we've lost. More than a million people are serving time in our prisons and jails for nonviolent offenses, most drug-related, at a cost to the public of some $9.4 billion a year. Many billions more are spent by the states and the federal government on drug interdiction, drug-law enforcement and drug prosecutions. Harsh laws that require lengthy minimum sentences for the possession of even small amounts of drugs have created a boom in the incarceration of women, tearing mothers away from their children. Much of the country's costly foreign-policy commitments—especially in Latin America and the Caribbean—are determined by drug-war priorities. And yet drug use has actually soared, with twice as many teenagers reporting illegal drug use in 2000 as in 1992.

The idea of putting more and more Americans in prison, a great number of them for crimes related to drug addiction, grew out of "broken windows" social theories developed by criminologists such as James Q. Wilson in the 1970s. Wilson and his acolytes believed that unless police and the courts aggressively cracked down on crime, the social compact would degenerate into anarchy. They argued that even nonviolent offenses, such as breaking windows or possessing small amounts of marijuana, contributed to an anything-goes climate in which more serious crimes would proliferate. By the 1980s, these theories had entered the political mainstream, allowing Presidents Reagan, Bush, Clinton and now George W. Bush to score political points by denouncing addicts and appearing tough on crime all at the same time. Though politicians may have embraced this framework because it sold well to voters, its implications for the nation's health have been extreme. The drug war exiled addiction from the realm of public health, placing it almost exclusively in the hands of law enforcement and the courts.

At the philosophical core of this war on drugs, as fought by the likes of Bush Sr.'s drug czar, Bill Bennett, are twin ideas: Drug use is a moral wrong in itself, and drug use makes people more likely to commit a host of other crimes, from prostitution to burglary to murder. To fight drugs, the drug warriors have insisted, it isn't enough to go after the narco-kingpins; government agencies and courts must disrupt the drug supply-and-demand by prosecuting, and imprisoning, increasing numbers of low-level street dealers, even users themselves.

In the past few years, however, these policies have come under attack from surprising quarters. Opponents range from public health activists to libertarian-minded political figures such as former Secretary of State George Shultz. On the one hand, the critics have argued, these policies have failed to make progress toward a drug-free America. On the other, the war has proved to be too expensive to sustain. In an era of shrinking state resources, legislators have come to understand that budgets cannot be balanced, and needed social programs cannot be maintained, unless the country's bloated prison system is shrunk back down to a more realistic size. These two concerns have converged to create a window of opportunity for drug-policy reformers to push their case where it matters most: in the states.

Winter is hesitatingly giving way to spring, and New Mexico's former Governor Gary Johnson is tending to a broken leg in preparation for an expedition to climb Mount Everest. His daredevil athleticism is a marker of the same temperament that allowed Johnson, a Republican, to become the only governor ever to publicly support drug legalization while in office. The significant progress he made on drug-policy reform during his eight-year tenure helped to turn the tide for state reform movements across the country. "Johnson was a huge advocate," says Jerry Montoya, who runs a county needle-exchange program in the state, "ahead of federal policy in terms of thinking, in terms of philosophy."

In 2002, the last year of Johnson's tenure, state legislators voted to limit the ability of state police to seize the assets of those accused of drug-related crimes; to return a certain degree of case-by-case discretion to judges trying nonviolent drug cases; and to waive the federal ban on welfare benefits for former drug offenders who have completed their sentences.

During his tenure, Johnson, a fiscal conservative, made enemies of liberals through his hostility to tax-and-spend policies and his fondness for privatizing government functions—including prisons. He frequently vetoed the creation of new government programs, using, in his words, "an iron fist" on the state budget. But he made enemies of conservatives as well, primarily over his outspoken views on drug policy. He combatively declared the war on drugs "a miserable failure" and ambitiously investigated alternatives, including legalization.

Although he abstains now even from caffeine, sugar and alcohol, Johnson admits that he once inhaled—quite often. "I didn't hide it," he says. "Growing up [in the 1960s], I smoked marijuana regularly in college and a little bit after college. And I experimented with other drugs." This experience, combined with a strong libertarian streak, allowed him to be an iconoclastic thinker on drug policy. "If we legalized all drugs tomorrow, we'd be better than we are now regarding death, disease and crime reduction," he says. "There'd be more money into education; and more money into treatment for those who want or need treatment. At present rates, I'm going to see, in my life, 80 million Americans arrested for illegal drugs. The human cost of what we're doing is untold."

Johnson concluded that policies such as distributing clean needles to addicts and opening up regulated heroin-maintenance programs would do more to manage addiction than simply sending the police out to round up addicts; he also concluded that legalizing some categories of drugs and carefully regulating their sale would remove a huge pool of money from organized-crime cartels, boost government tax revenues and free up large amounts of money to be invested in drug education and health centers.

Retired Judge Woody Smith, who served on the bench in   10
Albuquerque in the 1980s and '90s before joining a Johnson task force on drug law reform, says, "He believes our approach [to the war on drugs] was wrong, from a personal liberty standpoint and a pragmatic standpoint." Smith, too, was eventually persuaded that the country's approach to drugs needs to be drastically overhauled. "Legalization and regulation are the only answer," he says now. "It's not a perfect solution, but it's a hell of a lot better than what we're doing now."

This evolution of thinking in New Mexico has spread across the country in recent years. Increasingly impatient with the costly combination of policing and prosecution, voters, along with a growing number of state and local elected officials, have abandoned their support for incarceration-based antidrug strategies and have forced significant policy shifts. From conservative states like Louisiana to traditionally progressive states like Michigan, from small states like New Mexico and Kansas to large states like California, all the big questions are up for debate: Should marijuana be decriminalized, at least for those with pressing medical needs? Should mandatory minimum sentences for low-level drug offenders be abandoned? Should prison terms for crimes of addiction be replaced by mandated treatment? Should governments fund needle exchanges and other harm-reduction programs for drug users as a way of controlling epidemics? Increasingly, at the local level, the answers are yes, yes, yes and yes.

In 1996 voters in Arizona passed Proposition 200, transferring thousands of drug offenders into treatment programs. In California, a similar initiative passed in 2000, Proposition 36, channeled tens of thousands of addicts into treatment—and reduced the number of inmates imprisoned on drug-possession charges from almost 20,000 at the time of the law's passage to just over 15,000 in June 2002.

In 1998 Michigan repealed its notorious "650-lifer" laws, which decreed a mandatory life sentence for those caught in possession of more than 650 grams of certain narcotics. Then, last

Christmas, Governor John Engler signed legislation rolling back the state's tough mandatory-minimum drug sentences and its equally tough "lifetime probation," which had been imposed on many drug offenders following their release from prison.

Early this year North Dakota repealed its one-year mandatory-minimum sentence for those convicted on a first-time drug-possession charge, as did Connecticut in 2001. Indiana and Louisiana have repealed some of their statutory sentences, and Louisiana has restored parole and probation options for inmates convicted of a host of nonviolent offenses.

15   In Kansas a sentencing commission has proposed major reforms of the state's mandatory sentencing codes coupled with an expansion of treatment provisions. Despite opposition from conservative legislators, these recommendations were accepted in late March. "It's definitely a change of philosophy regarding how you deal with drug offenders," says Barbara Tombs, executive director of the Kansas Sentencing Commission. "With the state budget cuts and [many] drug treatment programs in prisons being eliminated, there is an urgent need to look at alternatives to incarceration for drug prisoners."

At the same time, a clutch of states, including California, Washington, Oregon, Hawaii, Alaska and Nevada, have adopted medical marijuana legislation, legalizing the drug's use for specific medical conditions such as AIDS wasting, and a similar measure in Colorado was invalidated on a technicality.

Taken as a whole, these reforms represent the biggest change to state drug policies in more than a generation.

But while state legislatures have opened up the financial and moral debates about drug policy at the local level, the federal government is having none of it. The most recent Bureau of Justice Statistics data show that the number of people charged with drug offenses in federal courts rose sharply, from 11,854 in 1984 to 29,306 in 1999. During roughly the same period, the amount of time a federal drug prisoner could expect to serve in prison more than doubled, from thirty months to sixty-six months.

On many issues, from gun ownership to environmental regulation, the Bush team has backed the conservative cause of states' rights. But the Administration has blocked even mild attempts at state drug-law reform and has challenged state reformers over issues such as medical marijuana and needle exchange. The Justice Department has fought medical marijuana laws in court and launched a massive PR campaign against pot use. It has even pursued federal prosecution of those who legally distribute medical marijuana under state laws. Attorney General John Ashcroft is "willing to push even the smallest cases," says David Fratello, political director of the Campaign for New Drug Policies. "We're seeing a new level of pettiness and aggression."

Clinton's drug czar, Gen. Barry McCaffrey, was criticized by drug policy reformers for his refusal to discuss legalization initiatives and his zeal for militarizing the drug wars overseas. But these advocates find Bush's czar, John Walters, to be even worse. Under Walters's reign, the Office of National Drug Control Policy (ONDCP) has encouraged state prosecutors to go after medical marijuana providers, especially in California, and has driven underground virtually every medical-marijuana buyers' club in the country. It has held press conferences against citizens' reform initiatives. And it has sponsored extravagant advertising campaigns in state and local papers and on television stations—with $180 million earmarked for antimarijuana ads alone—that demonize teen drug use by linking it to terrorism.

Walters has also put pressure on state legislators, declaring that many drug-law reforms would contravene federal laws. In the fall 2002 elections, he traversed the country, stopping in Arizona, Michigan, Nevada and Ohio, campaigning against medical marijuana efforts and meeting with newspaper editors to push his case. The House version of the ONDCP Reauthorization Act originally included a provision that would have brought such politicking to a new level, allowing the White House to spend almost $1 billion in public money on ads attacking state and local ballot measures that promote drug-law reform. Interestingly, a Republican-led House committee removed that provision before approving the bill.

Yet in many ways Walters may be fighting yesterday's war on drugs. States like California, with its extensive system of medical-marijuana buyers' clubs, and New Mexico, with its public support for needle exchange, are beginning to shape up as the vanguard of a whole new approach to drug addiction.

In the poorest barrios of Albuquerque, teams of workers with Youth Development, Inc. (YDI) take their vans from one addict-client to another. Late into the night, they visit shooting galleries, ordinary private homes and the cardboard shelters constructed in alleyways by some of the city's homeless. At each, they reclaim dirty needles, fill in forms identifying the numbers returned, give out an equivalent number of clean needles, provide bottles of needle-cleaning solutions and also offer their clients HIV tests.

This was once a fairly underground operation. But now groups like YDI operate across the state with strong support and funding from New Mexico's Department of Health. All told, they distribute hundreds of thousands of clean needles per month to almost 7,000 card-carrying clients—and retrieve hundreds of thousands of dirty needles.

New Mexico's harm-reduction approach seems to be bearing fruit. A study from 1997 found that while the majority of the state's injection-drug users had been exposed to hepatitis C—suggesting that considerable needle-sharing was taking place—less than 1 percent of injection-drug users tested positive for HIV. Health experts saw a brief window of opportunity in which to create workable needle-exchange programs that could prevent HIV from spreading, as hepatitis C already had. So far, the programs appear to have worked: In a state with one of the largest per capita injection-drug-using populations in the country (New Mexico recorded 11.6 heroin deaths per 100,000 between 1993 and 1995, compared with a national average of 5.4 deaths per 100,000), the needle-exchange program has kept HIV to a bare minimum within the close-knit community of users. Department of Health experts estimate that even today, that number is around 11 percent—a low rate, compared with data from the federal Centers for Disease Control and Prevention showing that 27 percent of injection-drug users are HIV-positive in cities like Boston, Miami and Washington.

"My whole attitude about drugs and drug users has changed," says Rosie Clifford, a nurse who works in a public health center in the hardscrabble community of Los Lunas, twenty miles south of Albuquerque. "I used to be very conservative, very law and order. But even if you're really conservative, and you look at needle exchange, you ought to see it as a good way to stop the further spread of HIV and hepatitis and any blood-borne disease."

Danny, a twentysomething heroin addict, has been a client of YDI since 1999 and speaks with gratitude about the group's services. "I don't have to worry about used needles, about diseases," he says. "There was a time if I needed a new syringe I'd have to buy it for five bucks, and you don't know if it's new or not." YDI has provided Danny with health information, and, if he needs it, the group will arrange for a doctor to visit him at home.

Elsewhere in the state, in Rio Arriba County, near the nuclear laboratories of Los Alamos, public health workers are distributing not only needles but Narcan, an injected medication that can reverse the effects of a heroin overdose. So far, they believe they have saved about a dozen lives by training addicts in its use.

Many of the communities in this beautiful mountainous region are desperately poor. Often the roads are dusty and unpaved, dotted with impromptu altars set up in memory of those killed in car accidents—or murdered in battles over drugs and drug money. Heroin and methamphetamine addiction is so widespread here that in some houses, three generations of users share drugs with one another. Yet, while the police in many parts of the country routinely arrest users—and even level paraphernalia charges against addicts bringing dirty needles into exchange programs—in the town of Española, police chief Richard Guillen allows harm-reduction coordinators into his jail and encourages his officers to coax addicts to seek treatment.

Guillen believes that the old approach to drug addiction has failed: "All we're doing is interdiction at the federal level," he says, "and we haven't been successful in reducing demand." By contrast, he says, his local police have recognized that "an addiction to drugs is just like any other illness. Let's try to get them treatment, counseling. Without treatment, all we have is a revolving door."

In the 1980s and early '90s, faced with a growing crack epidemic and the attendant media reports of out-of-control drug gangs and waves of violent crime, the public threw its support behind extremely coercive antidrug policies. Then the crime rates began falling and, gradually, public attitudes began to soften. High-profile research projections and a growing cadre of advocacy groups—many, like the Lindesmith Center and the Drug Policy Foundation, funded by billionaire philanthropist George Soros—encouraged this shift in attitudes by suggesting that treatment was more effective than prison at lowering both addiction and crime. The advocacy groups drafted model reform legislation and promoted ballot initiatives like those that have diverted nonviolent drug offenders away from prisons in Arizona and California. The researchers produced numerous studies showing that it costs far less to place an addict in treatment than in prison—and that treatment has a higher success rate in breaking the addiction cycle. A survey conducted by the Pew Research Center in 2001 found that fully 73 percent of Americans favored permitting medical marijuana prescriptions; 47 percent favored rolling back mandatory-minimum sentences for nonviolent drug offenders; and 52 percent believed drug use should be treated as a disease rather than a crime. Faced with this grassroots shift, local elected officials, too, began to re-examine the beliefs and theories underlying America's antidrug strategy.

Ever since recession hit two years ago, these changes in thinking have been bolstered by fiscal realities. While the Bush

Administration may think it can fight a war on terror and run an occupation of Iraq while also cutting taxes and continuing the drug-war imprisonment boom, states are dealing with a more bitter reality. The Administration may want to devote resources to shutting down medical-marijuana buyers' clubs set up legally under new state laws, but states are no longer so enthusiastic. They are realizing that their budgets, buffeted by declining tax revenues, simply can't support major domestic-security spending and, at the same time, continued high expenditures on drug-war policing and mass incarceration. With drug treatment cheaper than incarceration and increasingly viable in the court of public opinion, drug-law reform is gaining ground despite federal intransigence. More and more elected officials are beginning to conclude that it's time to bring home the troops in the war on drugs as we know it. "Treatment instead of incarceration across the whole country has become a political safe ground," former Governor Johnson says. "It could not have been said safely prior to three years ago. Now it's totally safe."

Stabilizing the Text

1. Describe the tone of Abramsky's essay. Does it seem to you more like an objective report of facts or an opinion piece? Point to specific features or points in the essay to explain your answer.
2. What do you take to be Abramsky's overall point? How does the organization of the body of the essay—moving from state reform efforts to federal persistence in the drug war—work in favor of, or against, that point?
3. What attitudes toward drugs does Abramsky's essay reveal? How do attitudes toward drugs relate to overall attitudes toward crime in the United States? What are the consequences for our communities of our attitudes toward crime?

Mobilizing the Text

1. What circumstances or pressures does Abramsky indicate are most forcefully encouraging reform of drug laws? What pressures are discouraging reform? What do you think will become of attitudes toward drugs and drug laws in the future? Why?
2. Why does Abramsky believe it is time to think of the drug war as "one war we've lost"? What do you think of the proposal that we should come up with an alternative vocabulary for war through which to talk about our collective efforts to avoid the ill effects of drugs and addiction on individuals

and on society? Given Abramsky's description of reform efforts already under way, what key words might an alternative vocabulary feature?
3. Focusing on the views of political leaders at the state and federal levels, whose perspectives and attitudes has Abramsky neglected? How might inclusion of neglected voices support or undermine the view that it is time to call the war on drugs approach a failure?

Masked Racism: Reflections on the Prison Industrial Complex
ANGELA Y. DAVIS

Angela Y. Davis is a professor in the History of Consciousness Department at the University of California, Santa Cruz. In 1994, she received the distinguished honor of an appointment to the University of California Presidential Chair in African American and Feminist Studies. She has lectured throughout the world, and her articles and essays have appeared in numerous journals and anthologies. She is also the author of several books, including Angela Davis: An Autobiography; Women, Race, and Class; Blues Legacies and Black Feminism: Gertrude "Ma" Rainey, Bessie Smith, and Billie Holiday; The Angela Y. Davis Reader; *and* Are Prisons Obsolete? *In "Masked Racism: Reflections on the Prison Industrial Complex," which appeared originally in* Color Lines, *Davis analyzes one of the key consequences of current views of crime: an alarming expansion of incarceration. As you read Davis's essay, pay attention to her arguments concerning the social and economic costs of prisons. What does she think, and what do you think, causes people to choose to spend our limited public funds on prisons rather than on schools, drug programs, housing, and health care initiatives? What does she think, and what do you think, are the results of our attitudes and priorities when it comes to crime?*

◆

Imprisonment has become the response of first resort to far too many of the social problems that burden people who are ensconced in poverty. These problems often are veiled by being conveniently grouped together under the category "crime" and by the automatic attribution of criminal behavior to people of color.

Homelessness, unemployment, drug addiction, mental illness, and illiteracy are only a few of the problems that disappear from public view when the human beings contending with them are relegated to cages.

Prisons thus perform a feat of magic. Or rather the people who continually vote in new prison bonds and tacitly assent to a proliferating network of prisons and jails have been tricked into believing in the magic of imprisonment. But prisons do not disappear problems, they disappear human beings. And the practice of disappearing vast numbers of people from poor, immigrant, and racially marginalized communities has literally become big business.

The seeming effortlessness of magic always conceals an enormous amount of behind-the-scenes work. When prisons disappear human beings in order to convey the illusion of solving social problems, penal infrastructures must be created to accommodate a rapidly swelling population of caged people. Goods and services must be provided to keep imprisoned populations alive. Sometimes these populations must be kept busy and at other times—particularly in repressive super-maximum prisons and in INS detention centers—they must be deprived of virtually all meaningful activity. Vast numbers of handcuffed and shackled people are moved across state borders as they are transferred from one state or federal prison to another.

All this work, which used to be the primary province of government, is now also performed by private corporations, whose links to government in the field of what is euphemistically called "corrections" resonate dangerously with the military industrial complex. The dividends that accrue from investment in the punishment industry, like those that accrue from investment in weapons production, only amount to social destruction. Taking into account the structural similarities and profitability of business-government linkages in the realms of military production and public punishment, the expanding penal system can now be characterized as a "prison industrial complex."

THE COLOR OF IMPRISONMENT

5   Almost two million people are currently locked up in the immense network of U.S. prisons and jails. More than 70 percent of the imprisoned population are people of color. It is rarely acknowledged that the fastest growing group of prisoners are black women and that Native American prisoners are the largest group

per capita. Approximately five million people—including those on probation and parole—are directly under the surveillance of the criminal justice system.

Three decades ago, the imprisoned population was approximately one-eighth its current size. While women still constitute a relatively small percentage of people behind bars, today the number of incarcerated women in California alone is almost twice what the nationwide women's prison population was in 1970. According to Elliott Currie, "[t]he prison has become a looming presence in our society to an extent unparalleled in our history—or that of any other industrial democracy. Short of major wars, mass incarceration has been the most thoroughly implemented government social program of our time."

To deliver up bodies destined for profitable punishment, the political economy of prisons relies on racialized assumptions of criminality—such as images of black welfare mothers reproducing criminal children—and on racist practices in arrest, conviction, and sentencing patterns. Colored bodies constitute the main human raw material in this vast experiment to disappear the major social problems of our time. Once the aura of magic is stripped away from the imprisonment solution, what is revealed is racism, class bias, and the parasitic seduction of capitalist profit. The prison industrial system materially and morally impoverishes its inhabitants and devours the social wealth needed to address the very problems that have led to spiraling numbers of prisoners.

As prisons take up more and more space on the social landscape, other government programs that have previously sought to respond to social needs—such as Temporary Assistance to Needy Families—are being squeezed out of existence. The deterioration of public education, including prioritizing discipline and security over learning in public schools located in poor communities, is directly related to the prison "solution."

PROFITING FROM PRISONERS

As prisons proliferate in U.S. society, private capital has become enmeshed in the punishment industry. And precisely because of their profit potential, prisons are becoming increasingly important to the U.S. economy. If the notion of punishment as a source of potentially stupendous profits is disturbing by itself, then the strategic dependence on racist structures and ideologies to render mass punishment palatable and profitable is even more troubling.

10   Prison privatization is the most obvious instance of capital's current movement toward the prison industry. While government-run prisons are often in gross violation of international human rights standards, private prisons are even less accountable. In March of this year [2000], the Corrections Corporation of America (CCA), the largest U.S. private prison company, claimed 54,944 beds in 68 facilities under contract or development in the U.S., Puerto Rico, the United Kingdom, and Australia. Following the global trend of subjecting more women to public punishment, CCA recently opened a women's prison outside Melbourne. The company recently identified California as its "new frontier."

Wackenhut Corrections Corporation (WCC), the second largest U.S. prison company, claimed contracts and awards to manage 46 facilities in North America, U.K., and Australia. It boasts a total of 30,424 beds as well as contracts for prisoner health care services, transportation, and security.

Currently, the stocks of both CCA and WCC are doing extremely well. Between 1996 and 1997, CCA's revenues increased by 58 percent, from $293 million to $462 million. Its net profit grew from $30.9 million to $53.9 million. WCC raised its revenues from $138 million in 1996 to $210 million in 1997. Unlike public correctional facilities, the vast profits of these private facilities rely on the employment of non-union labor.

THE PRISON INDUSTRIAL COMPLEX

But private prison companies are only the most visible component of the increasing corporatization of punishment. Government contracts to build prisons have bolstered the construction industry. The architectural community has identified prison design as a major new niche. Technology developed for the military by companies like Westinghouse is being marketed for use in law enforcement and punishment.

Moreover, corporations that appear to be far removed from the business of punishment are intimately involved in the expansion of the prison industrial complex. Prison construction bonds are one of the many sources of profitable investment for leading financiers such as Merrill Lynch. MCI charges prisoners and their families outrageous prices for the precious telephone calls which are often the only contact prisoners have with the free world.

15   Many corporations whose products we consume on a daily basis have learned that prison labor power can be as profitable as third world labor power exploited by U.S.-based global corpora-

tions. Both relegate formerly unionized workers to joblessness and many even wind up in prison. Some of the companies that use prison labor are IBM, Motorola, Compaq, Texas Instruments, Honeywell, Microsoft, and Boeing. But it is not only the hi-tech industries that reap the profits of prison labor. Nordstrom department stores sell jeans that are marketed as "Prison Blues," as well as t-shirts and jackets made in Oregon prisons. The advertising slogan for these clothes is "made on the inside to be worn on the outside." Maryland prisoners inspect glass bottles and jars used by Revlon and Pierre Cardin, and schools throughout the world buy graduation caps and gowns made by South Carolina prisoners. "For private business," write Eve Goldberg and Linda Evans (a political prisoner inside the Federal Correctional Institution at Dublin, California) "prison labor is like a pot of gold. No strikes. No union organizing. No health benefits, unemployment insurance, or workers' compensation to pay. No language barriers, as in foreign countries. New leviathan prisons are being built on thousands of eerie acres of factories inside the walls. Prisoners do data entry for Chevron, make telephone reservations for TWA, raise hogs, shovel manure, make circuit boards, limousines, waterbeds, and lingerie for Victoria's Secret—all at a fraction of the cost of 'free labor.' "

DEVOURING THE SOCIAL WEALTH

Although prison labor—which ultimately is compensated at a rate far below the minimum wage—is hugely profitable for the private companies that use it, the penal system as a whole does not produce wealth. It devours the social wealth that could be used to subsidize housing for the homeless, to ameliorate public education for poor and racially marginalized communities, to open free drug rehabilitation programs for people who wish to kick their habits, to create a national health care system, to expand programs to combat HIV, to eradicate domestic abuse—and, in the process, to create well-paying jobs for the unemployed.

Since 1984 more than twenty new prisons have opened in California, while only one new campus was added to the California State University system and none to the University of California system. In 1996–97, higher education received only 8.7 percent of the State's General Fund while corrections received 9.6 percent. Now that affirmative action has been declared illegal in California, it is obvious that education is increasingly reserved for certain people, while prisons are reserved for others. Five times as many black men are presently in prison as in four-year colleges and universities. This new segregation has dangerous implications for the entire country.

By segregating people labeled as criminals, prison simultaneously fortifies and conceals the structural racism of the U.S. economy. Claims of low unemployment rates—even in black communities—make sense only if one assumes that the vast numbers of people in prison have really disappeared and thus have no legitimate claims to jobs. The numbers of black and Latino men currently incarcerated amount to two percent of the male labor force. According to criminologist David Downes, "[t]reating incarceration as a type of hidden unemployment may raise the jobless rate for men by about one-third, to 8 percent. The effect on the black labor force is greater still, raising the [black] male unemployment rate from 11 percent to 19 percent."

HIDDEN AGENDA

20   Mass incarceration is not a solution to unemployment, nor is it a solution to the vast array of social problems that are hidden away in a rapidly growing network of prisons and jails. However, the great majority of people have been tricked into believing in the efficacy of imprisonment, even though the historical record clearly demonstrates that prisons do not work. Racism has undermined our ability to create a popular critical discourse to contest the ideological trickery that posits imprisonment as key to public safety. The focus of state policy is rapidly shifting from social welfare to social control.

Black, Latino, Native American, and many Asian youth are portrayed as the purveyors of violence, traffickers of drugs, and as envious of commodities that they have no right to possess. Young black and Latina women are represented as sexually promiscuous and as indiscriminately propagating babies and poverty. Criminality and deviance are racialized. Surveillance is thus focused on communities of color, immigrants, the unemployed, the undereducated, the homeless, and in general on those who have a diminishing claim to social resources. Their claim to social resources continues to diminish in large part because law enforcement and penal measures increasingly devour these resources. The prison industrial complex has thus created a vicious cycle of punishment which only further impoverishes those whose impoverishment is supposedly "solved" by imprisonment.

Therefore, as the emphasis of government policy shifts from social welfare to crime control, racism sinks more deeply into the economic and ideological structures of U.S. society. Meanwhile, conservative crusaders against affirmative action and bilingual education proclaim the end of racism, while their opponents suggest that racism's remnants can be dispelled through dialogue and conversation. But conversations about "race relations" will hardly dismantle a prison industrial complex that thrives on and nourishes the racism hidden within the deep structures of our society.

The emergence of a U.S. prison industrial complex within a context of cascading conservatism marks a new historical moment, whose dangers are unprecedented. But so are its opportunities. Considering the impressive number of grassroots projects that continue to resist the expansion of the punishment industry, it ought to be possible to bring these efforts together to create radical and nationally visible movements that can legitimize anti-capitalist critiques of the prison industrial complex. It ought to be possible to build movements in defense of prisoners' human rights and movements that persuasively argue that what we need is not new prisons, but new health care, housing, education, drug programs, jobs, and education. To safeguard a democratic future, it is possible and necessary to weave together the many and increasing strands of resistance to the prison industrial complex into a powerful movement for social transformation.

Stabilizing the Text

1. In the sections of this essay, Davis explains several dimensions of the prison system that she believes can contribute to a full understanding of the role of prisons in U.S. society. What point or points does she make in each section? Combined, what kind of picture do they paint of prisons? As a reader, how effective do you find her strategy of breaking her view into sections with subheadings to be? What are the strengths and dangers of such an approach?

2. Using Davis's essay, explain her view of crime. How does her view compare to what you think is the dominant view of crime? What do you think are the strengths of each view?

3. Davis concludes her essay by arguing that we live in a time of "cascading conservatism . . . whose dangers are unprecedented. But so are its opportunities." What do you think of these conclusions? What unprecedented dangers do we face and what unprecedented opportunities? How are these evident in your communities?

Mobilizing the Text

1. Are you persuaded by this essay that prison expansion, rather than crime it-self, is the true threat to a secure, peaceful democracy? What parts of Davis's argument are or are not especially convincing to you and why?

2. Davis uses "magic" and words associated with it throughout this essay to describe the cultural work performed by prisons. Make a list of her uses of these terms. How do they work to support her perspective?

3. In this essay, Davis offers a view of prisons that challenges fundamental assumptions about a taken-for-granted part of our society. Is this kind of questioning valuable? In what ways do you think it demonstrates the purpose of public writing in a democratic society? In what ways do you think it fails to fulfill the purposes of public writing?

CHAPTER 3

Cities and Suburbs

By the 1920s, most older cities in the United States had spawned a handful of close-lying suburbs. By the 1950s, the baby boom was in full swing and suburban areas encircled all major American cities, providing affordable homes for a new generation of families. Between the 1920s and 1950s, little new housing had been built in the United States. Cities such as New York City, Chicago, St. Louis, and Atlanta had become overcrowded, making any kind of housing both difficult to find and very expensive. The suburbs as we know them today were first developed in the 1950s to ease overcrowding and to accommodate the increased demand for single-family homes among veterans returning from World War II. As many families moved to the new suburbs for a chance to live the American dream, many of them also looked to the suburbs as an escape from the social problems of big cities.

The quality of life in suburban areas has changed dramatically in the past 50 years. During the 1950s, the suburbs were primarily places where people lived, while cities remained places where people worked. Today, the suburbs are places where people live and work, where they shop, where they visit the doctor, where they do all the things they once did in cities. Today, suburban areas have grown so large that they often seem like cities unto themselves. As more and more people move into suburban areas, and as the suburbs move farther and farther away from old city centers, we increasingly view suburban areas less as suburbs and more as the new American cities. As the new American cities, suburban areas divert businesses and tax dollars away from older cities, such as Pittsburgh, Indianapolis, and Baltimore. In fact, many people who live in the suburbs now rarely, if ever, go into the major urban center in their area, avoiding the old city be-cause it appears abandoned and crime-ridden, or run-down with nothing to offer. While it may be true that many urban centers are struggling, the urbanization of suburban areas has introduced ur-ban problems into the suburbs as well—problems such as crime, poverty, and overcrowding. Where people once moved to subur-ban areas to escape urban problems, people now move away from closer-in suburbs, farther and farther out into newly developed areas in an attempt to escape the problems that seem to follow them. Doing so, they create additional problems by encroaching on rural environments and habitats and by altering rural lifestyles.

Today, suburban development stretches for many miles around major American cities. If you live in an area such as Atlanta or San Diego, you know the suburbs stretch for miles in every direction, reaching into other counties, into other states, or, in the case of San Diego, into another country. We have all heard the term "urban sprawl." The term expresses the common percep-tion that the spread of urban spaces has gotten out of hand. The term also expresses the fact that, as a result of widespread and rapid growth, the suburbs are now the cultural, professional, and residential centers of contemporary life. So, when you read and write about cities and suburbs and their relationship, you are in-vestigating a topic significant to everyone. The writers whose es-says are collected in this chapter examine both the history and current state of cities and suburbs and their relationship. Through their discussions of the impact of suburbanization on the lifestyles of Americans, these authors consider such issues as sense of community and beliefs about political responsibility.

In "Stressed Out in Suburbia," Nicholas Lemann provides a historical perspective on the evolution of the suburbs through his description of Naperville, Illinois. Comparing Naperville in the 1950s to Naperville in the 1980s, Lemann finds parallels between increased urbanization in suburbia and rising stress among sub-urban residents. David J. Dent provides a different historical per-spective in "The New Black Suburbs." Dent describes the emergence of black suburbs in the 1980s and 1990s in terms of the continuing struggle for civil rights among middle- and upper-middle-class African Americans.

David Moberg describes the negative consequences of subur-banization on major American cities, such as Dallas, Philadelphia, and New York City. He argues for a recommitment to community in "Separate and Unequal." Moberg documents how the suburban separation from cities generates inequalities that spell economic and social loss for both cities and suburbs. He concludes that suburban reinvestment in cities is to everyone's mutual benefit.

Finally, Jan Rosenberg blurs the line between city life and suburban life in "Park Slope: Notes on a Middle Class 'Utopia.' " She describes her gentrified Brooklyn neighborhood as "postsuburban." Rosenberg sees in Park Slope a neighborhood representing an improvement on both traditional urban and suburban lifestyles.

In reading these essays, you will have an opportunity to consider several questions about suburbanization and urban sprawl: What forces have caused suburbanization in the United States? How do these forces continue to shape our lives and influence the choices we make? Also, how and why have the suburbs changed over the past few decades? What impact do changes in the suburbs have on our perceptions of cities? What are the relationships created between cities and suburbs by the processes of suburbanization? Does it make sense for us to talk about cities being left behind or abandoned? Or, does it make more sense for us to talk of large metropolitan areas, consisting of center cities and surrounding suburbs, as the new cities? You will also have an opportunity to reflect on people's reactions to suburbanization. For instance, do suburban residents have an economic or moral responsibility for what happens in inner cities? Is suburbanization in the United States a change for better or for worse? Or is change just change, neither good nor bad?

As you read the essays in this chapter, it will be useful to reflect on these and other questions, providing for yourself tentative answers to important issues of how we talk and write about our lives together and what that talking and writing do. Overall, the authors of these essays are asking you to think about how language—such as "pursuing the American dream" or "abandoning cities"—shapes what we think suburbanization means. The authors are also encouraging you to consider how our uses of such language persuade others to have certain beliefs about the changes suburbanization has wrought on American metropolitan areas.

Stressed Out in Suburbia
NICHOLAS LEMANN

Nicholas Lemann is a national correspondent for the Atlantic *and Henry R. Luce Professor at the Columbia University Graduate School of Journalism. He is a prolific essayist and author of several books, including* The Promised Land: The Great Black Migration and How It Changed America *and* The Big Test: The Secret History of the American Meritocracy. *In "Stressed Out in Suburbia," originally published in the* Atlantic, *Lemann describes Naperville, Illinois, a suburb 30 miles west of Chicago. Comparing and contrasting the suburbs of the 1950s with Naperville in the 1980s, Lemann emphasizes the lifestyle changes that have occurred in suburban America over the last 40 years. In particular, Lemann finds that people today move to the suburbs for many of the same reasons people moved to the suburbs 40 years ago. Despite their motivations, Lemann concludes that life in the suburbs has changed dramatically, leaving people less than satisfied with their lifestyles. As you read this essay, keep the title, "Stressed Out in Suburbia," in mind. Use it to help you identify the main points of the essay. This is one way for you to evaluate the kinds of stresses documented by Lemann.*

--- ✦ ---

I recently spent some time in Naperville, Illinois, because I wanted to see exactly how our familiar ideas about the suburbs have gotten out of date. Naperville is thirty miles west of the Chicago Loop. It had 7,000 residents in 1950, 13,000 in 1960, 22,600 in 1970, and 42,600 in 1980, and just in this decade it has nearly doubled in population again, to 83,000. . . . Driving there from Chicago, you pass through the West Side ghetto, the site of riots in the late sixties, and then through a belt of older suburbs at the city limits. Just when the suburbs seem to be dying out, you arrive in Oak Brook, with its collection of new shopping malls and office towers. The seventeen-mile stretch from Oak Brook west through Naperville to the old railroad city of Aurora has the look of inexplicable development common to booming areas that were recently rural. Subdivisions back up onto cornfields. Mirrored-glass office parks back up onto convenience-store parking lots. Most of the trees are saplings.

The history of Naperville as an urban village begins in 1964, when AT&T decided to build a major facility there for its research division, Bell Labs, along the new Interstate 88. Before that, as the next-to-last stop on the Burlington & Northern line from Chicago, Naperville attracted some hardy long-distance commuters, but it was mainly an independent small town, with frame houses and streets laid out in a grid.

Bell Labs opened in 1966 and is still by far the largest employer in Naperville—7,000 people work there, developing electronic switching systems, and another 3,000 work at a software-development center in the neighboring town of Lisle. In 1969 Amoco moved its main research-and-development facility from the industrial town of Whiting, Indiana, to a site in Naperville along the interstate, near Bell Labs. Today more than 2,000 people work there. All through the seventies and eighties businesses have built low-slung, campus-style office complexes up and down I-88, which Governor James R. Thompson in 1986 officially subtitled "The Illinois Research and Development Corridor." There are now four big chain hotels on the five-mile stretch that runs through Lisle and Naperville. In Aurora, Nissan, Hyundai, and Toyota have all established distribution centers, and four insurance companies have set up regional headquarters.

In the fifties the force driving the construction of residential neighborhoods in the suburbs was that prosperity had given young married couples the means to act on their desire to raise children away from the cities. In the eighties in Naperville there is still some of this, but the real driving force is that so many jobs are there. Dozens of new residential subdivisions fan out in the area south of the office complexes and the old town center. In this part of town, whose land Naperville aggressively annexed, the school district has built three new elementary schools since 1984 and added to seven others. A new junior high school opened this fall, another one is under construction, and last spring the town's voters passed a bond issue to build another elementary school and additions to two high schools.

In *The Organization Man*, William Whyte was struck by how 5 removed the place he studied—Park Forest, Illinois, the fifties equivalent of Naperville, brand-new and also thirty miles from the Loop—was from Chicago and from urban forms of social organization. Naperville is even more removed, mainly because downtown commuters are a small minority of the new residents. Nearly everybody in Park Forest worked in Chicago. Only five thousand people take the train from the Naperville station into

Chicago every day; most people work in Naperville or in a nearby suburban town. The people I talked to in Naperville knew that they were supposed to go into Chicago for the museums, theater, music, and restaurants, so they were a little defensive about admitting to staying in Naperville in their free time, but most of them do. Though Naperville has many white ethnics (and a few blacks and Asians), it has no ethnic neighborhoods. There are ethnic restaurants, but many of them are the kind that aren't run by members of that ethnic group. Naperville is politically conservative but has no Democratic or Republican organizations active in local politics. Nobody who can afford a house lives in an apartment. There are only a few neighborhood taverns. Discussions of Chicago focus on how much crime is there, rather than on the great events of municipal life.

In distancing itself from Chicago, Naperville has continued a trend that was already well under way in Whyte's Park Forest. Otherwise, most of the ways in which Naperville is different from Whyte's Park Forest and places like it were not predicted by the suburbia experts of the time.

Naperville is much more materially prosperous, and at the same time more anxious about its standard of living, than Park Forest was. The comparison isn't exact, because Park Forest was a middle-middle-class community dominated by people in their late twenties and early thirties; Naperville is more affluent and has a somewhat fuller age range. Nonetheless, since Naperville is the fastest-growing town in the area, it can fairly be said to represent the slice of American life that is expanding most rapidly right now, as Park Forest could in the fifties. The typical house in Park Forest cost $13,000 and had one story (the most expensive house there by far, where the developer lived, cost $50,000). The average house in Naperville costs $160,000 and the figure is higher in the new subdivisions. Plenty of new houses in town cost more than $500,000. Most of the new houses in Naperville have two stories; in fact, the small section of fifties and sixties suburbia in Naperville is noticeably more modest than the new housing.

Obviously one reason for the difference is that Park Forest in the early fifties was only a very few years into the postwar boom, which left the middle class vastly better off than it had been before. Another is that the consumer culture was young and undeveloped in the fifties. Middle-class people today want to own things that their parents wouldn't have dreamed of.

The affluence of Naperville is also a byproduct of what is probably the single most important new development in middle-class life since the fifties (and one almost wholly unanticipated in the fifties), which is that women work. Park Forest was an exclusively female town on weekdays; when Whyte wrote about the difficulty of being a "superwoman," he meant combining housework with civic and social life. In Naperville I heard various statistics, but it seems safe to say that most mothers of young children work, and the younger the couple, the likelier it is that the wife works. When *Business Week* did a big story on the "mommy track" last spring, it used a picture of a woman from Naperville. What people in Naperville seem to focus on when they think about working mothers is not that feminism has triumphed in the Midwest but that two-career couples have more money and less time than one-career couples.

In the classic suburban literature almost no reference is made to punishingly long working hours. The Cheever story whose title is meant to evoke the journey home at the end of the working day is called "The Five Forty-Eight," and its hero is taking that late a train only because he stopped in at a bar for a couple of Gibsons on the way from his office to Grand Central Station. In Naperville the word "stress" came up constantly in conversations. People felt that they had to work harder than people a generation ago in order to have a good middle-class life. In much of the rest of the country the idea holds sway that the middle class is downwardly mobile and its members still never live as well as their parents did. Usually this complaint involves an inexact comparison—the complainer is at an earlier stage in his career, works in a less remunerative field, or lives in a pricier place than the parents who he thinks lived better than he does. In Naperville, where most people are in business, it's more a case of people's material expectations being higher than their parents' than of their economic station being lower. A ranch-style tract house, a Chevrolet, and meat loaf for dinner will not do any more as the symbols of a realized dream. Also, a changed perception of the future of the country has helped create the sense of pressure in Naperville. Suburbanites of the fifties were confident of a constantly rising standard of living, level of education, and gross national product in a way that most Americans haven't been since about the time of the 1973 OPEC embargo. The feeling is that anyone who becomes prosperous has beaten the odds.

It is jarring to think of placid-looking Naperville as excessively fast-paced, but people there talk as if the slack had been taken out of life. They complain that between working long hours, traveling on business, and trying to stay in shape they have no free time. The under-the-gun feeling applies to domestic life as

well as to work. It's striking, in reading the old suburban literature today, to see how little people worried about their children.
Through many scenes of drunkenness, adultery, and domestic
discord, the kids seem usually to be playing, oblivious, in the
front yard. Today there is a national hyperawareness of the life-
long consequences of childhood unhappiness (hardly an issue of
People magazine fails to make this point); the feeling that
American children can coast to a prosperous adulthood has been
lost; and the entry of mothers into the work force has made child
care a constant worry for parents. The idea that childhood can
operate essentially on autopilot has disappeared.

The most reliable connection between subdivision residents
and the community is children. Adults meet through the children's activities. I often heard that new neighborhoods coalesce
around new elementary schools, which have many parent-involv-
ing activities and are also convenient places to hold meetings. The
churches (mostly Protestant and Catholic, but the town has
places of worship for Jews and even Muslims) have made an effort to perform some of the same functions—there is always a
new church under construction, and eight congregations are operating out of rented space. The Reverend Keith Torney, who recently left the First Congregational Church in Naperville, after
eighteen years, for a pulpit in Billings, Montana, told me, "We try
to create a community where people can acquire roots very
quickly. We divided the congregation into twelve care groups.
Each has twenty to thirty families. They kind of take over for
neighbors and grandma—they bring the casserole when you're
sick. People come here for a sense of warmth, for a sense that
people care about you."

There isn't any hard information on where new Naperville
residents come from or where departing ones go. Most of the people I met had moved to Naperville from elsewhere in the Chicago
area, often from the inner-ring suburbs. They came there to be
closer to their jobs along I-88, because the schools are good and
the crime rate is low, and because Naperville is a place where the
person who just moved to town is not an outsider but the dominant figure in the community. If they leave, it's usually because of
a new job, not always with the same company; the amount of
company-switching, and of entrepreneurship, appears to be
greater today than it was in the fifties. Several of the new office
developments in the area have the word *corporate* in their names.
(I stayed in a hotel on Corporetum Drive.) Since the likes of AT&T
and Arnoco don't call attention to themselves in this way, the use

of the word is probably a sign of the presence of new businesses. People's career restlessness, and companies' desire to appear regally established right away, are further examples of the main message I got from my time in Naperville: the suburbs and, by extension, middle-class Americans have gone from glorifying group bonding to glorifying individual happiness and achievement.

The bad side of this change in ethos should be obvious right now: Americans appear to be incapable of the social cohesion and the ability to defer gratification which are prerequisites for the success of major national efforts. But a good side exists too. Representations of middle-class life in the fifties are pervaded with a sense of the perils of appearing to be "different." William Whyte wrote a series of articles for *Fortune,* and the photographs that Dan Weiner took to illustrate them (which are included in *America Worked,* a new book of Weiner's photographs) communicate this feeling even more vividly than *The Organization Man* does: the suburban kaffeeklatsch and the executive's office come across as prisons. There can't be much doubt that the country is more tolerant now than it was then.

Stabilizing the Text

1. What specific stresses does Lemann identify? Are these some of the same stresses you can either imagine or have experienced as associated with living in suburbia? What additional stresses can you associate with suburban living today? Are these stresses enough to "stress someone out"?

2. Lemann argues that the stresses created by extra activities involved in living in the suburbs stress people out. Find a passage in the essay in which Lemann relates activity to stress. What is the connection between doing something and experiencing stress? Is it an explicit connection? Or is it more implicit? Does the relationship make sense to you as a reader? Why?

3. Lemann concludes his essay by claiming that suburbs such as Naperville have become both better and worse than they were in the 1950s. How can the suburbs be both better and worse at the same time? How do you understand Lemann to be using the words "better" and "worse"? Do you consider his conclusion ambivalent? Or is he being ironic? Do you find this kind of conclusion satisfying? Is it somehow more appropriate to have an ambivalent or ironic conclusion than to have a direct and decisive declaration?

Mobilizing the Text

1. A lot of things stress people out. Many of the stresses are built into the environment around us. At the same time, there are a lot of things in our environments that we desire, such as easy access to parks or favorite

restaurants. Can we ever find a balance between putting up with the things that stress us out and getting the things that help us relax? According to Lemann, the people of Naperville could not find a satisfactory balance between what they put up with and what they wanted. Why is that? Where did they go wrong?

2. Lemann traces the evolution of the suburban dream as it is lived in Naperville over the course of 40 years. What is that dream? Do you think that it is still with us today? We may no longer call it the suburban dream, we might call it something else, but what we long for could still be some version of what the people in Naperville long for. What do the similarities and differences in our dreams and theirs say about us and the choices we make?

3. Does Lemann give us any indication of the strategies used by Naperville residents for coping with stress? What indication does Lemann give of these strategies getting woven into the fabric of daily life in Naperville? What kinds of coping strategies do you use or have you observed used by people who live their life at a fast pace? How successful would you say these coping strategies are? In the essay and in real life, are people simply doing what they need to do to get by or are they making significant changes in their lifestyles? What sense do you make of these choices?

The New Black Suburbs
DAVID J. DENT

David J. Dent teaches journalism and mass communication at New York University. He publishes frequently on African-American culture, education, and media in such publications as Black Renaissance Noire *and the* New York Times Magazine. *"The New Black Suburbs" was originally published in the* New York Times Magazine *and won the New York Association of Black Journalists Award for Excellence in Magazine Journalism in 1992. In "The New Black Suburbs," Dent describes the predominantly African-American suburbs that have grown across the country since the 1970s. His discussion of one predominantly African-American suburb, Prince George's County, Maryland, provides one explanation for the choices made by many middle- and upper-middle-class African Americans to not move into white suburbs. As you read "The New Black Suburbs," pay particular attention to the tensions between assimilation and segregation that pull at financially successful African Americans. Think as well about the nature of the suburban dream in the real world.*

———————— ✦ ————————

Ageneration ago, peaceful civil rights demonstrators faced violent resistance in the fight for a racially integrated society. Years later, Barron and Edith Harvey, who are black, would embody the hopes of that struggle. In 1978, the couple moved into a white, upper-middle-income neighborhood in Fairfax County, Va., a suburb of Washington. During their seven years there, no crosses were burned in their yard and no racial epithets were muttered at them within earshot. There were a few incredulous stares, a few stops by the police, who had mistaken Barron for a criminal, and a run-in with an elementary school principal over the absence of blacks in the curriculum at the Harveys' daughter's school.

"You expect those kinds of things in a white neighborhood, and, all things being equal, we would have stayed," says Barron Harvey, chairman of the accounting department at Howard University and an international business consultant.

But the Harveys left in 1985—not because Fairfax was inhospitable, but because they wanted to become part of another Washington suburb, Prince George's County in Maryland. Prince George's—a county that George Wallace won in the 1972 Presidential primary—was fast becoming the closest thing to utopia that black middle-class families could find in America.

What some consider the essence of the American dream—suburbia—became a reality for a record number of blacks in the 1980's. In 1990, 32 percent of all black Americans in metropolitan areas lived in suburban neighborhoods, a record 6 percent increase from 1980, according to William H. Frey, a demographer at the University of Michigan Population Studies Center specializing in population and racial redistribution patterns. As an increasing number of black Americans head for the suburban dream, some are bypassing another dream—the dream of an integrated society. These black Americans are moving to *black* upper- and middle-class neighborhoods, usually pockets in counties that have a white majority.

The growing popularity of these neighborhoods over the past 5 decade has coincided with the increasing enrollment at black colleges and booming interest in African and African-American history, art, music and literature. These trends seem to represent a retreat from the days of the early post-civil-rights era, when status in the black community was often tied to one's entree into the once-forbidden worlds of white America.

Black suburbs have sprung up across the country. In the Miami area, there is Rolling Oaks in Dade County. Around St. Louis, black suburbs exist in sections of Black Jack, Jennings, Normandy and University City in St. Louis County. In the Atlanta suburbs, black majority communities include Brook Glen, Panola Mill and Wyndham Park in DeKalb County. And in the Washington area, Prince George's County itself has a black majority.

Racial steering, though illegal, may lead some blacks in the Washington area to the predominantly black neighborhoods of Prince George's. But for most, it is a deliberate, affirmative choice.

"I don't want to come home and always have my guard up," says David S. Ball, a senior contract administrator who works on railroad projects in the Washington area. Ball and his wife, Phillis, moved from Washington to a predominantly black subdivision in Fort Washington, Md. "After I work eight hours or more a day," he says, "I don't want to come home and work another eight."

Ball says his family didn't have to live in an *all*-black neighborhood. Currently, Ball says, his block comprises seven black families and three white families.

10   Barron Harvey adds: "We always wanted to make sure our child had many African-American children to play with, not just one or two. We always wanted to be in a community with a large number of black professionals, and to feel part of that community. We never really felt like we were part of Fairfax."

For some Prince Georgians, like Radamase Cabrera, 39, one reason for the move was a profound sense of disillusionment.

"I think the integration of black folks in the 60's was one of the biggest cons in the world," says Cabrera, an urban planner for the city of Washington. Cabrera was one of a small number of blacks attending the University of Connecticut at Storrs in 1970. "I was called a nigger the first week there and held by the police until this white girl told them I hadn't attacked her. You want to call me a separatist, so be it. I think of myself as a pragmatist. Why should I beg some cracker to integrate me into his society when he doesn't want to? Why keep beating my head up against a wall, especially when I've been there."

While the racial balance of Prince George's population of 729,268 may indicate an integrated county—50.7 percent black, 43.1 percent white, 6.2 percent other—census data suggest a segregated county. More than half of all the census tracts in Prince George's are at least 70 percent white or 70 percent black. Some experts predict the county will be two-thirds black by the end of the century.

Some white residents prefer to see the county serve as a model for true integration.

"Here we have a place that is nearly 50-50," says Margery A. 15
Turner, a white resident and senior research associate, specializing in housing for the Urban Institute. "We should be using this opportunity to show the country there are places where integration can work. I'm not suggesting we limit blacks. But I do think we should avoid resegregating. Separateness sustains prejudice, which sustains inequality."

Cabrera, however, disagrees. "What I reject is this notion that we are aiming toward an integrated county," he says. "African-Americans should be aiming toward an ability to control our own destiny."

The changing racial composition of Prince George's is not immediately evident when entering the county on Route 495, known throughout the Washington area as the Beltway. Many of the exits off the Beltway lead to neighborhoods with names like Enterprise Estates and Paradise Acres—subdivisions stocked exclusively with single-family houses for middle- and upper-income families. The county's transformation becomes clear when you enter those neighborhoods and see that most of the girls jumping rope on the sidewalk and most of the boys dribbling basketballs in driveways are black.

Ben Jones, a real-estate agent who lives in Prince George's County, is riding by the manicured lawns and well-kept colonial and ranch-style houses of Paradise Acres. He identifies house sales he has made by the profession of the buyer: a vice president of the World Bank, an assistant superintendent of schools, lawyers, professors and doctors.

Jones went on his own search for a black neighborhood in 1980. While riding through a then-undeveloped Mitchellville section, he saw four elaborate full-brick, four-bedroom ranch houses, a trailer and a black man walking out of the trailer. He decided to stop and introduce himself to the man, who turned out to be a realtor. "I assumed it would become a black neighborhood because there was a black real-estate agent," Jones says. Today all but a handful of the 83 families in that subdivision, Paradise Acres, are black.

Jones, a nuclear-weapons specialist at the Department of 20
Energy at the time, had been living in an all-white working-class neighborhood in Upper Marlboro, the county seat, for a decade. When he moved to Mitchellville, he saw a business opportunity in the large number of blacks moving into the county and eventually quit his government job to become a full-time real-estate agent.

He has sold 355 homes throughout Prince George's County—all to blacks, with the exception of about four sales to whites. "I don't exclude whites," says Jones. "But most of my sales come from contacts and referrals. There are few whites who will come to a black agent."

The black presence in Prince George's County can be traced to the late 17th century, when blacks were forced into the county as slaves. "Many eventually owned land, and many of their children are still here," says Alvin Thornton, a professor of political science at Howard University who has lived in the county for 20 years.

Descendants of those original black families have lived through segregation, the county's resistance to open housing laws in the late 1960's, court-ordered busing and fears of violence. David Ball remembers that Prince George's was viewed as a rural county full of "rednecks" in which the few pockets of blacks were subjected to police brutality and a citizenry that lived by a brand of justice loaded with "good old boy" rules. Ball never thought he would cherish living in the county he once regarded as racist. Even three years ago, when he and his wife began looking seriously at suburbia, Prince George's County wasn't on the list. They first looked at houses in Montgomery County, but they couldn't find a neighborhood that combined good value for their money and a neighborhood with a significant black presence.

"I really wasn't interested in moving into an all-white neighborhood and being the only black pioneer down there," Ball says.

Harold and Patricia Alexander have grown with Prince George's County. Patricia Alexander's mother, Claudia Sims, bought a town-house condominium in Prince George's County in the early 1970's. Harold Alexander was a premed student at Howard University at the time; Patricia was supporting them both with her salary as a secretary at the university. The couple moved into the county, and the second bedroom of Claudia Sims's town house became the Alexanders' home.

25   Their migration was part of a population boom, stimulated by the rapid construction of garden apartments and condominiums in the late 1960's and early 1970's. Like the Alexanders, many of the new black residents didn't go deep into the county. Instead, many moved to communities closer to the predominantly black Southeast Washington border.

"When we first moved into the county, it was very uncomfortable," says Patricia Alexander. "We heard stories about the police and racism. So, you know, you go to work, you come home and lock the door."

The new black residents of the 1970's laid the base that eventually drew large numbers of blacks in the 1980's. "You have to look at it in two stages," says Thornton, who has studied the county's migration patterns. "The great surge in the 70's came because many blacks were doing what other people were doing. They wanted better schools, more space, a backyard and less density. But that first period was met with massive white resistance, police brutality and court-ordered busing."

The second stage was inadvertently propelled by the county's Economic Development Corporation. It tried to entice developers to create industries and build houses that would woo white-collar professionals. The selling points of the county were these: the cheaper rural land of Prince George's contrasted with the overdeveloped tracts in neighboring counties; Prince George's road-improvement plan, and the presence of the Goddard Space Flight Center, the world's largest space research facility, Andrews Air Force Base and the University of Maryland at College Park. The campaign reaped $10 billion in new investments in the county, which included the construction of homes for mid- to high-level executives.

Diana V. Jackson, director of development for the corporation, says the majority of those new homeowners were blacks—something that startled the county's white leadership, according to many political activists and black realtors.

"The county officials underestimated the money within the black middle class in Washington," says Larry Lucas, a Washington lobbyist and former minority-population specialist for the Census Bureau. "It's one of the largest concentrations of middle-class blacks in the country. A lot of the subdivisions were really built for whites, but before whites could come out and buy them, black folks were coming in and buying them and when blacks started buying them, whites wouldn't look at them."

After four years of living in the county, the Alexanders, who by now had two children, were comfortable with the idea of moving farther from the Washington border. In 1977 they moved into a middle-income neighborhood of new four-bedroom split-level homes, and found virtually all the residents on their block were like them.

"The second stage was not met with that resistance because you had some white flight and a coming of age of black identity in the county," says Thornton. "There was a critical enough mass of black people by the 80's so blacks could feel they were a part of the county. That's when you get people who move here because they want to live in a black community."

Harold Alexander has benefited from the influx of blacks. His medical practice has increased, and four months ago, the Alexanders made another move inside the county—this time into a $1 million mansion.

The increasing number of blacks in the county and pressure from the N.A.A.C.P. have led to major changes in the police department, where 37 percent of the force is now black, compared with 8 percent in 1978. For many, fear of police brutality has nearly vanished.

35   Hodarl Abdul-Ali, who owns a chain of bookstores in the area, says, "I know that what happened to Rodney King can happen anywhere, but there's much less likelihood of it happening here."

Abdul-Ali's main store had been located near Howard University in Washington. Two years ago, after Abdul-Ali noticed an increasing number of customers were coming from Prince George's County, he opened a store there. It outsells his four other stores.

Barron Harvey visits the store at least twice a month, and the books he buys often become grist for conversations at the family's summer pool parties, when the Harveys' backyard is full of neighborhood friends. Edith Harvey, who lived in predominantly white towns all her life, says that in Prince George's, neighbors have comprised the core of her social life for the first time. The Harveys seldom entertained when they lived in Fairfax, but today they have people over at least twice a month.

"When I'm socializing with people who are not African-American, I have to do a lot of explaining," says Edith Harvey, an education specialist for the Department of Education. "It's stressful because you know it's your responsibility to educate whites who have a sincere interest in understanding an issue. But it's more like work when you should just be socializing. If it's a black social setting, it's more like sharing ideas than educating."

The social networks that provide a forum to share ideas in Prince George's have grown over the past decade. Churches and traditional black middle-class social and professional organizations—like the Links, Jack and Jill and graduate chapters of black fraternities and sororities—have increased their membership in the county, some by as much as fourfold.

40   The Ebenezer African Methodist Episcopal Church has revitalized itself by moving its congregation to Prince George's.

Membership at the 136-year-old church had dwindled to fewer than 100 members. Since the relocation from Washington in 1983, membership has grown to nearly 7,000, and donations have provided $10 million for the construction of a new church building.

Ebenezer holds forums every month, during which many Prince Georgians hear about the latest news and battles in the county's school system. The school system is now 66 percent black, compared with 22 percent in 1971–72. There is widespread agreement among black and white parents to move away from busing as a means of achieving racial balance, which doesn't occur naturally, because of residential separation in Prince George's. Many parents want the school system to continue to build its nationally lauded magnet programs, which feature specialized classes meant to attract a diverse student population.

But there is dissension over the new multicultural curriculum: many white parents object to it, while some black parents are pushing for an Afrocentric approach.

"I believe it's the next step in the battle," says the Rev. Dr. Granger Browning, pastor of Ebenezer and an advocate for an Afrocentric curriculum in the public schools. "It's a fight for our children, and we will win."

Radamase Cabrera and his wife, Denise, a reporter for The Associated Press, moved to Prince George's County in 1987, settling in a formerly all-white working-class neighborhood where blacks were becoming the majority. "It was about 50-50 then, and I knew it was only a matter of time before the white folks would leave and you'd have yourself a nice suburban African-American community."

For Cabrera, life in Prince George's County has become part 45 of a mission. Though he works in Washington, he has become an outspoken activist in his community—consumed with its demographic, political and economic statistics. "Prince George's County will be, if it is not already, the most educated and affluent African-American community on the planet, and it has the opportunity to be a model of how black folks can control their political, economic and social institutions," Cabrera says. "This place is unique because usually black folks inherit things like a Newark or a Gary when it's depressed and all the wealth is gone and it has no potential."

Prince George's now has more than 8,000 black-owned businesses. Financing for the smaller businesses—beauty parlors and home-based companies—often comes from a black-owned bank and a black-controlled savings and loan in Washington. Some of the county's larger black-owned companies—high-tech firms and a million-dollar-a-year trash-hauling business—have received financing for expansion by established banks in the county.

Although commercial development in the county has grown, many retailers have declined the county's invitations to open stores there while entering counties with a lower median income but a larger white population. Nordstrom and Macy's have opened stores in Baltimore County, which had a median household income of $38,837, compared with $43,127 in Prince George's County in 1989. But Baltimore County is 85 percent white. Many Prince George's shoppers, like Linda Williams-Brown, often ride two counties away to shop, pouring tax dollars into other communities. "For me to go to a nice mall with a Saks and a Macy's, I have to go all the way to Virginia," Williams-Brown says. "When they put new stores in the shopping centers here, they put in a T.J. Maxx, in a place like Mitchellville, across the street from $200,000 and $300,000 homes that black people own. Why?"

Daniel Russell, who spent 20 years as a private developer based in the Washington area and who now runs a development-training institute and consulting firm, has spent the past five years meeting with retailers, trying to bring them into the county. "In meetings, they say they don't know how to merchandise to a market like this or how to do promotion for this market or other excuses, like the people won't buy the merchandise, when what you have is people going to other counties to buy the merchandise."

An editorial in *The Prince George's County Journal* last year implied retailers like Saks Fifth Avenue and Bloomingdale's were snubbing the county. Spokesmen for both stores deny race is a factor. Some white county officials say the county's image still carries the baggage of its blue-collar days. "We've just now become a white-collar community with a large expendable income," says Prince George's county executive, Parris N. Glendening, who is expected to enter the 1994 Maryland race for governor. "The market hasn't caught up to us. But it will."

50   However, Douglas Massey, a professor of sociology at the University of Chicago, would not be surprised if it did not. "I think that a group that raises residential segregation to be an ideal is going to cut itself off from many of the benefits of society," he says. "You make it easier for the larger white population to eventually decapitalize it, and it basically becomes an easy target for racist attitudes. It becomes isolated politically.

"It's not a matter of liking whites. You don't have to want to live near whites or like whites. If you talk to Mexicans, who are more integrated than blacks residentially, they may not like Anglos and may prefer to live in Mexican neighborhoods, but they realize services are better in integrated neighborhoods than in Mexican neighborhoods."

Economics aside, the rapid racial change has created a sense of political uncertainty for many white politicians. Alvin Thornton led a citizens' group that lobbied to carve a new Congressional district. Two black candidates won the primaries in March, thereby guaranteeing that Prince George's will have its first black Congressman this November. Thornton's group also lobbied for the redrawing of the county council lines that will give five out of nine districts a black majority in the 1994 election. Currently only two of the nine council members are black.

Some black activists in the community have complained that the council makes zoning decisions to benefit developers who don't live in the county. "We need to look at this zoning process and get the council members who allocate the county's financial resources, to distribute that wealth with the business people who live here and care about the county's future." Thornton says. "Otherwise Prince George's will become like cities where banking and commercial corridors are owned and controlled by people who don't live there. All we'll own are our nice houses."

However, some black Prince Georgians don't live in nice houses, but in rundown apartments. These pockets of poverty, inside the Beltway, closer to the Washington border, seem far away from the well-kept lawns of Enterprise Estates. "This is now one of the wealthiest black Congressional districts in the country," says Thornton. "If the county wants to maintain that image, it's going to have to redevelop many of the inner-Beltway communities. If it doesn't, you are going to have the same separate cores of poverty and affluence that you find in many inner cities."

The distance between the two worlds of the county leaves 55 many in the middle class with a false sense of comfort, according to State Representative Michael E. Arrington, 36, who grew up in Prince George's.

"What's missing is a sense of activism," Arrington says. "Part of the problem is that you have a lot of people here doing well, and they don't see the problems in other communities firsthand."

Some black middle-class Prince Georgians say inner Beltway problems are thrust upon them, no matter how many miles separate the two communities. One week after Jack B. Johnson, a

Prince George's County prosecutor, spent hours discussing the Rodney King verdict with his three children, his 13-year-old son came to him with another incident. One of his classmates, Joseph, a straight-A student from an inner Beltway neighborhood, was gunned down, caught in the crossfire between two drug dealers.

Johnson, an active member of the Coalition of 100 Black Men and the graduate chapter of his fraternity, often spends hours in mentoring programs for low-income males. "There are so many programs here to help teenagers," he says. "There are a substantial number of black middle-class people who are out in the poorer community."

Other black middle-class parents say they must first keep *their* children free of the racism and peer pressure that leads to social alienation; crime and teen-age pregnancy. Those parents are reaching back to the days of segregation to extract the elements of black culture that nurtured self-esteem and a commitment to family and community.

60   Both Frank and Kathryn Weaver grew up in segregated black communities. Frank Weaver, who holds a B.S. from Howard and an M.B.A. from the University of North Carolina at Chapel Hill, says his academic and professional successes are rooted in the intellectual grooming, pride and discipline instilled in him by his parents, his church, his segregated neighborhood and his high school in Raleigh, N.C., from which he graduated in 1968. "I was always taught I could compete with the best," says Weaver. "Out of the top 10 of my class, two became Harvard lawyers, one a Duke medical doctor. All of us went on to college and graduate school. I find today many of us are searching to rediscover what some of us took for granted while growing up in a segregated society."

Frank and Kathryn Weaver say they don't want to re-create a segregated society for their daughter, but they do want their daughter to grow up with an appreciation of her heritage and culture as they did. They fear she will not be able to compete with others as equals if she is conditioned to see herself as a subordinate American. "Although we mix and mingle in the mainstream culture, we are proud of our African past," says Frank Weaver. "Our daughter does not have to shade everything black or wear a dashiki or kente cloth, but I want her to develop a sense of pride in her identity as a black person."

Could sheltering black middle-class children from racism and the inner city produce black adults with a vision of the world as narrow as that of many upper- and middle-income whites? The Alexanders have struggled with that question. They say they don't worry about their children's ability to interact with whites, since their daughters attend private, predominantly white schools. They did send their youngest daughter, Starsha, 11, to dance classes in the heart of Washington so that inner-city culture wouldn't seem alien to her. While accompanying Starsha to class one day, her mother and older sister, Shelique, 14, passed a group of winos sitting on the street outside the school. Shelique turned her nose up at the winos. Her parents were stunned. "That's when it hit me," Patricia Alexander says. "She said she had never seen anything like that."

Harold Alexander adds: "We both grew up in single-parent working-class situations. We are sensitive to problems in the inner city, and we want our children to have that same sensitivity."

Parents say their children do need protection from racism, poverty and the negative images of blacks that flood the media. "Two doors down from us is a black cardiologist," says Barron Harvey. "There's a dentist on the block, a couple of lawyers, an airline pilot, a college professor, an entrepreneur. My daughter needs to be exposed to that."

Ball adds, "If my son grows up to be a knucklehead, it won't   65
be because I didn't expose him to other possibilities."

In some ways, the need for black role models embodies the powerful impact of racism in defining achievement in America, according to Bart Landry, a sociologist and the author of "The New Black Middle Class." Landry says the sight of a white achiever doesn't offer strong signs of encouragement to many black children. "In this country, where we are polarized along racial lines, seeing a white cardiologist doesn't reaffirm their abilities. That's those people achieving. That's not us achieving. What their parents want them to see is us achieving."

The decision to live in a black community should not be equated with a desire to live in a one-race world. While many black Prince Georgians say integration shouldn't be a priority, they also say they wouldn't move away if more whites moved into the county.

"If they want to come and enjoy, help build the county and take advantage of the economic benefits of living here, that's great," says Fred Sims, who owns a management and secretarial company that grosses $5 million a year. "But we are not begging them to come."

Most residents of the black neighborhoods in Prince George's County work or function in other ways in the integrated American culture. "One of the things black folks never really have to worry about in America is being outside the realm of integration," says Harvey. "We will always have to interface with the other culture."

70   The rise of affluent black neighborhoods could enhance the relationship between the races, Landry says. "I think to the extent that it strengthens feelings of self-worth, it's good for integration, because you have to believe you are O.K. first before you can mingle with others."

Even Radamase Cabrera can see a slight ray of hope for the cause of integration in a strong black community. "Creating black wealth, black power and black stability will enable my children to go hand in hand in society with little white children. My children can integrate society from their own cultural taste, their own historical base, and meet on a level playing field. Right now, there is no level playing field. How are you going to successfully integrate something that is historically disparate?"

For the Harveys, the move to Prince George's may not be a step away from the Rev. Dr. Martin Luther King Jr.'s dream, but a step toward the realization of that dream. "We are advancing," says Barron Harvey. "We were fighting for the right to go where we want to go, to make the choice to live where we want to live. We have the freedom of choice, which we have exercised."

Stabilizing the Text

1. What does Dent mean by the term "new black suburb"? What are the defining characteristics of a black suburb? More must be involved than the race of the people living there. What else is involved in characterizing a suburb in this way?

2. Do the residents of Prince George's County sound familiar to you? Do they say things about their homes and community that you have heard before? If so, what does Dent find so interesting about their stories? If not, how does Dent make their stories relevant to us as readers?

3. More often than not, the suburbs are places described as devoid of values. Citing passages in Dent's essay, describe the values promoted in black suburbs. How and why are these values different from the values associated with white suburbs?

Mobilizing the Text

1. Does it make sense anymore to continue to talk of the suburbs in terms of the race of the people who live there? Are there still black suburbs? Are there still white suburbs? Why do you think race persists as a defining feature of certain suburban communities?

2. Dent proposes that the rise of black suburbs follows the successes of the civil rights movement and the emergence of a large African-American middle-class population in the 1970s. Keeping in mind the comments of people interviewed by Dent, how are the civil rights movement of the 1960s and the rise of the black suburbs in the 1980s related? In what ways do the black suburbanites continue the civil rights movement? In what ways do they not continue it?

3. What does the rise of black suburbs tell us about the current state of race relations in this country? Do they represent greater African-American empowerment, and so greater racial equality? Or do they represent greater racial segregation, and so a deepening of racial divisions?

Separate and Unequal
DAVID MOBERG

David Moberg is a senior editor at In These Times *and a senior fellow of the Nation Institute. He has written extensively and published widely on issues of urban life. "Separate and Unequal" first appeared in* Neighborhood Works, *a magazine devoted to covering policy issues, projects, events, and people impacting urban life at the community and neighborhood levels. In "Separate and Unequal," Moberg explains how the traditional outward growth of the suburbs devalues the suburbs themselves by devastating inner cities. Drawing from urban analysts as well as from the urban growth policies of such cities as Portland, Oregon, and Minneapolis-St. Paul, Minnesota, Moberg proposes alternatives for cities and suburbs to mutually benefit from integrated growth and renewal. As you read Moberg's essay, apply what he says to examples of suburban growth and decay you know about or have experienced. Can his proposals be made to apply to your examples? As you read, also watch for the way Moberg transitions form talking about economics to talking about community. What do his transitions say about how economic value and community values are joined?*

━━━━━━━━━━ ✦ ━━━━━━━━━━

For years, organizers and advocates have chipped away at the corrosive forces of urban decline. They market old factories, offer job training, rehab housing, preserve mass transit, reform local schools, and much more. Yet it's clear that saving the city requires something more.

Perverse government subsidies (especially for housing and transit) and uncoordinated, balkanized government encourage development that draws away from the urban core. National trends—such as economic globalization, mass computerization, the decline of labor unions and the conservative drive to deregulate business—are likely to increase metropolitan disparities and deprive central cities of crucial federal dollars.

But cities and suburbs form a metropolitan whole that rises and falls together. Many blue collar suburbs are losing factories; resegregated poor black suburbs are emerging; and old satellite cities don't share in the suburban boom around them. Recent research demonstrates that even wealthy suburbs' incomes and growth rates flow in tandem with those of the central city.

The central problem is uneven development, which is linked to the broader issue of inequality. Metropolitan areas are most likely to flourish if social and economic inequality between the central city (or poorer suburbs) and rich suburbs is reduced.

5   Consider the evidence of metropolitan economic health in relationship to that of the central city: A 1993 study by Cleveland State University professor Larry C. Ledebur and National League of Cities researcher William R. Barnes demonstrates clear income connections between city and suburban jobs. From 1979 to 1989, when central city incomes rose by $1, incomes in surrounding suburbs rose $1.12. Where suburban incomes declined, central city incomes dropped as well. They found these links grew stronger over the period they studied, even as the gap between suburban and central city poverty and unemployment grew. Indeed, the greater the region's gap in per capita income, the slower its job growth.

Conversely, the most economically integrated metro areas have the highest incomes, finds Hank Savitch and fellow researchers at the University of Louisville. Suburbanites in the healthiest one-fourth of the nation's metropolitan areas earn $2,000 more each year when compared with suburbanites in the lowest quartile, Savitch says. "Healthier cities make for healthier metropolitan regions."

Suburbanites prosper from a healthy central city in part because they claim a growing share of the city's best jobs and income. Savitch found that while real per capita income rose in the cities in the 1970s and 1980s, suburbanites took more of the city jobs. "A decade ago," Savitch wrote in 1993 in *Economic Development Quarterly*, "47 percent of suburban income could be attributed to the density and income of the core city. Today, that number has risen to 61 percent."

These links arent immediately apparent to those fleeing the city. Traditionally, the city itself redistributed income among varied neighborhoods, forcing the rich to share in providing services for the poor. But the rapid suburbanization and sprawl of the past 50 years have amounted to class conflict played out in suburban space. In flight from the city and its problems, suburbanites search for comparative advantage over others by banding together with people of similar income. They pay only for services, especially education, to serve a narrow slice of society.

This is in itself a perverse redistribution benefitting the suburbs. Poverty—and related crime, blight, high tax rates and low tax bases—pushes job-creating investments from the center, leaving cities with less revenue to deal with a disproportionate share of problems, notes Henry R. Richmond, chairman of the Washington, D.C.-based National Growth Management Leadership Project.

The opposite attractions pull investment to the suburbs: good schools, low crime, strong tax bases, cheap and clean industrial sites and high levels of new public investment, Richmond adds. This push and pull simply deepens existing inequality, making it harder for the city to pull itself up.

Current statistics show this trend is accelerating. The fringes of Chicago metro population growth move out at about five miles per decade, according to a recent study by Chicago's nonprofit Metropolitan Planning Council, which used statistics released by the Northeast Planning Commission. While population in the six-county Chicago region grew 4 percent from 1970 to 1990, the region used 46 percent more land for housing and 74 percent more for business.

Throughout the process, general tax revenue subsidizes sprawl. First, there's the home mortgage interest deduction and other supports for home ownership. In 1988, the federal government spent $35 billion on subsidies for families making $50,000 or more through the interest deduction, aid that primarily built more suburbs. During the same period it spent a total of $10 billion on all forms of government housing assistance for families making less than $10,000 a year—people now disproportionately living in the cities.

Similarly, infrastructure spending and transportation policy favor the affluent and the suburbs. For example, in the 1980s, 85 percent of the capacity of the more than $1 billion in new high-ways built in the Twin Cities served an affluent southwest quad-rant of Minneapolls suburbs, according to Minnesota State Representative Myron Orfield. Central city residents paid $6 mil-lion a year in the early 1990s to build new sewers in those same wealthy suburbs.

Richmond notes that, to the extent that public subsidies pay for amenities in the suburbs, the houses are more valuable. This benefits the local suburban government, because it permits tax rates to stay low yet still provide adequate income. Thus public subsidies and metro area structures both reflect and reinforce a stark class contrast. "In Europe, for example, you don't see the kind of wasted urban landscape and extensive chunks of urban solid waste and ghettoes that we allow in cities because we subsi-dize growth at the fringe," he explains.

15   But, how does that inequality hurt the metropolitan *region?* First, there's the fiscal contradiction: The jurisdictions within a metro region (especially rich suburbs) with the greatest resources frequently have the fewest problems, and vice versa. And even growth areas have problems of equity. Research released in January 1995 by the Federal Reserve Bank of Chicago showed that suburban communities near centers of commercial and in-dustrial growth often suffered from rapidly rising tax rates. The influx of people brought by nearby growth increased demands on government without the requisite revenue.

One of Chicago's outlying suburbs, Schaumburg, had strong commercial and industrial development in the 1980s and saw its taxes as a percent of income decline from 4.11 percent in 1981 to 3.05 percent in 1991. In nearby Roselle Village, which shared in the costs of population growth but not revenue development, the tax share as a percentage of income rose during the same period from 4.12 percent to 4.49 percent.

There is a second mechanism that is harder to measure but may be quite important, especially in education and perpetuation of social class inequality: Different communities provide mem-bers varied amounts of what sociologists refer to as "social capi-tal," analogous to financial capital or human capital (knowledge and training). This includes role models, peer relations, "old boy" networks, community associations such as churches and clubs, and recreational and cultural amenities.

Much of the "new regionalist" research on urban inequality emphasizes education and such informal community influence as key mechanisms for perpetuating and deepening inequality.

University of Wisconsin economist Steven N. Durlauf has found that the combination of differences in formal education and in community social capital, which is unequally distributed through residential segregation, results in "persistent income inequality."

"As income inequality gets worse," he observes, "society organizes itself to increase stratification, and that increases intergenerational inequality even more. You get these cycles, and the long-run outcomes are ugly."

Now all this might seem to work to the advantage of the upper middle class or rich, and to some extent it does. But New York University economist Roland Benabou's recent research questions that conclusion. Benabou observes that minor differences in education and wealth lead to high stratification, which increases inefficiency in the region. In the short run, Benabou writes, mixing of income could lead to slower growth, but in the long run, mixing yields higher output and productivity growth, eventually raising everyone's income, even that of the affluent.

"As an individual, I always have an incentive to make myself better off and to go with the select group," Benabou says, but "the pursuit of rational private interest collectively may hurt everyone. It always hurts the ones left behind."

Research by Mark Dynarksi of Mathematica Policy Research, Inc., a Princeton firm, largely confirms Benabou's ideas. He concludes that when children of different backgrounds and abilities are mixed in a classroom, the highest achievers are not held back as much as the lowest achievers gain. "The net result is a higher average outcome," he says, noting that it is not even clear that the higher achievers lose anything. "Higher-income people have a vested interest that may not be obvious to them in the well-being of lower-income people," he says, "because if society frays at the lower end, it hurts everyone. On the part of individuals it may be rational [to move to homogeneous suburbs and their schools], but what's the social perspective? Maybe it's better for everyone to take an interest in eliminating inequality. It's the tension between private choice and public good."

There are other ways equality may help efficiency and productivity. Workers may be more motivated to work or to cooperate with management if they believe rewards are fair. Also, high wages encourage investment in productivity-enhancing equipment. Finally, greater equality leads to more spending on education and health, since everyone shares in the same education or health-care system and has a stake in its success.

What can a metropolitan area do about inequality? First, it could move away from relying so heavily on property tax for local school financing—an American anomaly—and adopt income or other broad-based taxes covering the metropolitan area, or draw from state or federal funds. Yet, precisely because the informal social capital of neighborhoods (and families) is important, equalization of financing would still not be adequate. Dynarski concludes that the local differences "can only be offset by large variations in spending." The well-to-do have a compound advantage—more money for schools as well as informal educational privileges. Only extraordinary efforts on behalf of the poor or working class kids can begin to level the playing field.

25   Some cities—Tucson, Ariz., Albuquerque, N.M., Columbus, Ohio, and Madison, Wis., to name a few—were able to annex parts of their growing fringe and retain a more stable tax base. Other metropolitan strategies include urban growth boundaries.

For example, since 1979 Portland has enforced boundaries to limit growth of the metropolitan area, including provisions to encourage mass transit and affordable housing.

"Urban growth boundaries deflect growth inward to the region, though not necessarily to the core, but it does reduce the outward flow," Richmond says. "By having urban growth boundaries in Portland and affirming that development is desired in certain locations inside the boundary, all controversy about development is eliminated. When residential or industrial developers want to build, they just need a building permit," which they typically get within 60 days.

Two decades ago in Minnesota, the St. Paul and Minneapolis metro area began sharing a portion of the growth in local government tax bases and established a weak metropolitan council that was—and still is—dominated by developers. Orfield recently forged a coalition of the central cities, older suburbs and low-tax base suburbs to strengthen those metropolitan structures. Orfield proposed greater tax base sharing, strong metropolitan land use planning, fair housing, and a combination of urban reinvestment, job creation and welfare reform.

Through state legislation, the young Minneapolis politician has expanded responsibilities of the metropolitan council, enlarging its authority over sewer and transit systems and thereby expanding its budgetary responsibility from $35 million to $800 million per year. He also strengthened metropolitan land use planning: Now local communities have to submit comprehensive plans to the metropolitan council, which must review and approve how those plans fit into a metropolitan strategy. He also pushed through fair housing goals after several defeats. If metropolitan communities do not take steps toward the fair housing goals, such as reducing zoning barriers or accepting subsidies that are offered, the communities could lose sewer, road and other funding they want.

Since 1971 Twin Cities suburbs and central cities have 30 shared in a fund generated by taxes on 40 percent of the growth in the business tax base. As a result, the metro region now shares in slightly less than one-fourth of property tax revenue. Though the Minnesota legislature approved Orfield's plan, which would have gradually boosted tax sharing to nearly half of all property tax revenue over 15 years, the Republican governor vetoed the legislation.

Orfield's welfare reforms, which link work requirements with New Deal-style central city public works projects, were undermined by Republican cuts that eliminated job creation programs. But he did win $30 million in funds to reinvest in the city for environmental cleanup and removing blight to prepare land for redevelopment. By uniting disadvantaged suburbs and the central cities, while relying on church support to temper opposition in the richer suburbs, Orfield has rallied a coalition that is successfully fighting the trend toward metropolitan inequality.

Inequality is both a symptom of unsustainable social patterns underlying the development of America's metropolitan areas and a cause of slow growth, educational shortcomings and a wide range of other urban social problems. Making cities work will involve reversing both inequality and its causes. That requires forging new, regional political alliances and strategies, but such local efforts are only the start of a task that ultimately is national in scope.

Stabilizing the Text

1. According to Moberg, how are the fates of cities and suburbs joined? In what ways do actions in one have consequences in the other?

2. Moberg uses economic evidence to support his claim that the suburbs benefit more when they sustain the economic growth of cities. At what point in the essay does he turn from economic evidence to making claims about social consequences? Does the transition persuasively join economic issues to social outcomes? Explain why you find his connection more or less persuasive.

3. Moberg concludes his essay with examples of local reform efforts, such as those in Minneapolis-St. Paul. What do you think the examples contribute to the overall argument of the essay? For instance, do you think the examples

make his claims for urban-suburban cooperation more concrete? Or, do the examples make his claims seem unrealistic?

Mobilizing the Text

1. We are all generally aware of the coexistence of affluent suburban areas with economically depressed urban areas. What does Moberg's essay add to your awareness? Identify a passage in which he makes a point you had not considered before. Describe how this point alters your awareness of inequality.
2. Just what is the relationship between separation and inequality as described by Moberg? Do you think that separate necessarily means unequal? Do you think there are commitments to equality none of us can or should separate ourselves from?
3. Moberg identifies a global problem and suggests only local solutions. What makes the problem of separation and inequality of cities and suburbs exist globally but only to be resolved locally? Why can't a global solution, such as a national policy, resolve this global problem? Is it the nature of the problem that makes it resolvable only in this way, if at all? Or is it the nature of the local and global solutions that limits what works?

Park Slope: Notes on a Middle Class "Utopia"

JAN ROSENBERG

Jan Rosenberg lives in New York City and teaches sociology at Long Island University. She has written essays on a variety of topics, including workplace rights, the women's movement, and family issues. She is also author of the book Feminism into Film. *"Park Slope: Notes on a Middle Class 'Utopia' " was first published in* Dissent. *In this essay, Rosenberg briefly describes a Brooklyn neighborhood, Park Slope, which declined during the rise of the suburbs in the 1950s and 1960s, but became gentrified in the 1970s and 1980s. Throughout her description, she emphasizes the things that have recently brought people back to Park Slope. Rosenberg's description explains the urban lifestyle Park Slope offers, a lifestyle that is "distinctly not suburban." While reading her essay about Park Slope, pay attention to the language she uses to evaluate people, places, and trends. How does that language contribute to your evaluation of Park Slope as a place to live?*

———————————— ✦ ————————————

A familiar story, playing itself out in city after city: skyrocketing housing costs send upscale urban dwellers looking for new areas to "pioneer" (some would say invade) and to reshape to their taste. In Manhattan, it has transformed areas once filled with machine shops and printing plants into the luxury lofts and art spaces of Soho, Noho, and TriBeCa. And across the East River, similar changes march through Boerum Hill, Carroll Gardens, Cobble Hill, and particularly Park Slope—the "brownstone" neighborhoods ringing downtown Brooklyn.

Stroll through Park Slope on a warm Saturday night, past young middle-class crowds patronizing a cornucopia of chic new restaurants offering the latest in trendy cuisine: sushi, Tex-Mex, "continental," five types of Chinese, Thai, and various gourmet take-out shops. A lone shoemaker hangs on, but for a dime store or bodega where you can still get an ice cream sandwich for under a dollar, you have to literally go down the Slope, an avenue or two away. Interspersed among the restaurants are numerous real estate offices and nearly as many "new wave" florists (there's almost a florist a block in the heart of the Slope's Seventh Avenue). New craft shops display expensive, elegant *objets*. Completing the ambience are those emblems of yuppiedom, Benetton's, a nearly-completed D'Agostino's, and a recently arrived "closet designer." (Those from Wall Street who specialize in restructuring corporations can now hire someone to restructure their closets, though some spouses have been known to view this as a hostile takeover.) These Saturday-night sidewalks are filled with well-dressed, well-coiffed people in their twenties, thirties, and forties (hardly any are beyond their forties). A tennis pro from Sheepshead Bay, accountants and teachers from Bensonhurst, are drawn to the shops, the people, the élan of Park Slope, where they encounter the full range of young professionals priced out of the Village and the Upper West Side, searching for an affordable "outer borough" alternative. The atmosphere is thick with style and expectation; this is a place to be, and to be seen. This is *New York Magazine*'s Park Slope.

But there are other Park Slopes flourishing, in ways less familiar, less commercial. One is the Park Slope of neighborhood day-care centers and nursery schools, of after-school programs and Little League, of PS 321 and JHS 51, of religious institutions, nearly moribund only a few years ago, revitalized by the in-migration of families since the early 1970s. This child-centered, family-oriented Park Slope, anchored in its own institutions, has its own landmarks and symbols: the area around "the monument" at Ninth Street and Prospect Park West on Saturday spring mornings is one of these. Awash in a maroon and yellow sea of St. Saviour's and St. Francis's baseball uniforms, elementary school kids (mostly boys, despite some organizers' best efforts) embody the neighborhood's vitality and—since many if not most are not Catholic—its ecumenical spirit. The kids, drawn from public, private, and parochial schools, wait at the monument for their teams to assemble and games to begin.

A six-year-old boy worries about his orthodox jewish neighbors seeing him in his St. Saviour's uniform, and dons a yarmulke to offset his St. Saviour's shirt before visiting them on the Sabbath after his game. The priests ask the non-Catholic parents and children in the league to participate in and respect their preseason service, now nearly purged of specifically Catholic references. Congregation Beth Elohim (the Garfield Temple) also typifies the neighborhood. Faced with dwindling membership and bleak prospects in 1970, its former grandeur faded, temple members had the good sense and good luck to create one of the early neighborhood nursery schools. Its early-childhood programs helped revitalize the temple, drawing Jewish families into (or back into) Jewish institutional life. The churches and synagogues have made themselves centers of many family-oriented activities, from sports to preschool and after-school programs, potluck dinners and week-end retreats, that knit together some of the baby boomers with children.

5   Parking is nearly impossible ("double Park Slope," my older son calls it) as I zoom up on a Saturday morning to drop off my child for his nine o'clock game. I pull away quickly to park and get back before the first inning, thinking of my friend, Fred I., the envy of the "silent majority": while most of us quietly grumble that our weeks are dominated by Little League (in our own case, practices on Wednesday, Thursday, and Friday afternoons and "official games" all day Saturday), Fred courageously manages to sneak off to his country house with his brood in tow every weekend.

It's a cold, drizzly Saturday in April and the parade to officially open the neighborhood baseball season is about to begin. Hundreds of kids and their parents huddle together by team, waiting to march up Union Street and over to "the monument." Mayor Koch is going to inaugurate the newly renovated playing fields near Prospect Park's new concert area and playground at Ninth Street, only a stone's throw from the beautifully restored Picnic House and Tennis House—all of which border the Park Slope side of Prospect Park. The southern and eastern sides of the park, bordered by predominantly black neighborhoods, seem a distant land. The park serves as more of a barrier than a meeting ground between white upper-middle-class and black and Hispanic Brooklyn. Connections between private neighborhood gentrification and the careful restoration of once-treasured, then-deteriorated public space suggest themselves to even the most casual visitor. But for even the most apolitical of Slopers, there is nagging doubt that their good fortune can endure in a Brooklyn increasingly overwhelmed by an underclass as cut off from prosperity as they are connected.

The 1950s and 1960s brought hard times to urban neighborhoods all over the country; Park Slope was no exception. This middle-class family neighborhood was losing out to newer, more promising suburban areas. Clashes between rival Hispanic and Italian gangs made the area inhospitable to the middle class. The park block residents of Third Street, always one of the Slope's most beautiful and desirable blocks (and Sidney Hook's home through the 1940s and 1950s) organized the Park Slope Betterment Committee to promote the neighborhood's revival. They pressured the banks to give mortgages and held meetings to advise prospective neighbors on buying and remodeling homes.

A trickle of newcomers, led by artists seeking affordable housing and studio space, flowed into the Slope. One early "pioneer," a writer-editor who moved to Park Slope with her artist husband in 1968, left Manhattan for the Slope's beautiful, ample space, and affordable homes. A *New York Times* article had trumpeted the neighborhood's virtues: its distinguished architecture and undervalued homes, its beautiful park, and the nearby presence of other artists. The couple bought a prime park block house, though it was occupied by numerous tenants and the neighborhood was still redlined by the banks, and converted it from a rooming house to a triplex for themselves and a floor-through rental. The single-room occupants they displaced have long since been forgotten by the current owners and their neighbors. Built in the 1890s as a one-family house with ample room for servants, the brownstone adapted quite readily to the changed circumstances of middle-class families in the 1970s.

Like artists, 1960s radicals were another important trickle in the early 1970s migration stream. They, too, were drawn by the affordable space, the park, and the presence of others like themselves. Veterans of the antiwar, civil rights, and feminist movements quickly found each other in, and drew each other to, this budding urban community.

10   Many came in couples, expecting to settle in and eventually to have and raise their children here. Not surprisingly, these 1960s veterans remain central to community politics in Park Slope. Over the years, personal, community, and political interests have converged around issues of housing and education.

Early antiredlining campaigns were organized by people experienced with bankers' power to make and break neighborhoods. Ready but unable to buy houses in Park Slope, a neighborhood the banks did not yet believe in, activists successfully challenged the then-standard diversion of neighborhood resources to finance suburban and Sunbelt development. Ironically (but predictably) the end of redlining sped up the gentrification, which was soon to work against middle-class housing/investment opportunities. By the mid-1980s, despite considerable expansion of gentrified Park Slope's boundaries, only highly paid professionals, bankers and the like (and those lucky enough to have queued up on time), could afford to own a home in Park Slope.

School politics reflect the neighborhood's concentration of leftists and liberals. Several leading elementary schools have adopted the "Peace Curriculum"; the Community School Board has committed its resources to establishing an "alternative school" similar to the ones in Manhattan's District 4 founded by Deborah Meier.

To the middle class among a generation wary of suburbia's soured promise, places like Park Slope came to be seen as a contemporary alternative, the chance to build a family-centered urban life that is distinctly not suburban. The mix of people in public institutions, the subway rides to and from "the City," the architecture, the shared public grandeur of a partially restored Prospect Park—these eddies against the tide of privatization are reminders that one has embraced a post-suburban dream of a vital, complex, dynamic urban life.

Stabilizing the Text

1. What features of Rosenberg's description give you the best sense of Park Slope as a desirable place to live? What features of her description leave you unimpressed with Park Slope as a community?

2. In what senses is Rosenberg using the word "utopia" to characterize Park Slope? Do you understand her to mean it is an ideal community? Or do you get the sense that she is saying it is a vision of community that cannot be realized?

3. Rosenberg discusses suburbanization and gentrification to provide a wider context for her description of the resurgence of Park Slope. Carefully read that contextualization. How do the details of Park Slope relate to the larger trends of suburbanization and gentrification? Is Park Slope simply an example of those larger trends? Or is Park Slope something else?

Mobilizing the Text

1. Would you choose to live in a neighborhood like Park Slope? Why or why not? What do you think our choices about where we live say about who we are?

2. Do you read Rosenberg's essay as encouraging or discouraging future projects like the Park Slope renewal? Are there details of the story of Park Slope that resonate with stories of renewal projects in your area? What do these resonances tell us about the adequacy of our renewal talk?

3. Rosenberg provides vivid descriptions of people and activities in the Park Slope community. Choose any one of those descriptions and compare it to a similar person or activity you have experienced. In what ways is Rosenberg's description similar to and different from your own experience? What do those similarities and differences tell you about your experience in relation to the essay? Are you more postsuburban than you thought? Or is Park Slope not as unique as Rosenberg describes it? In the end, just how different can communities be from each other?

CHAPTER 4

Cities and Race

Living in the United States means living a life shaped by race. Throughout our history, many Americans have hoped and worked to diminish the degree to which race would matter to each American life. Because they bring together all kinds of people, cities often show the ways in which these efforts have paid off, the ways that these hopes have been and have not been fulfilled. In cities, for example, we are likely to find many examples of success, high achievement, and good fortune that cross boundaries of skin color. Individual doctors, lawyers, professors, and elected officials today come from all groups. In addition, the open racial animosity and violent white supremacism that characterized public life in American cities until relatively recent times is now considered unacceptable. At the same time as this progress should be celebrated and used as a foundation for further developments, race, and especially racism, is almost always a taboo topic for public conversation today. As a result, while individualized racism has proven to be impossible to defend, institutionalized racial privilege has proven to be almost impossible to discuss.

While the relationships between race and city life are in ways very complicated, they can also be very direct. In many U.S. cities, there are racial ghettos that present a reality in stark contrast to areas of wealth and privilege. In the absence of out-in-the-open discussion of the truths of race—that race is a fiction invented to justify power relationships, that institutional racism and white group privilege are products of our collective history and continue despite the waning prevalence of individualized racial animosity—the subtle, or perhaps not so subtle, messages our cities send to us are in part messages about the continuing tragedy of race.

Race is a continuing tragedy because of the ways that institutionalized racial dynamics of privilege and oppression shape public life. Despite individual success stories, group-level disparities in critical life areas such as health, education, employment, and safety persist in the United States. As an example, John A. Powell, a researcher at the University of Minnesota, has compiled data on racial disparities in Minnesota:

- Seventy-seven percent of white families own a home, while homes are owned by only 32% of African-American families and 43% of Latino families.
- While African Americans make up 10% of the adults in St. Paul, they comprise 26% of the drivers stopped by law enforcement officials and 43% of the individuals searched.
- An African-American man is 27 times more likely than a white man to be incarcerated.
- African-American and Native American infant mortality rates are two to four times higher than those of whites.
- In 1999, 83% of whites graduated within four years from Minnesota high schools, compared with 39% of African-American and 48% of Latino students.

These group-level racial disparities reveal the profound effects of policies and practices that automatically accumulate advantages and privileges in the lives of white people. Faced with the reality that individual lives and accomplishments—personal connections, good jobs, college degrees, homes, and businesses—are, in part, the result of the whole group's greater access to social goods, which is a continuing legacy of racial injustice, whites have tended to respond defensively. Yet the discussion of race continues to reemerge as an important piece of unfinished business for all American cities.

Whether or not we engage it publicly, race matters in cities. In schools, boardrooms, neighborhoods, and streets we live together and do our best to observe Rodney King's once famous suggestion to "just get along." Because we get along much better than we get to the bottom of complex issues, public discussion of race usually begins with an explosion: a police beating, or a hate crime, or a large protest. As a result, some of the most important public discussion of race has been anchored in discussion of public explosions in which feelings of frustration, disadvantage, and hopelessness gain expression. While the insights we are able to express at such times are valuable in themselves, their value is diminished unless we use them to help us improve our lives together—unless we use them as opportunities to learn. The essays in this chapter all seek improvement of race relations by seeking to help readers understand the specific challenges of racial justice in the United States. Each thus seeks to help us transform the lessons of race we learn from and through our lives in and around cities.

As you read and consider the essays presented here, you will notice that they reflect important developments in efforts to deal openly with issues of race. They include white people as participants in the racial landscape and efforts to change it. They also address the impersonal power of institutional forces that produce racially inflected experiences. And they begin the important process of thinking of race in terms that include but go beyond black-and-white issues.

Each of the essays in this chapter begins from a distinct, explosive, moment: a lynching in 1930, the 1992 Los Angeles "riot," and the 2002 Cincinnati "riot." The writings gathered here each claim that making sense of such moments is important because those moments resonate with all of American history and suggest our possible lives together. Thus, in the opening essay, C. Carr's "An American Tale" explores how whiteness gets taught, learned, and possibly redefined. Carr explores the relationships between her own life and identity and those of her relatives and others involved in a 1930 lynching in her hometown. She tries to sort out how looking at the past might help us live differently in the future.

Also pursuing a better future, the Bloods and Crips article presented here responds to the 1992 Los Angeles upheavals. In the "Bloods/Crips Proposal for LA's Face-Lift," members of rival gangs offer a set of concrete plans for rebuilding the city. These plans explain the causes for violence and point to reasons for hope that can be compared by readers to the perspectives of more officially sanctioned voices.

Following the Blood/Crips proposal are two essays that launch from events in Cincinnati, Ohio. In "Building Democracy from Below," Manning Marable interprets events in Cincinnati for the lessons they teach about changing the forces that result in the tragedies of America's racial ghettos. For Marable, urban explosions of the sort experienced in Cincinnati point to the need for people to work collectively to put pressure on government to make the promises of democracy more real for everyone. Offering a very different view, Heather Mac Donald's "What *Really* Happened in Cincinnati?" argues that urban explosions reveal the pathologies of the urban poor rather than inadequacies of opportunity.

An American Tale: A Lynching and the Legacies Left Behind
C. CARR

C. Carr contributes frequently to the Village Voice *on topics ranging from race to art to popular culture. In "An American Tale," Carr combines aspects of personal narrative, social history, and cultural criticism to make sense out of how life as a "white" person today is related to the history of race relations. Discussing memories shared by a survivor of a 1930 lynching in Indiana, she shows how being "white" means very different things at different moments. While reading Carr's essay, think about the implications of the shifting meanings of race the essay reveals. Ask yourself about how Carr, and how you, would like to see the meanings of "whiteness" or other racial markers change and what roles writing might play in working toward those changes.*

◆

> *One day, sometime during your childhood or adolescence, a Negro was lynched in your county or the one next to yours. A human being was burned or hanged from a tree and you knew it had happened. But no one publicly condemned it and always the murderers went free. And afterward, maybe weeks or months or years afterward, you sat casually in the drugstore with one of those murderers and drank the Coke he casually paid for. A "nice white girl" could do that but she would have been run out of town or perhaps killed had she drunk a Coke with the young Negro doctor who was devoting his life in service to his people.*
>
> Lillian Smith, *Killers of the Dream*, 1949

I was an adult before I ever saw the picture. But even as a girl I knew there'd been a lynching in Marion. That was my father's hometown. And on one of many trips to visit my grandparents, I heard the family story: The night it happened back in 1930 someone called the house and spoke to my grandfather, whose shift at the post office began at three in the morning. "Don't walk through the courthouse square tonight on your way to work," the caller said. "You might see something you don't want to see." There was laughter at the end of the story—which puzzled me. *Something you don't want to see.* Then, laughter.

I now know that, in the 1920s, Indiana had more enrolled Ku Klux Klan members than any state in the union, and that my grandfather was one of them. Learning this after he died. I couldn't assimilate it into the frail grandpa I'd known. Couldn't really assimilate it and for a long time, didn't try. He had been an intensely secretive man, and certainly, there'd been other obfuscations. He always said, for example, that he was an orphan, that his parents had died in a wreck when he was three. I accepted this, but the grown-ups knew better. After grandpa's funeral, my father discovered there'd been a safe-deposit box and hoped at last to find a clue to the family tree. Instead, he unearthed this other secret: a Klan membership card. All my father said was. "I never saw a hooded sheet. He'd go out. We never knew where he was going."

So much of this story is about shame. My grandfather was a bastard, a fact that someone born in small-town Indiana in 1886 would rather die than discuss. And so he did. But if that particular humiliation seems foreign today, what about the other secret? A lot of us who are white come from . . . something, and it is not discussed. "That's in the past," we like to say, as if that did more than give us another hood to wear.

I remember, for example, when I first saw the picture a few years ago. Two black men in bloody tattered clothing hang from a tree and below them stand the grinning gloating proud and pleased white folks. I remember looking anxiously for my grandfather's face. But of course, he hadn't been there. I recalled the family story. There'd been *something you don't want to see.* Then, laughter. And as I began to tell people this story, that became the detail I left out because it shamed me: there was laughter.

5   For years now I've wondered if I should ever write about these things. Part of me thinks—why *my* family? I knew my grandfather well enough to feel sure that he was a follower, not a leader, not evil, not really different from other white men of his generation. Would "removing the hood" illuminate anything? Or merely cause pain? I discussed this with my brother, inconclusively, but shortly thereafter he sent a newspaper article he happened to see while visiting my sister. I seized, upon these coincidences, made them a sign.

Because there'd been a third man lynched in Marion that night—and he'd survived. He was living in Milwaukee.

Somehow a survivor hadn't made it into the family story. But the clipping my brother sent said that this man, James Cameron, had opened a museum devoted to the history of lynching. And I know it mentioned that Cameron's book, *A Time of Terror*, would soon be reissued by Black Classic Press. I reread the article many times, then lost it at some point along the swing shift of my ambivalence. Even so, I knew I would have to meet this man or regret it for the rest of my life.

James Cameron came so close to dying in Marion's courthouse square that he had rope burns around his neck from the noose. He'd been dragged from the jail and beaten bloody and carried to the tree where the other two men were already hanging. In those last moments—certain he was about to die—he had a vision. Then, miraculously, he didn't die. The mob let him go, just let him walk away. He was 16, and he believes he was saved by divine intervention, sent back to us with news—our Ishmael. *And I only am escaped alone to tell thee.*

Yet who would hear what he'd come back to tell? For over 45 years, Cameron tried to find a publisher for his story, probably the only written record by a lynching survivor. Finally, in 1982, he mortgaged his house for $7500 and published *A Time of Terror* himself. Now he's struggling to renovate his museum building, an old boxing school/fitness center donated by the city of Milwaukee. He doesn't have a working boiler. He pays electric and phone with his Social Security. He figures he needs $200,000 for renovations, and he's certain that this—more than the book, even—is the true work for which God saved him. But Cameron is worried. He is about to turn 80, and this time he won't have 45 years to get it done.

But here I get ahead of myself. First, you must hear the story 10 of the lynching—and the miracle.

It began on the evening of August 6, 1930. Cameron, 16, had been pitching horseshoes with a school friend, Tommy Shipp, 18, and an acquaintance, Abe Smith, 19. The three decided to go out for a joyride in Shipp's car. As they drove past the Marion city limits and into the countryside, Smith announced that he wanted to rob someone to get money for a new car of his own. Cameron wavered inside: he immediately wanted to get out, yet he didn't get out. They drove to Lover's Lane to look for a victim. Spotting one parked car, Smith pulled out a .38-caliber pistol, handed it to Cameron, and ordered him to tell the white man and woman inside to "stick 'em up." Cameron didn't even know Smith very well, and later he would tell the sheriff that he didn't know why he'd followed Smith's orders. But he did know: once more, he had wavered. While something inside him said "go back, go back" even as he approached the car, he had been pushed forward by someone with a stronger will. And it was a last but fateful moment that this would be true of him.

There he stood, pistol in hand, telling the driver and his girlfriend to get out. And when the driver did so, Cameron realized that he knew this man—Claude Deeter—a regular customer at his shoeshine stand, someone who'd always tipped him, someone who'd always been decent to him. Now he knew he couldn't go through with it. He handed the gun back to Smith, and ran. A few minutes later, he heard shots, and he wondered what had happened back there, but he never stopped running. As it turned out, Deeter had been mortally wounded.

Cameron arrived home with new eyes, because he saw the gulf that had opened between past and present. He saw his mother differently, feeling sorry for her for the first time in his life, though he lied when she asked him why he was so agitated. He couldn't sleep. He kept telling himself he hadn't really done anything wrong: he'd just been foolish. "The trouble was," he wrote in his memoir, "this was Marion, Indiana, where there was little room for foolish Black boys." Cameron hadn't been in bed long when the police arrived—guns drawn, surrounding the house, raking it with searchlights. He could hear his mother getting up from the sofa bed to answer the pounding at the door.

Shipp and Smith had already been locked in separate cells on the first floor of the jail by the time Cameron got there. He remembers the three hours of interrogation, the kicks and punches delivered when it was over, the confession he then signed without even reading it. The officers tossed him into an upstairs cell block with 30 black men arrested for riding a freight train.

15   By the next morning, rumors were circulating through Marion that the white woman in the car had been raped. She would later testify in court that she hadn't been touched, but the spark had been lit. Cameron writes that there was no particular "race problem" in the town, just the strictly enforced segregation common to so many towns, just an everyday sense of limits, if you were black. "And once the boundary was crossed, anything might happen to the trespasser. . . . The realization dawned on me that I had crossed the boundary into the most sacred area of all, the world where white women lived."

He noticed a crowd of white people gathering outside the jail right after breakfast, some pointing to the windows of the cell, some shaking their fists. He could feel the tension among his older cellmates, who'd abandoned their usual card games to pace. Small groups of white people kept coming up the steps to stare into the cell block. A white prisoner assured Cameron that "people in this part of the country wouldn't lynch anybody," but a black prisoner countered that the white guy was "nuts." Hadn't Cameron been charged with the rape of a white woman?

The mob outside the jail grew steadily larger. Then, sometime during the afternoon, Deeter died. His bloody shirt was hung from a flagpole. As Cameron learned later, local radio stations announced that a lynching was imminent, and white people began to stream in from surrounding small towns, while entire black families fled Marion. Around 5:30, a reporter from the *Marion Chronicle* came by to interview Cameron. He told the journalist his story, but he could see that he wasn't being heard, that the truth didn't matter. "Ask the girl." Cameron finally implored him. But the reporter just smirked. "You'll never get out of this."

In his book, recalling how he felt as that day built toward its violent climax, Cameron can't quite fit the dimensions of his fear into words. "At times, even now," he writes, "I awaken in the middle of the night, reliving that whole day—and night. . . . I can never return to sleep. I suffer headaches all through the night. I just lie there, thinking, praying, saying my rosary, hoping, reassuring myself that it all happened a long, long time ago. I am not the same man. I am somebody else now."

At dusk of that fateful day, August 7, Cameron could peer out from his second-floor cell block and see white faces for as far as he could look in any direction. He could hear people demanding "those three niggers." And they began to throw rocks at the windows of the jail. Some carried shotguns. Some carried pistols. Some carried bats, clubs, crowbars, or stones. And among them, Cameron recognized people he knew: customers from his shoeshine stand, boys and girls he'd gone to school with, people whose lawns he'd mowed. He saw Klan members in robes and headgear, faces unmasked, who seemed to be monitoring the crowd. He sensed a carnival air. And there, laughing and talking with them all, were the scores of policemen ostensibly protecting the jail.

The assault on the building began at nightfall. Some men ran into the alley with gasoline cans and doused the brick wall, but they couldn't get it to burn. Then, for the next hour, men took   20 turns pounding with a sledgehammer on the steel door of the jail and the brick casement around it, while the mob chanted itself into a frenzy, and, as the frame began to give, people pulled bricks out with their bare hands and four men—adrenalized by hatred—lifted the entire door jamb out of the wall. Cameron could hear Sheriff Jacob Campbell ordering, "Don't shoot! There are women and children out there!"

The ringleaders burst in and pulled Shipp outside first. As Cameron wrote, "I could see the bloodthirsty crowd come to life the moment Tommy's body was dragged into view. It seemed to me as if all of those 10 to 15 thousand people were trying to hit him all at once." Clubbed and stoned and then garrotted at the bars of a jailhouse window, Shipp was dead long before the hysterical mob ever got him to the tree. So was Smith. Someone rammed a crowbar through his chest, while souvenir hunters cut off Shipp's pants and distributed the pieces. Shipp was then dressed in a Kluxer's robe, and the crowd dragged both bodies over to the courthouse square and strung them up. Cameron couldn't stop watching: the delirium, the sadism, and finally, a weird ecstasy. Over at the tree, "people howled and milled around the lifeless bodies, their voices a mumbo jumbo of insane screams and giggles." He could see them posing for pictures with the bodies.

And then he could hear the men coming up the steps to get him. Cameron remembers what they carried—ropes, swords, rifles, a submachine gun. He remembers the chanting outside: "We want Cameron!" But when the ringleaders rushed into his cell block, they couldn't pick him out. At first, none of the other prisoners would identify him either, but the white mobsters threatened to "hang every goddamn one of you niggers," and Cameron watched in horror as about half of his black cellmates dropped to their knees groveling. "Don't hurt us, Mister White Folks." Finally, one old black man pointed him out.

He remembers the white men gripping him viselike, and the chorus of voices yelling "Nigger! Nigger! Nigger!" as they got him outside. He remembers the bricks and rocks and spit that hit him as they carried him toward the courthouse, and the crowbar glancing across his chest, and the pickax handle hitting his head, and children biting his legs. "Once or twice. I thought I saw a kind face in the press around me. To each of them I called out for some kind of help. . . . But nothing happened." Police began clearing a path to the tree where the other two bodies were hanging, and someone called out for the rope.

Cameron felt numb, encased in ice, and as someone put the noose around his neck and snaked the other end up over a branch, he remembered what his mother had told him about sinners facing death, about the thief on the cross, and he prayed, "Lord, forgive me my sins. Have mercy on me." In his mind and body and soul, he was dead at that moment, and he stopped thinking.

Suddenly a woman's voice called out, sharply and clearly. "Take this boy back! He had nothing to do with any raping or killing!"

A silence fell over the mob, as Cameron remembers it. Or perhaps, it was part of his vision—because he recalls that the people around him were struck dumb, that everyone froze, and that he suddenly felt himself surrounded by what seemed to be a film negative and on it were the images of the people in the crowd, and he couldn't tell anymore if they were black or white.

Then the spell broke. "And hands that had already committed murder, became soft and tender, kind and helpful," he wrote. "I could feel the hands that had unmercifully beaten me remove the rope from around my neck. Now, they were caressing hands!"

Then the crowd drew back. He saw that many bowed their heads. They couldn't look at him as he staggered back to the jail.

In the years since the lynching, Cameron has spoken to many white people who were present in the square that night. And no one heard any voice. No one but him. "You were just lucky," they tell him. But something had stopped the rampage cold, and Cameron knows he didn't imagine the voice. Sometimes, he can still hear it.

And at what point in that evening did someone call my grandfather? To tell him there was something out there he didn't want to see. Perhaps that's the problem: we don't want to see. I was thinking about Cameron's vision. And that's my term for it, not his. For in this story of signs and wonders, why should there *not* be a "vision." I mean that moment of suspended animation when everyone around him froze and became an image, a negative, and he could no longer tell if those people were black or white. But why didn't this "vision" appear to the white people—who needed to see it? Maybe it was something they didn't want to see. Or maybe it had to be entrusted to someone whose life depended on it.

25

30   In the first hours, days, months following his narrow escape, however, Cameron had a heightened sense of black and white—as the blacks got angrier and the whites got more cruel, or more ashamed.

The four detectives who drove him out of Marion right after the lynching, to a jail in nearby Huntington—they were white. They ordered this beaten and traumatized kid to lie on the floor of the back seat the whole way, for safety, while they cracked jokes like "this nigger back here is as white as a sheet." Then, in Huntington jail, there was the old man in the facing cell who began apologizing to Cameron—he was white too. He told Cameron he'd had a fight with his own son about going to Marion. The son wanted in on the lynching. "For all I know, he might have been one of the people in the mob. He might have been the one who put that rope around your neck, and caused that rope burn. He had me arrested and put in jail. Told everybody I was crazy. I am sorry, son, sorry to my heart."

Next day, the white detectives drove him back to Marion. He lay down on the floor beneath a mat while they cruised the courthouse, where part of the lynch mob remained on guard. The cops crowed gleefully that "those niggers are still hanging on the tree" "and look how their necks have stretched." One detective called out to a newsboy, bought the day's paper, and pulled the mat back to show Cameron the front page. There he saw for the first time the infamous photograph of his dead companions surrounded by celebrating white people.

Copies of the photo sold briskly to sightseers that day for 50 cents apiece. And the bodies hung in the courthouse square till late afternoon when the state attorney general, a notorious Klan opponent, arrived from Indianapolis and personally cut them down.

Cameron, meanwhile, had been delivered to the state reformatory, where white guards gathered around to laugh at his clothing, shredded during the beating, and to ridicule his ashen complexion. But then Cameron saw another group of white guards come in and stare from a distance, tears running down their cheeks. Sorrowful, immobilized, they were unable to be more than Greek chorus to the tragedy.

35   Sympathy was apparently in such short supply among white people in the Indiana of 1930 that Cameron has never forgotten those who gave it to him. Like those guards. And the old man in Huntington jail. "They are etched in my memory, stamped upon my heart," he would later write. But at the time, tears weren't enough to case his growing hatred of all whites. For months,

Cameron felt sick with rage and wanted to kill a white man, any white man. His stepfather actually lived this out for him within a week of the lynching, going crazy to "kill some white folks," and managing to shoot nine policemen (none fatally) during a night-long battle. (He then spent a year in prison.) Naturally, the lynchers went free. A grand jury ultimately concluded that Marion authorities had acted "in a prudent manner" on the night of August 7. Cameron was never even asked to testify.

Granted a change of venue for his own trial, he moved from the state reformatory to a cell in Anderson, Indiana, a town about 30 miles from Marion. Word soon spread that Klansmen from Marion planned to storm the Anderson jail, lynch Cameron, and "break in" the sheriff who'd just taken office there. But Anderson's new sheriff, Bernard Bradley, turned out to be the first white person in Cameron's life to make a positive difference. First, he promised his young prisoner that if those Kluxers showed up, he and his deputies would shoot to kill. Bradley had patrols in the streets every night, for weeks. Rumor had it that he had even armed the town's black residents. Cameron writes that that clinched it for the Klan leaders, who decided not to try anything.

Once the tension eased, Sheriff Bradley called Cameron to his office and announced that he was going to make him a turnkey trusty, which would allow him to leave jail during the day. The sheriff said he didn't believe Cameron guilty of any rape or murder. "I want you to treat me like a father," Bradley told him, "and I'll treat you like a loving son." Utterly shocked, Cameron studied the sheriff's eyes and body language, "because no white man had ever spoken to me like that before." But he decided that "my concentration, my scrutiny, could detect no deceit or falsity." He came to love this sheriff, this anomaly who'd grown up in an all-white town near Anderson. Cameron could only conclude in retrospect that Sheriff Bradley must have been "a weird sort of person, because he was mysterious and apparently outside natural law. By his nature, he seemed to have belonged to another world."

Then, one day while Cameron was out in the town of Anderson, he saw a man on a bicycle, riding with a little blond girl perched on the handlebars—both of them laughing. Suddenly Cameron realized that this was one of the raging men who had grabbed him in the Marion jail and pulled him out into the street. And he felt a flicker of intense anger, but mostly he felt confounded by the purely human mystery of it. How could it be that this "happy-go-lucky man with that equally happy child had been capable of doing the things I knew he had done"?

I couldn't help but notice that, after the lynching, many of the white people in Cameron's story were either laughing or crying. As you'll remember, I'm from the lineage of those who laughed. Though personally, I never got the joke. And when I think of my grandfather, who died when I was 16, I share Cameron's sense of bewilderment. I ask myself—how could it be?

40   Of course, how much can one know about a man who never even told his own family about the circumstances of his birth? All he ever said of his childhood was that he'd seen Buffalo Bill then. He had no family stories, while my grandma told so many. I remember once asking her about his parents, and she said, "We don't talk about that, because it makes him very sad."

One day when I was eight or nine, I found his mother's obituary in a desk drawer. I didn't know that that's what it was. Just saw that certain lines had been cut out with a razor blade. Curious, I walked into the living room where everyone was seated, blurting out "Who's Josie Carr?" No one spoke, but my grandpa got up and took the clipping from my hand. None of us ever saw it again. A search of every little newspaper in and around Marion never turned up another copy. Nor is there a record anywhere of her death. Or for that matter, her life. *And certain lines had been cut out with a razor blade.*

Now it's been more than 25 years since I last visited Marion. Months after my grandpa's death, my father drove us out of the town into farm country to see the little house where my grandpa had been born. Somehow my father had managed to find it again, after visiting once as a child. Sort of. My grandpa hadn't shared this either, leaving my little dad at the end of a dirt road, telling him, "I want to see that house one more time before I die." And my father remembered that while he waited, he could see a church in the distance with its graves. Now our car was parked at the foot of a rutted road from which we could see that church, its graves. And we were walking through knee-deep grass. Then we came to the little house. Or shed. Some horses were living in it.

My grandfather had a sixth-grade education. He hated cars, airplanes, speed—modernity. He never learned to drive. There was still a shiny black hitching post out in front of the house. For a hobby, he studied railroad timetables, and knew which trains rode on what tracks all over America. He was always walking to the tracks to watch a train. He named my father after Eugene

Debs, the Socialist and trade union man. He did not allow any liquor in the house. He wore a long-sleeved shirt with cuff links every day of his life, and he'd wear the same necktie until it wore out, before he bought another. Always parsimonious, he did the grocery shopping rather than give my grandma any money—buying tongue, green-fried tomatoes, mush, hominy, the fatty cuts of meat. And when he took the family on vacation, it was always the same thing: one day in either Cleveland or Chicago to window-shop and ride the elevated.

He was part of the intolerance in the town, a narrow man. Yet I can also see him joining the Kluxers for the most painfully human reasons. The Klan made him respectable. For awhile there, all the "right people" belonged.

The Klan took over the Indiana Republican Party in 1924 and elected a majority of the state legislature. One open Klansman became governor, another the mayor of Indianapolis. Cameron thinks a prominent lawyer ran the Marion group. I read Kathleen M. Blee's *Women of the Klan*, because most of her research focuses on Indiana in the '20s, where, she concludes, the Klan was an integral part of white Protestant culture: "Far from the popular media image of people with weaknesses of character or temperament or intellect as the Klan's only adherents, the Klanswomen and Klansmen of the 1920s were more often—and perhaps more frighteningly—normal. Scholars disagree on the number of enrolled members, but it ranges between a quarter million and half a million at a time when Mississippi (for example) initiated 15,000. The indisputable fact is that in the '20s Indiana had more Kluxers than any other state, though it was 97 per cent white and Protestant.

The Klan had developed over the years from a raw expression of hate to a more convoluted expression of hate. After the Civil War, it had been a purely terrorist organization. But in the '20s, the Invisible Empire sold itself as a morality crusade redolent of today's "traditional values" campaigns. The Klan claimed that Jews, blacks, and Catholics were purveyors of vice and social decay.

Possibly the only white writer to examine what it meant to be white in a segregated society, and this in the '40s, Lillian Smith analyzed the signs and signifiers of the KKK, pointing out that no one could have dramatized the Return of the Repressed more vividly. These were men dressed in sheets and pillowcases, stalking through the darkness, intent most often on "the symbolic killing of a black male who, according to this paranoid fantasy, has 'raped' a 'sacred' white woman. It is a complete acting out of

45

the white man's internal guilt and his hatred of colored man and white woman."

Perhaps it should come as no surprise then that the Invisible Empire in Indiana collapsed in a sex scandal at the end of the '20s. Apparently, the state's charismatic Grand Dragon, D. C. Stephenson, had long been notorious among the Klan elite for sexual harassment, attempted rapes, deserted wives, and late-night orgies. But his exploits didn't become public until 1925, when he was arrested for the rape and murder of a young woman. Once Stephenson was convicted, many Klan members never attended another meeting, and political infighting began to discourage many of those who remained. Again, scholars disagree on an exact figure, but by 1928 membership had declined to somewhere between 4000 and 7000.

The most bizarre stories I found in my research relate to the Indiana Klan's fixation with Catholics, who were much more of a focus in the Hoosier State than either blacks or Jews. "Escaped nuns" and former "priests" often appeared at Klan rallies to regale their audiences with tales of Romanist sadomasochism, kidnapped white Protestant girls turned sexual slaves, and "abortions forced on nuns by the priests who fathered their babies." It's almost funny—these porn fantasies of the rubes, but they are a reminder of another fact: everyday life back then was determined in ways we can't imagine by phantoms, rumors, and myths. Many Klan members anticipated the imminent invasion of the pope, who, it was believed, already had a papal palace under construction in Washington, D.C. Given their loyalty to the "dago on the Tiber," Catholics were simply not good Americans. Blee recounts this incredible story from an anonymous informant: "Some Klan leader said that the Pope was coming to take over the country, and he said he might be on the next train that went through. . . . Just trying to make it specific. So, about a thousand people went out to the train station and stopped the train. It only had one passenger [car] and one passenger on it. They took him off, and he finally convinced them that he wasn't the Pope. He was a carpet salesman."

50   My grandfather had a particular hatred for Catholics. I still remember the worried dinner conversations over the possible election of John F. Kennedy—who would most likely be turning the country over to the pope. Maybe this antipathy helped push him to join his local klavern. I'll never have an answer to that mystery. When I first learned that he'd been a member, I remembered that his was the only one of my relatives homes in which I ever saw

black people—women from my grandma's Sunday school class. And I remembered that my grandma herself was one-quarter Indian. But these are the paradoxes of American racism.

Last august I went to Milwaukee to meet James Cameron.

It was a way to begin to find what had been hidden from me. At the time, I didn't analyze it beyond that. Certainly there was nothing I could do about my grandfather's choices, or about a lynching that took place decades before I was born, but somehow I felt I was still living the wages of that sin. *A human being was burned or hanged from a tree and you knew it had happened.* Or maybe you knew that someone you loved had even participated in it, or condoned it, or laughed at it. The moment embodied in that infamous Marion photograph was a tragedy for everyone there. And I didn't see a way to set it right. But I could go to Milwaukee.

When I met Cameron, I would have to acknowledge my own connection to that defining moment in his life, and I considered this with some apprehension. As I drove into the neighborhood near his museum, I realized I must also be near the parochial school where I attended kindergarten and first grade. I was born in Milwaukee, and back then, this area was undergoing "white flight."

America's Black Holocaust Museum sits on a quiet street between a public school and a soul food restaurant. Greeting me at the museum's locked steel door, Cameron is more robust than I expect. He is a soft-spoken man, a down-home Midwesterner who in many ways has lived an ordinary life. He puts in six days a week at the museum, by himself. As we sit in his small makeshift office, I ask him to talk about his life between the lynching and the present.

First came four years in prison, as an accessory before the fact to voluntary manslaughter in the death of Claude Deeter. Ordered to serve his parole outside Indiana, he moved to Detroit, then returned to Anderson, and finally moved to Milwaukee in 1953, working a series of blue-collar jobs. He worked at a shoeshine parlor, the Delco factory, then a cardboard-box factory. Went to night school to learn air conditioning and steam combustion. Worked at a big shopping mall. Retired. Then, went into business for himself as a rug and upholstery cleaner. He attends mass daily. In 1953, he converted to Catholicism, a faith he attributes to the example of Sheriff Bernard Bradley. He's been married for 55 years and raised five children.

But mostly what he's done for over 60 years is struggle obsessively to bear witness. He began writing *A Time of Terror* in prison, but authorities confiscated the manuscript when he was paroled. By early the next year, he'd written it out again. Once he'd moved to Anderson, he began going back to Marion to interview white people who'd witnessed the lynching. Cameron then rewrote the book about 100 more times as he accumulated nearly 300 rejections before self-publishing. He pulls out pamphlets he's produced on the Klan, the Confederate flag, the Thirteenth Amendment, slavery, Reconstruction, the first civil rights bill, the second civil rights bill . . . he's written hundreds. The latest is "Definite and Positive Proof that Free Black Men Did Vote Right Along With Free White Men in the Formation of the Constitution of the United States of America." Neither an academic nor an activist, he's out of the loop in which these messages usually get advanced, self-publishing as much as he can afford at $20 per copyright.

He hasn't even begun to renovate the ex-boxing school. His exhibits have been packed away for over a year. But Cameron points into the gymnasium where I notice basketball hoops and piles of chairs: "That'll be my Chamber of Horrors." That will be the room with, for example, the photo taken in Marion's courthouse square. Cameron intends to exhibit large pictures in the style of the Jewish Holocaust Museum. That's what inspired him, when he visited during a trip to Israel with his wife, Virginia, in 1979. "It shook me up something awful," he recalls. "I said to my wife, 'Honey, we need a museum like that in America to show what has happened to us black folks and the freedom-loving white people who've been trying to help us.' " He shows me where he intends to put his bookstore, his contemplation room, his lecture and screening room. The spaces are still filled with old weightlifting machines, lockers, a pool table.

This building is his third location. With $5000 of his own money, he opened the museum in 1988 on the second floor of Milwaukee's Black Muslim headquarters, then moved to a storefront around the corner, but he never had room to exhibit more than 10 photos or to store many of his 10,000 books on race relations. And, to his utter frustration, he would sometimes go for days without a single person coming in. *And I only am escaped alone to tell thee.*

The approach of his 80th birthday has kindled a sense of urgency. "I got one foot in the grave and the other one got no business being out," he chuckles, then sobers. "I wish that book would hurry up and come out so I can get some speaking engagements under my belt and then I can get my money to put that boiler in."

Cameron is part of that tradition of African Americans who 60
would hold this country to her ideals. He would like to replace the
word "racism" with "un-American." He pulls out a copy of Ralph
Ginzburg's *100 Years of Lynchings*. "This should be in every home
just like the Bible." I ask him if he's ever studied history—noting
*The Rhetoric of Racial Revolt, The Negro Since Emancipation,
Writings* by W. E. B. Dubois and stacks of other books in his clut-
tered office. "Yes," he replies. "I live in history."

"My grandparents were from Marion," I tell him.

"They probably remember it," says Cameron.

This benign assessment of what I know to be shameful slows
me down. "My father remembers it too, even though he was only
seven when it happened."

"Yeah, that made an impression on him. Sure."

He begins to tell me his story, even though he has said that he 65
doesn't like to do this one-on-one. It's still too emotional for him.
Showing me a postcard of the Marion jail, he points out where
Tommy was, where Abe was, where he was. Almost compulsively,
he describes how they were beaten, how he'd found out later that
the Marion sheriff, Jacob Campbell, was in the Klan, and how,
when the mob was about to hang him, he prayed. "And then this
voice spoke from heaven. It was from heaven. No human voice
could have quelled the fury of that mob." Then a great silence fell
over the crowd, and he entered what seemed like a room made of
film negatives, where he and everyone else was "petrified," and he
couldn't tell anymore if they were black or white.

I tell him my family's story, leaving out the cruel part—the
laughter. "Then, after he died, we found out that my grandfather
was in the Klan."

"That happens," he replies.

"All my father said was he never saw a hooded sheet."

"You know what?" Cameron tells me. "During the roaring
'20s, Indiana had over a half million Klansmen and Marion had
the first chapter. They were called the mother den of all the Klans
in Indiana. It was an upgoing thing. If you weren't in the Klan,
you were nobody, and that's what gave them the liberty to lynch
black people with impunity. Sure."

"My grandfather may well have known about the lynching 70
and may well have approved of it."

"Sure." He gets up, saying that he has something special to
show me, a new artifact for the museum. Someone in Marion had
sent him one of the Klan's infamous "souvenirs." The ropes used
to hang Tommy Shipp and Abe Smith had been cut into pieces

and distributed as mementos. Now, from a business envelope, Cameron pulls a piece of nondescript and fraying rope. A handwritten document says that it was obtained from the original owner by the man elected sheriff several years after the lynching, and that it was unknown which of the two ropes it came from. "I'm going to put that in a glass case with all kinds of padlocks on it," he says, handing it over for me to inspect. "You're the first one to have seen this."

In my conversations with Cameron, I found myself constantly astonished at things he mentioned in passing. I would stumble to rephrase a question, not sure I'd heard him right. Most of these little shocks related to his interactions with white people—not the brutal ones, the "nice" ones. Like the 200-plus white people Cameron found who'd been among the spectators at his near-death. The actual lynch mob probably numbered between 25 and 50. But thousands more had watched. Those Cameron interviewed were all happy to see that he'd survived the beating (rumor had it he'd died), but none of them had lifted a finger to ensure that he would survive. And they now demonstrated neither a reluctance to talk nor a wish to apologize.

Then there's the story about the mayor of Marion, who came to visit Cameron in jail the day of the lynching, bringing with him a red-haired man who had the bottom half of his face covered with a handkerchief. I think we can assume that the redhead was a ringleader, that he'd come to see which three prisoners they'd be taking from the jail, but he remained silent while the mayor asked Cameron how old he was and what his mother did for a living and had he ever been in trouble before. Then the mayor left town "on business" before the lynching began. In 1980, Cameron visited the old mayor and together they looked at the infamous picture taken that night while the mayor named for him nearly every person in it. They were photographed while doing this, for *Ebony* magazine.

In an old article from the Marion paper, I read a vehement denial from Sheriff Campbell's daughter about his allegiance to the Klan. Not only was he never allied with them, she asserted, but it was his voice that called out that night to save James Cameron.

75   When I related this to Cameron, he said. "Isn't that pitiful?"

These historic crimes are the ghosts still flitting through all of our lives. Perhaps if we white people could take responsibility, reconciliation could happen. But how do we do that? The further we get from these stories and their contexts, the easier it is to say: I wasn't there; I didn't do anything. We ignore how much the new stories grow out of old rot. And we can't acknowledge that we've done something that needs forgiving.

But in 1991, Cameron decided that *he* would ask to be forgiven. He wrote a letter to Indiana governor Evan Bayh, requesting a pardon "for the foolish role I played in the commission of a crime that resulted in the loss of three precious lives." Cameron said the idea to request a pardon just came to him. He wanted to clear his name before he died. He wanted to "wipe this whole thing clean." Bayh signed the pardon in February of last year, and Cameron went back to Marion. The mayor gave him a key to the city in a ceremony at a Marion hotel, and Cameron wiped away tears as the inscription on his pardon was read.

"Now that the state of Indiana has forgiven me for my indiscretion," he told the overflow crowd, "I, in turn, forgive Indiana for their transgressors of the law in Marion on the night of August 7, 1930. I forgive those who have harmed me and Abe and Tom realizing I can never forget the traumatic events that look place that night."

See, he did it for us. Wiped it clean.

In a racist society, a white person can not feel "whole." That 80 was the conclusion reached by Lillian Smith, and I keep going back to her because she is one of the very few to consider what whiteness means, and what its tragedy might be. "Only a few of our people are killers," she wrote in her analysis of lynching, but she noted the heightened level of violence, how usually the black man was killed several times over, becoming a receptacle for "dammed-up hate" and "forbidden feelings." There's a pathology there that leaks out into everyday relationships. Only a few of our people are killers, but we are dissemblers, dehumanizers, averters of eyes, enforcers of a rift in our psyches, and all because we're wearing the hood—to hide our guilt, our past, and our helplessness in the face of that past. This is why Smith analyzed lynching, in the end, as "a Sign, not so much of troubled race relations, as of a troubled way of life that threatens to rise up and destroy all the people who live it."

I remember my childhood disquiet with that Bible verse about "visiting the iniquities of the fathers upon the children unto the third and fourth generation." It was so unfair, yet I worried that it might be true. I no longer know this as the curse of a wrathful God but as the curse we've brought on ourselves by refusing to look at our histories. We white people don't want to feel guilty, of course. And guilt isn't useful. But, too often, we compensate by feeling nothing.

We can at least begin to tell the truth about the past. I decided to, hoping in some way to uplift my race.

Stabilizing the Text

1. Interpret the title of this essay. In what ways is Carr's tale "American" and not just personal? What are the legacies Carr discusses? In what ways are Carr's readers part of the legacies of lynching?
2. Identify the part of Carr's essay that made the strongest impression on you. Analyze Carr's writing in that part. Discuss at least three aspects of the writing and how those aspects contribute to the impression the writing makes on you.
3. "An American Tale" begins with an epigraph from Lillian Smith. How does that epigraph relate to Carr's article? Are hypocritical race/gender boundaries similar to those Smith describes still maintained today? In what ways is Carr's "American Tale" in keeping with, or a violation of, present-day expectations about the writing of "a nice white girl"?

Mobilizing the Text

1. Carr mentions her family's laughter several times in this essay. What do you think laughter means in the story? How does Carr's repetition of that detail affect the way that you as a reader make sense of the stories she tells? What are the alternatives to laughter that she offers?
2. How do Carr's final words relate to the rest of her article? Can her article "uplift her race" as she hopes? How so? As you reflect on this question, compare Carr's essay to other things you've read about cities and race and discussions of race. How is her message typical or unique and how is the manner in which she delivers it typical or unique?
3. In the conclusion of her essay, Carr discusses a "curse we've brought on ourselves by refusing to look at our histories." What does she mean? Thinking of your own experiences as a citizen, in what ways do you think she's right or wrong? What problems that we face as a society are made harder to deal with because of inattention to history? How so?

Bloods/Crips Proposal for LA's Face-Lift

BLOODS AND CRIPS

The uprising that followed the Rodney King verdict caused two long-time rival Los Angeles gangs to call a truce in their feuds. Working together, these gangs articulated the following proposal to restore the

*physical and emotional infrastructure of the inner-city neighbor-
hoods in South Central Los Angeles. The proposal, which was published in* Why L.A. Happened, *suggests a list of projects that
demonstrate the diversity of factors underlying the kind of insurrection that Los Angeles experienced. As you read this document, think
about the ways in which diverse aspects of experience come together
to influence how people feel about their reality and their prospects.
Pay attention to the diversity of problems and solutions that the document brings up and ask yourself throughout: What is the fundamental solution that the Bloods and Crips document is proposing?*

------------------- ◆ -------------------

Burned and Abandoned Structures

Every burned and abandoned structure shall be gutted. The city
will purchase the property if not already owned by the city, and
build a community center. If the structure is on a corner lot or is a
vacant lot, the city will build a career counseling center or a
recreation area, respectively.

Repavement

All pavements/sidewalks in Los Angeles are in dire need of resur-
facing. The Department of Transportation shall pay special attention to the pedestrian walkways and surface streets located in
predominantly poor and minority areas. Our organization will assist the city in the identification of all areas of concern.

Lighting

All lighting will be increased in all neighborhoods. Additionally,
lighting of city streets, neighborhood blocks and alleyways will be
amended. We want a well-lit neighborhood. All alleys shall be
painted white or yellow by the building owners and alley lights
will be installed at the cost of the owner.

Landscaping

All trees will be properly trimmed and maintained. We want all
weeded/shrubbed areas to be cleaned up and properly nurtured.
New trees will be planted to increase the beauty of our neighborhoods.

Sanitation

5 A special task force shall be assigned to focus on the clean-up of all vacant lots and trashed areas throughout the deprived areas. Proper pest control methods shall be implemented by the city to reduce the chances of rodent scattering. The city will declare a neighborhood clean-up week wherein all residents will be responsible for their block—a block captain will be assigned to ensure cooperation. Residents will clean up the block in unisys.

$2 billion shall be appropriated for this effort over and above existing appropriations.

BLOODS/CRIPS ECONOMIC DEVELOPMENT PROPOSAL

Loans shall be made available by the federal and state governments to provide interested minority entrepreneurs interested in doing business in these deprived areas. The loan requirements shall not be so stringent that it will make it impossible for a businessman to acquire these loans. These loans shall not exceed a 4% interest bearing charge per year. The businessman shall not be required to have security for the loan, however, the businessman must present at least two years of business operation and taxes, with a city license before funds will be allocated. The owner, must have either an established business desiring to expand or a sound business plan. Assistance for business plans shall be made available to these businessmen by the Small Business Administration. Additionally, the Small Business Administration will provide agents to help each business to develop a sound business plan from beginning to end. No one will be neglected in receiving adequate assistance. These business owners shall be required to hire 90% of their personnel from within their community and the monies shall not be distributed in a lump sum. Funds will be released in increments outlined by the business plan. Any businessman that doesn't conform to the hiring practices will have funding ceased until they conform.

$20 million shall be appropriated for this program over and above existing appropriations.

Please note all grants for these major reconstructions shall be granted to minority-owned businesses. While these minority-owned businesses are doing the work in our communities, they must hire at least 50% of their work force from within the community. *NO* front organizations will be tolerated!

BLOODS/CRIPS HUMAN WELFARE PROPOSAL

Hospitals and Health Care Centers

Federal government shall provide the deprived areas with three
new hospitals and 40 additional health care centers. Dental clinics
shall be made available within ten miles of each community. The
services shall be free and supported by federal and state funds.

Welfare

We demand that welfare be completely removed from our community and these welfare programs be replaced by state work and
product manufacturing plants that provide the city with certain
supplies. State monies shall only be provided for individuals and
the elderly. The State of California shall provide a child welfare
building to serve as day care centers for single parents. We would
like to encourage all manufacturing companies to vigorously hire
these low income recipients and the state and federal governments shall commit to expand their institutions to provide work
for these former welfare recipients.

Parks & Recreation

Los Angeles parks shall receive a complete face-lift, and develop
activities and programs in the parks throughout the night. Stages,
pools and courts shall be reconstructed and resurfaced, and the
city shall provide highly visible security 24 hours a day for these
parks and recreational centers. Programs at the park shall be in
accordance with educational programs and social exchange programs developed by the city for adults and young adults.

*$1 billion dollars shall be appropriated for this program over
and above existing appropriations.*

BLOODS/CRIPS EDUCATIONAL PROPOSAL

1. Maximizing education standards in the low income areas is
   essential to reduce the possibilities of repeated insurrection.
   The Bloods/Crips propose that:

   a. $300 million will go into the reconstruction and refurbish-
      ment of the Los Angeles Unified School District (LAUSD)
      structures,

b. $200 million will be donated for computers, supplies and updated books (each student shall have the necessary books),

c. All teachers' salaries shall be no less than $30,000.00 a year to give them an incentive to educate in our districts, and

d. Re-election shall be held for all Los Angeles Board of Education members.

2. Reconstruction shall include repainting, sandblasting and reconstruction of all LAUSD schools: remodeling of classrooms, repainting of hallways and meeting areas; all schools shall have new landscaping and more plants and trees around the schools; completely upgrade the bathrooms, making them more modern: provide a bathroom monitor to each bathroom which will provide freshen-up toiletries at a minimum cost to the students (the selling of toiletries will support the salary of the bathroom monitor).

3. A provision for accelerated educational learning programs shall be implemented for the entire LAUSD to provide aggressive teaching methods and provide a curriculum similar to non-economically deprived areas. Tutoring for all subjects will be made available to all students after normal school hours. It will be mandatory for all students with sub-level grades to participate.

   In these after-school tutorial programs, those students whose grades are up to par will receive federally funded bonus bonds which will be applied to their continued education upon graduation from high school. They will also receive bonus bonds for extra scholastic work towards assisting their fellow students. All institutions shall maintain a second shift of substitute teachers in the schools to enforce educational excellence.

   Special financial bonuses shall be given to students who focus on education beyond the school's requirement in the areas of applied math and sciences. High achievers in these areas shall be granted a free trip to another country for educational exchange. Fifty students from each school will be granted this opportunity each year for an indefinite period.

4. The LAUSD will provide up-to-date books to the neglected areas and enough books to ensure that no student has to share a book with another. Supplies shall be made plentiful and school-sponsored financial programs shall be instituted in order to maintain equipment and supplies for the institution after the first donation.

5. LAUSD will remove all teachers not planning to further their education along with teachers who have not proven to have a passionate concern for the students in which they serve. All teachers shall be given a standard competency test to verify they are up-to-date with subjects and modern teaching methods. Psychological testing will also be required for all teachers and educational administrators, including the Los Angeles School Board, every four years.

6. All curriculums shall focus on the basics in high school requirements and it shall be inundated with advanced sciences and additional applied math, English and writing skills.

7. Bussing shall become non-existent in our communities if all of the above demands are met.

$700 million shall be appropriated for these programs over and above existing appropriations.

BLOODS/CRIPS LAW ENFORCEMENT PROGRAM

The Los Angeles communities are demanding that they are policed and patrolled by individuals whom live in the community and the commanding officers be ten-year residents of the community in which they serve. Former gang members shall be given a chance to be patrol buddies in assisting in the protection of the neighborhood. These former gang members will be required to go through police training and must comply to all of the laws instituted by our established authorities. Uniforms will be issued to each and every member of the "buddy system," however, no weapons will be issued. All patrol units must have a buddy patrol notified and present in the event of a police matter. Each buddy patrol will be supplied with a video camera and will tape each event and the officers handling the police matter. The buddy patrol will not interfere with any police matter unless instructed by a commanding officer. Each buddy patrol will also be supplied with a vehicle.

$6 million shall be appropriated for this program over and above existing appropriations.

IN RETURN FOR THESE DEMANDS THE BLOODS/CRIPS ORGANIZATION WILL:

1. Request the drug lords of Los Angeles take their monies and invest them in business and property in Los Angeles.

2. Encourage these drug lords to stop the drug traffic and get them to use the money constructively. We will match the funds of the state government appropriations and build building-for-building.
3. Additionally, we will match funds for an AIDS research and awareness center in South Central and Long Beach that will only hire minority researchers and physicians to assist in the AIDS epidemic.

CONCLUSION

Meet these demands and the targeting of police officers will stop!!
You have 72 hours for a response and a commitment, in writing, to support these demands. Additionally, you have 30 days to begin implementation. And, finally, you have four years to complete the projects of construction of the major hospitals and restorations.
GIVE US THE HAMMER AND THE NAILS, WE WILL REBUILD THE CITY.

Budget Demands*

Proposal for LA's Face-Lift	$2,000,000,000
Educational Proposal	700,000,000
Law Enforcement Program	6,000,000
Economic Development Proposal	20,000,000
Human Welfare Proposal	1,000,000,000
TOTAL	$3,726,000,000

*To be appropriated over and above existing appropriations.

Stabilizing the Text

1. What does the Bloods/Crips proposal look like? In what ways do you think the Bloods/Crips document meets the expectations of different audiences? What aspects of the proposal's form can you associate with specific possible audiences?
2. How would you characterize the tone of this piece? What specific words or phrases are used in the Bloods/Crips proposal to maintain a consistent tone throughout the document?
3. The Bloods/Crips proposal first considers the physical environment, then the economy, human welfare, education, and law enforcement. How does this arrangement influence the ways you understand the objectives and priorities of the text?

Mobilizing the Text

1. Public policy proposals are typically offered by elected officials and government figures. In what ways do you think that it is good for "civilians" to offer proposals like the Bloods/Crips document? Does this text express values that you think are different from those expressed by government?

2. Which of the changes that the authors propose or demand seem most important for people to consider? Why is that proposal important? What underlying values does it stress?

3. Compare the terms "proposal," "program," and "demand" as they are used in this text. How do you think each of these terms would affect an audience? Which term seems to you to be the most accurate as a description of the text's content? What audience do you think would respond most positively to the text and why?

Building Democracy from Below
MANNING MARABLE

Manning Marable is professor of history and political science, and founding director of the Institute for Research in African-American Studies, at Columbia University. Marable is a prominent lecturer and interpreter of the politics and history of race in America. His most recent publications include Black Leadership; Black Liberation in Conservative America; Dispatches from the Ebony Tower, *edited volume;* Let Nobody Turn Us Around, *edited with Leith Mullings; and* The Great Wells of Democracy: The Meaning of Race in American Life. *He also writes "Along the Color Line," a radio and newspaper commentary series. In this excerpt from "Building Democracy from Below," a chapter in* The Great Wells of Democracy, *Marable situates the shooting of Timothy Thomas and its aftermath in Cincinnati within larger dynamics of race, opportunity, and the lessons to be learned from people's efforts to organize collective action to improve their lives.*

◆

I

Two hours after midnight on April 7, 2001, nineteen-year-old Timothy Dewayne Thomas left his apartment, which was located in Cincinnati's inner-city neighborhood called Over-the-Rhine, and walked to a nearby convenience store to buy some cigarettes. Although Over-the-Rhine was less than twelve city blocks from Cincinnati's central business district and impressive new Convention Center, it was generally considered by most of the city's white population a dangerous, drug-filled ghetto. For most African-American residents of Over-the-Rhine, the district's petty dealers, prostitutes, and grifters who came out after dark posed no threat to personal safety. Thomas's only worry was the possibility of running into the police, who had a habit of stopping and frisking black men out at night without probable cause. Thomas had been stopped eleven times since March 2000, mostly on suspected driving infractions, such as driving without a seat belt, and other petty misdemeanors. Twice he had managed to run away, darting into familiar neighborhood alleys and one-way streets. All he wanted was to pick up some cigarettes and go home to his girlfriend and their newborn baby boy.

Several Cincinnati police officers, including Stephen Roach, twenty-seven years old, saw Thomas returning home on foot and decided to check him out. When they confronted Thomas, the young laborer decided that the only prudent course of action was to run. Thomas bolted, and the police followed in pursuit. The foot chase lasted for nearly ten minutes. Thomas ran down an alley not far from the corner of Thirteenth Street and Republic. Officer Roach circled around the block and waited for Thomas at the end of the alley with his gun ready to fire. Thomas stopped suddenly and, according to one version of the events later offered by Officer Roach, appeared to reach into the waistband of his oversized pants. Roach fired, hitting Thomas once, killing him. No weapon was found on Thomas's body.

Thomas was the fifteenth African-American male who had been killed by the Cincinnati police, and the fourth in the previous six months. As word spread the next day about Thomas's killing, many residents of Over-the-Rhine and other black neighborhoods throughout the city were overwhelmed with grief and outrage. Spontaneously, people went into the streets, venting their hostility against the symbols of white power and property. Garbage cans were hurled through plate glass windows; fires were started in white-owned businesses along the central business district of the neighborhood; property and goods were looted. Cincinnati Mayor Charlie Luken responded by declaring a "state of emergency" and imposing an 11:00 P.M. curfew until the rebellion stopped. Police were outfitted in riot gear and armed with tear gas and bean bags filled with metal shot. As the rioting continued on April 10 and 11, businesses closed and the city buses in inner-city neighborhoods stopped running. Thousands of urban residents who relied on public transportation were unable to go to work. After four days of unrest, the police tactics succeeded in suppressing most of the urban unrest. Cops traveled in pairs or teams, never alone, and arrested black women, men, and even children, frequently without cause. As peace was restored, 837 people had been arrested and dozens injured.

The vast majority of black Cincinnati residents had not participated in the street disturbances, and a number of black elected officials, religious leaders, and community activists publicly urged African Americans to show restraint and not to violate the police curfew. On April 14, the funeral service for Timothy Thomas was held at the New Prospect Baptist Church. Attended by hundreds of people, the service attracted many who wanted to make a political statement against the epidemic of police brutality present in Cincinnati and throughout the United States. The new Black Panther Party, an eccentric group of black nationalists who bear little resemblance to the original group of African-American community activists, served as pallbearers. As the family and a small number of friends buried Thomas in a private service, more than 2,000 protesters marched quietly through the Over-the-Rhine district. A series of national civil-rights leaders attended the protest march or came to speak in the city within weeks after the civil unrest, including NAACP President Kweisi Mfume, the Reverend Al Sharpton, Martin Luther King III, and the Reverend Fred Shuttlesworth. Much of the attention on local leadership focused on a charismatic black minister, the Reverend Damon Lynch, an Over-the-Rhine activist whose constructive work with youth had earned him much respect.

On May 7, 2001, one month after Thomas's death, a Cincinnati grand jury indicted Officer Roach on only two misdemeanor counts, negligent homicide and "obstruction of official business," which together were punishable by less than one year in prison. Roach was tried in criminal court, and on September 26, 2001, he was found not guilty. About a hundred social-justice activists stood outside the courtroom awaiting the decision. When it was announced, they were stunned. The police anticipated a strong reaction to the decision and were prepared to use force if necessary to quell any spontaneous demonstrations. When some protesters attempted to organize a march outside the courthouse, they were quickly dispersed. Mayor Luken, taking no chances, imposed a curfew for several days.

The social unrest and public violence precipitated by the Thomas killing was the culmination of decades of structural racism and official indifference. In 1967, Cincinnati experienced a racial uprising in its ghetto areas that had resulted in hundreds of arrests and the destruction of several million dollars' worth of private property. Police relationships with the city's African-American population became tense again in the late 1970s, when four white officers and four black civilians were killed in a series of armed confrontations. The police demanded and were given the authority to carry .357 magnums with powerful exploding bullets, began to wear bulletproof vests, and acquired state-of-the-art weapons for crowd control and assault.

In the 1970s and 1980s, tens of thousands of middle- and upper-class whites moved out of the city. Over-the-Rhine, which for many years had been racially and ethnically diverse, became predominantly African American, and overwhelmingly poor. According to Cincinnati's City Planning Department, the total population of the city declined by 6 percent, or 21,417 people, from 1980 to 1990. Fourteen percent of all households were on public assistance, 18 percent were headed by females, and 24 percent fell below the federal poverty line. The median household income citywide in 1990 stood at $21,006, the ninth lowest out of the seventy-five largest U.S. cities. The rate of home ownership, at only 35 percent of all households, was also the ninth lowest of that group.

The statistics for Cincinnati's Empowerment Zones, impoverished urban districts targeted for development under federal legislation, were even more disturbing. About three out of four of the 50,000 residents living in these zones were African Americans. Their 1989 median income was $10,877; more than one-fourth survived on public assistance, 45 percent were defined by federal poverty criteria as poor, and six out of ten children were living in poverty. Nearly one-half of the adults over the age of twenty-five did not have a high-school diploma. Fewer than one-fifth of all households owned their own homes, and 44 percent of all adults were not in the paid labor force.

The political and corporate establishment's approach to addressing these expanding pockets of poverty and despair only made matters worse. The city spent millions of tax dollars to subsidize the construction of downtown sports stadiums and to advertise Cincinnati as a Midwestern mecca for tourism and convention gatherings. Relatively little was spent to enhance the quality and availability of housing for low-to-median-income families, to upgrade public schools, or to assist in the development of community-based, black-owned businesses. Major highway construction and downtown developments disrupted and divided neighborhoods and displaced the homeless and the poor. Yet the plight of Cincinnati's racialized urban poor was little different from the situation confronting black, brown, and oppressed populations elsewhere in the decaying cores of America's depopulated urban landscapes. And it was these socioeconomic conditions, the normal inequalities of daily life, that had fostered and perpetuated the volatile climate of black alienation, white anxiety, and excessive police force that caused Thomas's death.

There was a new determination in Cincinnati's black community not to allow the tragedy to go unanswered. On Tuesday, April 24, 2001, African-American leaders throughout the city met to devise a concrete plan of action. Notes from this remarkable discussion of "African American Grassroots Leadership" provided by black community leader Reginald Boyd indicate the profound soul searching in the black community in the aftermath of the urban uprising. The general discussion focused on generating practical strategies to foster community empowerment. Relatively few comments centered on the immediate issues of police brutality and the lack of governmental accountability, because a clear consensus about these issues was readily apparent to nearly everyone at the meeting. "What happened in Cincinnati was not a RIOT," one participant said, "it was a REBELLION and in SELF DEFENSE." The "police are out of control inside and outside the City of Cincinnati." Another participant suggested changing "the policy that pays suspended officers," because "if they are not paid then there will be fewer problems because suspension will stop their income." Others encouraged the group to "look carefully at the homicide investigations into the death of African-American children" and to contribute to a "legal defense fund to assist those who were arrested." Participants in the conference were clear that public safety was necessary for people to live and work in the neighborhoods, and that responsible law enforcement was necessary in the preservation of civil order. One black police officer expressed these sentiments by observing, "We want and need policing in our community, but we want GOOD POLICING."

In early 2002, the Cincinnati Black United Front, led by the Reverend Damon Lynch, came together with two other progressive groups, Stonewall Cincinnati and the Coalition for a Just

Cincinnati, to initiate a nationwide boycott against the city's economic elite. The boycott campaign urged celebrities, business and social groups, and others planning conferences or events in downtown Cincinnati to cancel their engagements. The coalition announced that the boycott would be terminated only when city leaders met its "demands for neighborhood economic development, police accountability, support and enforcement of civil rights, and government and election reform." At first, the politicians and the media largely ignored the boycott effort, stating that it would be ineffective. But within weeks, a host of prominent performers canceled their local engagements, including Wynton Marsalis, Bill Cosby, Whoopi Goldberg, Smokey Robinson, and the Temptations. Many civic and fraternal organizations pulled out. The city government responded by launching an ad campaign touting the area's incredibly rich "diversity" and pushing the banal slogan, "Cincinnati Can: You Can Too!"

In early February 2002, when I visited the Cincinnati area, I walked through the Over-the-Rhine community and spoke before the Black United Front. Local television stations were filled with stories about black workers who had been dismissed from their jobs at downtown restaurants and shops due to the boycott. Mayor Charlie Luken and several prominent blacks with ties to Cincinnati's largest corporate employer, Proctor and Gamble, charged that the economic campaign was destroying the city's reputation and damaging any hope for improving the material conditions of poor black people.

These and other shrill attacks against the Black United Front were largely ineffective. Not unlike the 1980s campaign to promote divestment of U.S. corporations from engaging in business in South Africa, the Cincinnati boycott created the necessary political pressure to force the city's corporate and political establishment to reach a settlement with their critics. Almost one year after Thomas's slaying and the urban uprising, Mayor Luken admitted to the press that Cosby's decision was a crucial blow: "Cosby gave it legs. . . . It had a negative effect on our image." A tentative agreement was soon reached between city government officials and representatives of the Black United Front and other African-American constituencies, the police union, and the American Civil Liberties Union. New guidelines were established, according to the *New York Times*, "to deal with decades of racial profiling complaints by African Americans." Luken "promised to get behind the new agreement with fresh job, education and housing opportunities for needier neighborhoods." Luken informed the media, "We want to be the model that other cities will look to and say, hey they put all their problems out on Front Street and they're dealing with them the right way." In the most stunning move, Luken appointed Valerie A. Lemmie, an African-American woman and the respected city manager of Dayton, Ohio, to become Cincinnati's city manager. As the city's highest-ranking official, Lemmie promised black residents, "There'll be no smoke and mirrors in getting this done. . . . This is all about respect for other human beings."

Despite these positive changes, many in the boycott coalition favored continuing the pressure on the local political and corporate elite to ensure that promises made would be kept. As Diskin and Dutton observed, "the coalition of non-profit community-based organizations and other groups that are supporting the boycott have called for economic inclusion, a greater political voice, police accountability, housing rights, and job production. This renewed and broad-based participation must translate into policies and practices that help build local communities."

II

An important lesson can be drawn from the events in Cincinnati 15 following the death of Timothy Dewayne Thomas: To challenge the effects of neoliberalism and revive those suffering from civil death, a black political project must be grounded in grassroots struggles around practical questions of daily life. Such struggles bring into the public arena diverse and sometimes contradictory ideological and social forces. In the Cincinnati grassroots resistance movement, a wealth of new ideas were brought out in public brainstorming sessions, especially in the areas of public-policy issues and economic development. It is at this grassroots level that blacks might begin the difficult task of constructing new social theory and political strategies, extrapolating from their collective experiences and practices of neighborhood and community-based activism. This approach to politics starts with the micro-battles of neighborhood empowerment to bring about change in the macro-contexts of national and international processes impacting African Americans.

During the period of Jim Crow segregation, any references to the "Negro community" could be immediately understood on both sides of the color line. "The black community" was a territorial, geographical, and sociopolitical site occupied by blacks. Its existence was simultaneously a product of coercion and voluntary activity. With the processes of desegregation, class stratification, and to some degree middle-class out-migration from the inner cities, the meaning of "community" for African Americans is less clear-cut. All communities are sites of collective imagination, social processes rather than mere locations for living and work. Within the concept of the black community, there is a social geography of blackness—a set of political, social, and economic experiences and relations with whites as a dominant group that to a large extent define and construct our collective understandings of daily life. Where we work, whether we obtain home mortgages, the quality of medical treatment we receive, and the encounters our sons may have with the police all contribute to a sense of membership and kinship to an "imagined" black community. In this larger sense, it is possible to talk about a black community's rituals, folklore, discourses, and contested forms of cultural construction that are independent of a territorial space.

It is helpful to consider black political theorist Adolph Reed's warnings about the pitfalls of black community-based politics. In a perceptive 1996 article, Reed argued, "The main internal obstacle to generating a popularly based progressive black political movement is the very concept of 'black community,' and the rhetoric of authenticity that comes with it." For Reed, "the ideal of community is a mystification, however, and an antidemocratic one at that." For decades, black activists provided critical support to a series of community-based "leaders" who in turn manipulated race to practice brokerage politics. "I suspect that black activists' continuing romance with political hustlers and demagogues ('Up with hope, down with dope!') stems from their seductive promise of connection to a real, mobilizable constituency," Reed suggested. "There are no significant forces on the ground in black politics attempting to generate any sort of popular, issue-based civic discourse, and the language of community is largely the reason."

Much of what Reed says I absolutely agree with. Community-based politics always reflect the many contradictions existing in all communities—homophobia, sexism, class elitism and privilege, anti-immigrant bias, and so forth. Conservative black nationalists like Farrakhan have historically manipulated the language of community for their own purposes. Liberal integrationist politicians may espouse the goal of black cultural and political advancement into the mainstream, but they also utilize the concept of community to mask their own class interests and support for the political establishment. That is exactly why a class-based, progressive intervention around community-based organizing is so urgently necessary.

Many community-based protests, as I have illustrated, are simultaneously class-based struggles around clear-cut economic justice issues. Community-based coalitions struggling for affordable public transportation, health care, decent schools, or an end to police brutality in their neighborhoods may all eventually contribute to black and multiracial progressive movements for democratic change. Even more important, community organizations are frequently the sites where many working-class and low-income black, Asian, and Latina women become actively engaged in day-to-day resistance. These neighborhood struggles led by women greatly enrich our understanding of the possibilities for change within the entire society and we should support them and learn from them. At the same time, we must consciously oppose the racial essentialism and antidemocratic trends that Reed correctly cited as inherent in many community-based formations and struggles.

One great difficulty in building black community-based capacity from below is the contradictory impact of racism on the oppressed. "Race" is constantly and continuously constructed from without and within the sites of human activity and experience. That is to say, "race" is not real, but "racism" is manufactured constantly by the formal institutional barriers that reproduce inequality, which in turn shape the texture and contours of the lives of the people living under such a regime. The sites of racialized existence become spaces for fighting back, for noncooperation, for hope and courage when the objective realities of one's situation appear to negate all possibilities for change. It is through the veil of race that the oppressed comprehend and interpret the social forces that impact their families, friends, and communities. But the strengths of racialized radicalism also produce cultural, social, and even psychological barriers to building movements across racial boundaries. As in the intense public debate recorded at the African American Grassroots Leadership conference in Cincinnati, there are real schisms within many black communities about how to relate to other racialized ethnic groups and immigrant populations that do not share our own history. Petty differences drawn from language, cultural traditions and mores, and codes of public conduct and courtesy can be misinterpreted in antagonistic ways, dividing communities who share in most respects common material and political interests.

The Over-the-Rhine neighborhood is more than 80 percent black—but about one in six community residents are white, Latino, or Muslim. There are several working-class neighborhoods in Cincinnati where white household median income falls below the national average and where chronically high rates of unemployment exist. The debate over the Cincinnati boycott, as it was projected in the national media, was presented solely in black versus white terms, which grossly misrepresented the real political dynamics in that city's struggle. There were prominent African Americans, including one NAACP local leader, who publicly opposed the boycott, and there were liberal, religious, and community activist whites who supported it. The same media distortions about the multiracial character of community-based coalition politics exist nationally.

If you watched commercial television twenty-four hours a day for an entire year, you'd never guess that poor whites existed in the United States. Poor white people are never depicted in television commercials, and only rarely are they mentioned in the electronic media. The great American national narrative, the story everybody learns, is that this country resolved the problems of disadvantaged whites sometime between the Great Depression and the Great Society. Exposés illustrating the impact of workfare requirements seldom profile white single mothers and their children.

In reality, there are several million white people who are trapped within what ideologically conservative sociologists call the "underclass," neighborhoods in which 40 percent or more of the residents live below the government's poverty line. These urban pockets of white poverty exhibit the same kinds of devastating socioeconomic statistics that Daniel Patrick Moynihan nearly forty years ago mistakenly attributed to the cultural and social pathology of black female-headed households—high percentages of school dropouts, teenage pregnancies, single-parent families, unemployment, and mass incarceration.

Using an extremely narrow definition of white underclass poverty—two contiguous census tracks in which at least 50 percent of the residents were non-Hispanic whites, at least 40 percent lived below the poverty line, and more than 300 were headed by single white females—U.S. News and World Report in 1994 identified fifteen areas that by any standard fell into William Julius Wilson's category of the "truly disadvantaged." In the eastside communities of La Grange-Central and Vestula in Toledo, Ohio, an area with 13,000 residents, nearly 600 households consist of white female-headed families with children, and 46 percent of all people exist below the federal government's poverty line. In the economically depressed area near the westside of Syracuse, a neighborhood of 11,800 residents, 49 percent are poor. In Flint,

Michigan, the home of thousands of unemployed white auto-workers, 56 percent of all households in the mostly white areas of the central city on the south and east sides are below the poverty line. In the depressed Whittier and Phillips neighborhoods in Minneapolis, which have a combined population of 22,000, two-thirds of all families live in poverty. And in the southern tip of South Boston, which is virtually all white, there were 453 white female-headed families with children, and the poverty rate was a staggeringly high 73 percent.

In 1994, Ronald Mincy of the Ford Foundation and re-   25
searchers at the Urban Institute found that black and white ghettoes are similar in several important respects: "Both white and black underclass areas are filled with men who abandoned the work force and residents who dropped out of high school." In these so-called "white underclass" census tracts, an average of 42 percent of all adults had failed to complete secondary school, 55 percent of all adult males were not in the paid labor force, and 53 percent of all households were single-parent, female-headed families. For many social liberals, these statistics seemed to validate the color-blind thesis that poverty, not race, was the principal factor in perpetuating the underclass.

As attractive as this thesis might be to neoliberals and class-based reformers, it fails to hold up for several reasons. First, in terms of the concrete realities and practical experiences of daily life, poor whites and poor blacks living side by side both know that blacks have it worse. African Americans consistently have higher rates of single-parent families, chronic unemployment and underemployment, secondary school dropouts, and substandard housing. Whites also have an important material asset that allows many of them to escape the greatest liabilities and disadvantages of poverty—their whiteness. White Americans who are homeless, unemployed, and/or uneducated for the most part still believe in the great American master narrative of opportunity and upward mobility. If they scrape together enough money to buy a new suit, they will find it relatively easy to obtain employment, albeit at subsistence wages. They know that with the same set of skills and level of educational attainment as the black householders across the street, they stand a superior chance of being hired. Whiteness creates a comfortable social and psychological safety net for the white poor: Everyday may not be a lucky day, but nobody has to sing the blues for too long.

A different situation exists for the Latino urban poor. With the significant exception of the white Cuban community, Latinos suffer from the same socioeconomic factors that make social mobility and neighborhood development so difficult for blacks. For example, the poverty rate for Latinos as an ethnic group rose significantly, from 19.8 percent in 1973 to 26.5 percent in 1991, a rate more than three times that of white households. One out of every four Mexican-American families and 40 percent of all Puerto Rican families lived in poverty. Millions of undocumented workers from Central America and the Hispanic Caribbean are trapped in low-wage jobs without benefits. Many Latinos who are gainfully employed encounter many of the same problems African Americans routinely experience, from their inability to obtain home mortgages or loans from banks and lending institutions, to being harassed and insulted by police in their own neighborhoods.

Inner-city neighborhoods like Harlem and south central Los Angeles, which have historically and culturally been identified as black, are becoming predominantly Latino. On the eve of the 1992 Los Angeles urban uprising over the Rodney King beating, 45 percent of the south central area was Hispanic. Although about 80 percent of Los Angeles's population was Mexican American, by 1990 there were also 200,000 Guatemalans and 600,000 Salvadorans living in the barrios of the "City of Angels." These neighborhoods were, and still are, plagued by high rates of poverty and unemployment. Thus, it should not have been surprising that the depths of alienation and resistance displayed by Southern California's black community after the verdict was announced were also present among several million Latinos living in the same depressed neighborhoods. For example, in the week immediately following the King verdict, 7,100 rioters were arrested in the City of Los Angeles on charges such as assault, looting, and violating curfew. About 850 of those arrested were white, more than 3,500 were Hispanic, and 2,600 were African American. Nineteen Latinos were killed during the 1992 Los Angeles uprising, only three less than the total number of blacks who died. About one in ten of the rioters who were arrested were undocumented immigrants. Hispanic grievances and bitterness against the Los Angeles Police Department ran as deep as those within the black community.

The example provided by Los Angeles in this context has been repeated in other major American cities. In 1991, for example, in the Mount Pleasant neighborhood of Washington, D.C., Salvadorans rioted and destroyed property after a Salvadoran man was killed by a police officer. In Miami's impoverished Wynwood section in 1990, hundreds of Puerto Ricans rioted in the streets following the acquittal of police officers who had beaten a Puerto Rican to death.

What do these major demographic shifts in the racialized ethnic composition of American cities mean for black Americans? The language of black resistance to police brutality, to poverty, and to hyper-unemployment must be expressed in Spanish as well as in English. It will even require the extremely difficult task of educating and liberating low-income whites from the bondage and blindness of their whiteness.

The old models of liberal integrationism and black separatist nationalism are unable to accomplish these tasks. A radical alternative, anchored in civil society and based on capacity-building and extensive networking between multiracial, multi-class constituencies, is now necessary to revive the Black Freedom Movement. A key first step in building this alternative is to popularize the essential idea that the masses, not charismatic leaders, are the fundamental force with the capacity to challenge American governmental and corporate power. As historian Clayborne Carson has reflected: "Waiting for the messiah is a human weakness unlikely to be rewarded more than once in a millennium. Careful study of the modern black freedom struggle offers support for the more optimistic belief that participants in a mass movement can develop their untapped capacities and collectively improve their lives."

The classical model of class-based organizing historically focused on issues located at the workplace: struggles over employment access, increases in wages and fringe benefits, and improved working conditions. In the postindustrial cities of America, however, the decisive battleground has shifted from the workplace to the living space. A significant number of the working poor, unemployed, and marginally employed people express their political activism through civil society rather than in trade unions or formal electoral political parties. These small-scale, ad hoc, grassroots organizations represent a "great well of democracy," an underutilized resource that has the potential to redefine our democratic institutions.

Stabilizing the Text

1. When dealing with long essays such as this one, it can be helpful to outline the flow of the discussion. Look again at Marable's essay. Identify the major sections and indicate what constitutes the focus in each section. How does each section contribute to the whole?

2. Analyze Marable's opening description of the police shooting in Cincinnati. What words, phrases, or writing techniques make it seem objective? What words, phrases, or writing techniques make it seem to represent a particular "side" of the story.

3. In the opening section of the essay, Marable moves back and forth between discussions of the police shooting and Cincinnati history and demographics. How does this dual focus encourage you as a reader to make sense of the shooting and the boycott movement? Does this organizational strategy lend legitimacy to the community-based boycott movement or not? In what ways?

Mobilizing the Text

1. In paragraphs 15–18, Marable discusses the meaning of the term "community" as it applies specifically to African Americans. What do you understand him to be saying about past meanings of community versus present, about Adolf Reed's concerns regarding community, and about his own conclusions on the usefulness and dangers of community as a concept? Use the text to support your answer.

2. In part II, Marable discusses the "veil of race" as a resource for, and, at the same time, an obstacle to people's ability to understand and change the "social forces that impact their families, friends, and communities." What is Marable's point here? What "social forces" is he referring to? What is "racialized radicalism"? How does it help people and what are its limitations? Give examples from your own knowledge or experience to explain.

3. Marable discusses demographic shifts in the composition of American cities and asks what these shifts "mean for black Americans." How does he answer this question? Can his answers apply to groups other than African Americans? How so or why not? When it comes to race, is Marable more of a separatist or does he value coalitions among groups? Use the text to explain.

What *Really* Happened in Cincinnati?

HEATHER MAC DONALD

Heather Mac Donald is a John M. Olin Fellow at the Manhattan Institute and a contributing editor to City Journal. *Her* City Journal *articles have addressed a range of topics, including policing and "racial" profiling, homelessness and homeless advocacy, educational policy, the New York courts, and business improvement districts. Mac Donald's writings have also appeared in the* Wall Street Journal, *the* Washington Post, *the* New York Times, *the* New Republic, Partisan Review, *the* New Criterion, Public Interest, *and* Academic Questions. *Her latest book is entitled* Are Cops Racist? *In "What Really Happened in Cincinnati?" originally published in* City Journal, *Mac Donald discusses events leading up to and following the police shooting of Timothy Thomas in Cincinnati. She proposes that the riots following the Thomas shooting resulted from what she calls the conventional approach to race in the United States, and that efforts to respond to riots are typically misguided. While reading this essay, think about what constitutes the conventional approach to race in the United States and pay attention to moments when you think Mac Donald is participating in or refusing to participate in assumptions about racially marked groups.*

❖

In April, when riots erupted in Cincinnati, the national media let out a glad cry: Black rage, that hottest of political commodities, was back! The subsequent post-riot drill, perfected over the last four decades, unfolded without flaw: instant discovery of the riot's "root causes"; half-hearted condemnation of the violence, followed immediately by its enthusiastic embrace as a "wake-up call" to America; warnings of future outbreaks if the "wake-up call" is ignored; and hurried formation of task forces promising rapid aid for Cincinnati's inner city.

"Riot ideology"—historian Fred Siegel's caustic phrase for the belief that black rioting is a justified answer to white racism—is alive and well in twenty-first-century America. Riots may be relatively rare, but the thinking that rationalizes them is not. It pervades the country's response to underclass problems and to race issues generally. The Cincinnati riots and their aftermath offer a peerless example of all that is wrong with this conventional approach to race. But in Cincinnati, too, if you look, are the clearest possible guideposts for how to get race issues right.

A fatal police shooting of an unarmed teenager, Timothy Thomas, triggered the riots. After 2 A.M. on Saturday, April 7, Thomas spotted two Cincinnati police officers and started running. Wanted on 14 warrants for traffic offenses and for evading arrest, Thomas led the policemen on a chase through the narrow alleys of Cincinnati's most drug-infested and violent neighborhood, Over-the-Rhine. The area's Italianate walk-ups, home in the late nineteenth century to one of America's most culturally rich and densely populated German-American communities, today often are either abandoned or given over to methadone clinics, drop-in centers, or Section 8 public housing.

Officer Steve Roach, hearing a radio alert about a fleeing suspect with 14 warrants, joined the pursuit and came abruptly face-to-face with the 19-year-old in a dark alley. When Thomas appeared to reach for his waistband, Roach shot him once in the chest. Three days later, Over-the-Rhine would be burning.

5   Cincinnati's riots hardly constituted a spontaneous outcry against injustice. A demagogic campaign against the police, of the kind common in American cities today, had already heated black residents almost to the boiling point. "Thirteen black men!—a tally of the suspects killed by the Cincinnati police since 1995— was the rallying cry of protesters in the City Council chambers last fall. Thomas's shooting (added to a January shoot-out death) brought the total to 15, and black politicians duly updated their cry to "Fifteen black men," in effect charging that Cincinnati's cops were indiscriminately mowing down black citizens. With robotic predictability, every national news account of the riots repeated the cry, to demonstrate Cincinnati's racism.

In fact, the list of the 15 police victims shows the depraved nature not of Cincinnati's cops but of its criminals. Harvey Price, who heads the roster, axed his girlfriend's 15-year-old daughter to death in 1995, then held a SWAT team at bay for four hours with a steak knife, despite being maced and hit with a stun gun. When he lunged at an officer with the knife, the cop shot him. Jermaine Lowe, a parole violator wanted for armed robbery, fled in a stolen car at the sight of a police cruiser, crashed into another car, then unloaded his handgun at the pursuing officers. Alfred Pope robbed, pistol-whipped, and most likely fired at three people in an apartment hallway, just the latest assault by the vicious 23-year-old, who had already racked up 18 felony charges and five convictions. He then aimed his handgun at close range at the pursuing officers, and they shot him dead in return.

To call such lowlifes martyrs to police brutality is a stretch. Besides the Thomas shooting, only three of the 15 cases raise serious questions about officer misjudgment and excessive force. The notion that race was the controlling element in the 15 deaths is even more absurd.

But it is perfectly in keeping with Cincinnati's racialized politics. Advocates of the city's status quo, whether opposing competitive bidding for city services or blocking the investigation of low-income housing fraud, can bring the City Council to its knees by playing the race card. For the last two years, black nationalists calling themselves the Special Forces have turned up regularly in the delicately carved council chambers of Cincinnati's Romanesque City Hall to spew anti-white and anti-Semitic diatribes. Two days after the Thomas shooting, on Monday, April 9, they were back, accompanied by hundreds of angry black residents, by Timothy Thomas's mother, and by her attorney Kenneth Lawson—Cincinnati's answer to Johnnie Cochran.

The Council meeting instantly spun out of control. Backed by constant screaming from the crowd, lawyer Lawson and another racial activist, the Reverend Damon Lynch III, masterfully inflamed the crowd's anger by suggesting that city officials were willfully withholding information about the Thomas shooting. Lawson, and doubtless Lynch, too, knew full well that disclosing Officer Roach's testimony after the shooting would jeopardize the investigation and possible prosecution of the case, yet both threatened to hold every chamber occupant hostage until Roach's testimony was released. Some of the Council Democrats seconded the threats. Three chaotic hours later, Lawson and Lynch grudgingly agreed to disband, Lynch demanding that the police chief "call off the dogs [i.e., officers] outside."

The crowd left City Hall and, swelling to over 1,000 along the way, headed toward the boxy, low-slung police headquarters. Protesters screamed at the officers protecting the station and snapped photos of them, promising lethal revenge for the 15 black "murders." Someone threw a rock that shattered the station's front door; others pulled the flag from its pole and hung it upside down; police horses were hit; officers were injured by flying glass—but the order was: "let them vent." The lieutenant in charge even gave a protester a bullhorn in the hope of calming the crowd. It didn't work.

Finally, at 1 A.M., police started arresting those who were hurling rocks and bottles at the station house. Too late: the violence had begun. Over the next three days, crowds would rampage through Cincinnati's poorest neighborhoods, beating white motorists, burning property, breaking hundreds of store windows, and making off with the appliances, furniture, clothing, and booze within. Gunmen fired thousands of shots, many at officers.

10

The police chief begged black clergy for help in restoring calm but got little response.

Though the police were outmatched and overworked, Democratic mayor Charles Luken refused to take additional measures against the violence. Then on Thursday, a bullet hit a cop, grazing off his belt buckle. That afternoon, Luken imposed an 8 P.M. curfew and announced a state of emergency. By then, the riot ideologues were in full cry. The NAACP's Kweisi Mfume flew in to declare Cincinnati the "belly of the whale" of police violence against young black men. Al Sharpton called for federal oversight not just of Cincinnati's but of the nation's police. *Time* magazine named Cincinnati a "model of racial injustice." The *New York Times* found pervasive economic discrimination against the city's blacks. White gentrifiers, pronounced The *New Republic*, lay behind the riots. The *Los Angeles Times* and ABC's *This Week* noted how salutary the violence had been.

Local leaders scrambled to contain the public-relations fiasco and to show their concern for black anger. The City Council hurriedly voted to submit a pending racial-profiling lawsuit to costly "mediation," rather than contest it, even though none of the suit's allegations had been shown to be credible. Mayor Luken invited in the Justice Department to investigate the police division, which could result in federal oversight of the kind that busts municipal budgets. But the city's main riot response was to form Community Action Now (CAN), a three-man panel dedicated to racial reconciliation through, as its members and promotional materials insist, action, action, and more action. Its three co-chairs are Ross Love, an ex-Procter & Gamble vice president who now heads a black radio empire; Tom Cody, an executive vice president of Federated Department Stores; and the Reverend Damon Lynch, the activist who calls the police "dogs."

At CAN's inception, Ross Love, the official spokesman, announced five task forces to "address the root causes of the recent unrest." The groups, manned by local civil rights figures, business leaders, and poverty advocates, would address "education and youth development, economic inclusion, police and the justice system, housing and neighborhood development, and image and media." But "root causes" have a way of proliferating: soon, Love created a sixth task force to look at "health care and human services." And as a harbinger of its future largesse, CAN then hired a former black city manager at $1,400 a day as "special counsel."

15   With the formation of CAN, and the media agitation that preceded it, we are ready to test the central tenets of riot ideology. In

place of "riots," any other element of underclass behavior, such as crime, can be substituted—the rationalizations are identical.

Start with the contention that riots are a response to white racism, since this is the mother of all "root cause" arguments, first popularized by the Kerner Commission Report on the 1960s riots. Ross Love gives this argument an economic spin: racially based "economic exclusion" is his mantra for explaining why blacks rioted in his city. The *New York Times* jumped on the "economic exclusion" bandwagon as well, claiming that Cincinnati has long "frustrated" blacks' justified demands for a "share of prosperity."

To test that hypothesis, walk around Cincinnati's poorest areas, from the river basin, spanned by John A. Roebling's first, beautiful suspension bridge, up to the city's seven surrounding green hills, which in Cincinnati's nineteenth-century heyday compressed its population into a greater density than anywhere but Manhattan. You will see knots of young men in their teens and twenties milling about on almost every street corner, towels draped over their heads, their shorts hanging far below their underwear. Heat has driven some out of their apartments, but many others are there to peddle drugs hidden in crevices in the old brick buildings. I approached a group of boys leaning against a tiny convenience store on a steep intersection called the Five Corners. One boy's T-shirt read: NO JUSTICE, NO PEACE, THESE OUR STREETS, F—K THE POLICE, 1981–2001—presumably Timothy Thomas's dates. I introduced myself and asked if they'd answer a few questions. "Hell, no!" In a blink of an eye, all but one of the boys had disappeared across the street and into a parking lot or down the steep incline.

Inside the tiny, dark store, a fortyish Jordanian with a mustache and a receding hairline stands squeezed behind the register. He will only give his name as "Mike." "We call the police five to ten times a day," he says quietly. "They drive through and tell them to move." What are they selling? He casts his eyes down. "I don't know; I don't want to talk about it."

At least Mike's store has not been shot at. Under the shredded red awning of Johnnie's Supermarket in the Walnut Hills neighborhood, spider-web cracks radiate across the window from a bullet hole. The bullet's target—a large red sign prohibiting loitering and giving the police the authority to come onto the premises at any time—is still visible under the cracked window. Until recently, up to 50 young men stood in front of Johnnie's, hawking drugs and extorting money from the market's customers. They are mostly gone now, thanks to an undercover operation that netted 19 indictments. But in front of an abandoned building kitty-corner from Johnnie's, ten young men in white T-shirts shift back and forth.

20   Now, remember the "economic exclusion" argument: Cincinnati's racist power structure is excluding hordes of qualified young black men. Well, here the men are, and it is ludicrous to attribute their joblessness to corporate bigotry, rather than to their own unemployability. The high school dropout rate in Cincinnati is between 60 and 70 percent. And will the young men across from Johnnie's show up every day to work on time and respond appropriately to authority? Has any of them even applied for a job and been turned down? Last summer, King's Island, an amusement park north of the city, had to import 1,000 young Eastern Europeans for summer jobs, because it could find no local youths to apply. Yet the well-intentioned CEO of Procter & Gamble, Cincinnati's beloved corporate titan, has called, in good riot-ideologue fashion, for the urgent creation of 2,500 government- and privately subsidized summer jobs to forestall another rampage.

     I asked Ross Love what evidence he had for "economic exclusion" in Cincinnati. "You have to look at the end result," he said. "The unemployment rate is four times higher for blacks than for whites; for 18- to 30-year-olds, it is an incredible 50 percent." But "looking at the end result" is the hallmark of bogus civil rights analysis, designed to shift attention from individual deficits onto the resultant disparate outcomes, which are then attributed to racism. We can argue about whether society is, in some structural way, still somehow to blame for Cincinnati's idle, functionally illiterate young dealers, but let's not brand employers as racist.

     Cincinnati's African immigrants have a different perspective from CAN on "economic exclusion." "We experience more resentment from African-Americans than from whites," says cabdriver Mor Thiam. "They don't want to see us in business. 'Man, go back to Africa! You come here and take our monies,' they say." Amy, a Senegalese cabdriver in a robin's-egg-blue ruffled cotton dress, has been teaching herself about riot ideology by listening to Ross Love's local radio station, WDBZ, "The Buzz." "They are angry on that station!" she exclaims. "A lot of them don't work; they go to your taxi, try to steal your money. When I came here, I earned $4.25 an hour, but I worked. I liked it. I paid my bills; I sent money home. If you want to get a job, you get a job. We see a lot of opportunity here."

The notion that this friendly, well-meaning town is denying employment to job-ready black men because of the color of their skin is ridiculous. To the contrary, Cincinnati's biggest corporations have long practiced affirmative action. Expect CAN's "economic inclusion" task force to recommend even more quotas, however, rather than honestly to address why young blacks are not working. . . .

Mayor Luken's swipe at the business community, with its faux sorrow and its faux facts, is a riot-ideology classic. "I am somewhat saddened that it takes this kind of situation to come together, [but] I'm happy that business leaders are finally engaged," he pontificated at the end of riot week. Finally engaged? Cincinnati's business community can perhaps be faulted for the dreary conventionality and naïveté of its philanthropic efforts but not for the scope of those efforts. Local corporations contribute millions to poverty agencies and civil rights groups. Fifth Third Bancorp and Procter & Gamble, for example, have been funding "economic development" in Walnut Hills, home of Johnnie's Supermarket, only to see their projects torn up by the recent riots. Loath to bear a grudge, the companies have only "redoubled [their] commitment to . . . improve the neighborhood," according to a spokesman. Too bad they haven't decided to rethink radically what Walnut Hills and other riot targets really need. . . .

Here is the hidden logic of race riots: supposedly a cry   25
against racial oppression, their implicit threat to destroy the city merely guarantees full employment for race hustlers and sensitivity trainers by driving the races further apart. If whites flee Over-the-Rhine, expect plenty of breast-beating in the future from the press and civil rights advocates about Cincinnati's enduring racial segregation. No one will recall why the integrators left. . . .

According to the riot ideology, the most authentic black leaders are angry black leaders, and the Reverend Damon Lynch, ever since his appointment as the city's Number One racial healer, has taken on the role with a vengeance. He drove out an annual rock festival from Over-the-Rhine by threatening boycotts and protests, and he tried to shut down one of Cincinnati's most moneymaking tourist attractions, its food festival. During a noisy sit-in at a downtown restaurant, he promised to "let people know that Cincinnati is not a place to bring your conventions or your business. Until there is justice, there will be no business as usual, no lunch as usual." (Lynch carefully refrained from defining the "justice" that would buy peace.) His choice of protest symbolism was fanciful, since no one has ever alleged that blacks cannot get service at downtown restaurants—but no more fanciful than his comparison of Cincinnati to South Africa in its "economic apartheid."

Lynch's rhetorical extremism guarantees his ongoing relevance as anointed black leader. Liberal whites need black anger to prove the persistence of racism among their unenlightened neighbors, which they alone can atone for by the noblesse oblige of liberal paternalism. Thus, to reinforce their own sense of moral superiority, they confer racial authenticity only on blacks like Damon Lynch, self-proclaimed angry victims of American bigotry. Lynch's ever more rash protests make a mockery of his mediator position on Community Action Now; if he wants to continue playing firebrand, he should resign from CAN. But no one dares suggest he leave, even though his boycotts are killing the very neighborhood he purports to represent. Ross Love's support of his co-chair reflects his grasp of the underlying dialectic: "Lynch's protests increase his authority," he told me. "They give him more credibility in the eyes of the people we need at the table."

And here, in a nutshell, is the tragedy of moral leadership in black America. Love merely states received wisdom in claiming that black moral authority derives from protesting white racism, and that the alienated youth who most respond to such protests are the most authentic representatives of the black community.

This logic consigns to silence many, many black Americans—law-abiding citizens, who see crime, not racism, as the biggest threat in their lives. Over-the-Rhine resident Sheila Randle, for example, doesn't buy Love's and Lynch's charges. A former manager of Salvation Army stores, the 50-year-old Randle is a prisoner in her own home. Young people smoke marijuana and crack on the street outside her apartment all night; they jeer at her husband when he asks them to get off his car. Addicts have started breaking into her building's entryway. "You never know who's going to be on the landing in the morning," she says. Randle is desperate to move, but her options are limited.

30 What about these stories of police racism? I ask her. "I have no problem with the police; they treat me respectfully," she answers. "It's the young people who are the problem." And the thesis that the police only care about white yuppies? "The police are there to protect all the people, not just the whites," she asserts. What about societal racism generally? "I've never experienced it."

Randle wanted to support the police in their time of trouble by attending the annual police memorial this May. The anti-police demonstrators frightened her off, however—demonstrators allegedly representing her interests as an oppressed black woman. As for the claim that the Timothy Thomas shooting is a sign of police racism, Randle will have none of it. "Thomas brought it on himself," she says. "He had [warrants] on him; if he had halted like they told him to, it wouldn't have happened."

This is no fringe view. In early May, a letter writer named Loretta Blackburn wrote to the *Cincinnati Enquirer:* "If I were in pursuit of a black youth and had cornered him in an alley, after what happened to Officer Kevin Crayon [dragged to death last year by a 12-year-old joyrider], the first thing in my mind would be, 'Someone is coming out of this alley; now who do you think it will be?' We as black people need to get back to the basics and help the police to police our neighborhoods. . . . When you are in the streets hollering how unfair black people are being treated, what are you teaching your children about respect for authority? If you don't like the job that [the police] are doing, then give them a helping hand, not a shot in the back."

Damon Lynch, Al Sharpton, and Kweisi Mfume have no interest in representing the Sheila Randles and Loretta Blackburns. Far more responsible leaders who do speak for such citizens are out there, though—but the opinion elites are not about to give them a platform. . . .

. . . If the media did pay attention to the racial nonconformists, it would find a large, untapped audience, frustrated with conventional black politics but also afraid of retribution for dissent. A downtown Cincinnati business figure who would only speak anonymously told me bitterly: "The civil rights leadership is killing us; it's absolutely killing us. As white exploitation is a sin, so is black waste. We are living in an unnatural state." Illustrator Galen Bailey blames Lynch and Lawson's pre-riot rabble-rousing for the violence: "All these young kids needed was for an adult to give them permission to riot," he says in dismay.

Riot ideology in Cincinnati has had its usual effect. In the month following the riots, violent crime of all kinds rocketed up 20 percent. This is not surprising. Not only did the riot ideologists romanticize assaults and theft as a long-overdue blow for justice, but they demonized the police as hard-core racists. Arrests for quality-of-life offenses, disorderly conduct, and drug possession—the firewall against more serious crime—have plummeted since the riots, as the police keep their heads down. 35

The next time an urban riot hits, the best response is: do nothing. Compensate the property owners, then shut up. Scurrying around with anti-racism task forces and aid packages tells young kids: this is the way to get the world to notice you, this is power—destruction, not staying in school, studying, and accomplishing something lawful. Even better, of course, would be to prevent the next riot before it happens by sending in police in force at the first sign of trouble.

But better even than this, political and business leaders who have not already sold out to the civil rights monopolists should try to break their cartel. They should find black citizens who are willing to speak about values and personal responsibility, and who embody them in their own lives. They should appear with these citizens at public meetings and put them on task forces, if task forces they must have. If they do it enough, the press will have to pay attention. And when the voice of hardworking black America becomes familiar, the riot ideology may finally lose its death grip on American politics.

Stabilizing the Text

1. Mac Donald opens her essay with the claim that events in Cincinnati "offer a peerless example of all that is wrong" with the "approach to race" in the United States. Using examples from her essay, explain how Mac Donald understands the U.S. approach to race and what she thinks is wrong with it. Discuss your sense of the strengths or weaknesses of her interpretation.

2. Mac Donald offers a relatively detailed description of the events leading up to the Cincinnati "riot." What characteristics of her description make it seem objective and what characteristics make it seem like she is writing from a certain "side"? In what ways does her description offer an alternative to, or participate in, the usual approach to race?

3. Analyze the historical contexts that Mac Donald provides to help readers understand the shooting and subsequent violence. How do these contexts shape the way you as a reader interpret the shooting and violence?

Mobilizing the Text

1. Whose "side" of the story do you think Mac Donald wants to be on? What in her essay makes you think that? Do you think she succeeds in putting herself on the side she wants to be on? Why or why not?

2. What does Mac Donald think is "the tragedy of moral leadership in black America"? Do you agree with her assessment?

3. Examine Mac Donald's conclusion in light of her opening claim that "in Cincinnati . . . are the clearest possible guideposts for how to get race issues right." What does Mac Donald think it means to get race issues right? Use her text to explain your answer. In what ways do you agree or disagree with her?

CHAPTER 5

Cities and
Citizenship

When most people think about their citizenship they think of themselves as being citizens of a country, such as the United States. They may also think about the duties of their citizenship, such as military service or paying taxes. Or, they may think about the rights and privileges of their citizenship, such as the freedom of assembly and the right to vote. Citizenship is all of this and more. In the context of city life, citizenship—complete with its obligations and privileges—describes the public acts of belonging to a community. Acts of citizenship include but are not limited to participation in school board meetings, in neighborhood watches, as well as in such youth activities as Little League baseball. Acts of citizenship both reaffirm and reflect attitudes of citizenship. People who consider themselves citizens of a particular city or town participate in civic activities for a variety of reasons, they are committed to the good of the community, they value the experience of being involved with others, or they believe it is their duty to be responsible in some way for the place they live.

Anyone who has ever attended a school board meeting knows that more often than not, people do not participate as citizens of a particular city or town. Either they are unaccustomed to understanding their roles as citizens, or too many obstacles prevent them from fully realizing their roles as citizens. Obstacles to active and full citizenship are many. Everything from the inconvenience of having another thing to do at the end of a long work day to seemingly endless bureaucracies become obstacles to participation in civic life. In addition to the obstacles to citizenship, we are faced with many distractions that draw our attention away from civic participation. It is often much easier, and in a way more immediately gratifying, to watch a movie, listen to music, or surf the Internet. These distractions are not bad in and of themselves. It is just that, combined with all the other things occupying our time, we are left with little sense of why our citizenship should matter to us.

Yet, many people want to say the experience of local citizenship is essential to the quality of public life in a democracy. Without citizenship, responsibility for our day-to-day existence shifts to others and we become subject to all their decisions. Without citizen participation, developers can remove residents from their homes and replace their neighborhood with a shopping mall or manufacturing facility. Citizen participation also keeps pressure on government officials to do such things as improve the quality of public schools and constantly monitor the actions of the police force. As citizenship becomes weak and thin in a particular place, it becomes more and more obvious that participation is a privilege as well as an obligation—that we are obligated to be a part of school board meetings, citizen police review boards, or neighborhood groups, in part, in order to protect the privilege of having a say in how our schools are run, how our police function, or how developers are able to change our neighborhoods.

The essays in this chapter explore some of the challenges to our citizenship as well as some of the advantages of our citizenship. They ask us to reflect on what individual practices of citizenship say about our overall view of our lives in relation to the privileges and obligations of democracy.

Exemplifying the power of people joining together, Iris Marion Young argues in her essay, "From Guilt to Solidarity: Sweatshops and Political Responsibility," that everyone has the capacity for citizenship and can take some responsibility, even in institutions beyond their control. Drawing from the recent tactics of the antisweatshop movement, Young describes a view of citizenship that can deal with the toughest issues of our time. She describes citizenship as looking past assigning blame and liability and toward individual participation in meaningful and transformative collective action.

Discussing an alternative definition of citizenship to the one Young describes is "Hate Radio," by Patricia J. Williams, which focuses on the views of citizenship that create popular radio shows. Her claim is that radio personalities such as Howard Stern, whose programs aim to offend, reinforce stereotypes that keep us from talking with and listening to each other.

The last two essays in this chapter discuss specific efforts to work together to address particular public challenges. In "Speaking for Ourselves," Makani Themba-Nixon and Nan Rubin discuss current struggles over control of the media. In "Pathfinders," Peter Medoff and Holly Sklar discuss how residents of an inner-city Boston neighborhood banded together to create a common vision for their community and to make powerful forces such as government and big developers hear and respond to their perspectives and dreams.

In the end, the essays collected here ask common questions for our thinking about cities, our writing about cities, and our lives in and around cities: What kind of life do we dream of living together and how do our thinking, writing, and actions pursue our dreams? What kinds of thinking, writing, and actions produce a public life of gated communities, security fences, prisons, and guns? What kinds of thinking, writing, and actions produce a public life of good schools for all kids, nice parks to play in, and a broad set of relationships with others that cross all boundaries? What kinds of thinking, writing, and actions do cities, democratic cities, depend on?

From Guilt to Solidarity: Sweatshops and Political Responsibility

IRIS MARION YOUNG

Iris Marion Young is a professor of political science at the University of Chicago. Her books include Throwing Like a Girl *and* Intersecting Voices. *Her most recent book is titled* Inclusion and Democracy. *Her writings have been translated into several languages, she has lectured widely around the world, and she has been involved internationally in justice issues at such places as the Institute for Human Sciences in Vienna and the Human Sciences Research Council in South Africa. The essay reproduced here, "From Guilt to Solidarity: Sweatshops and Political Responsibility," was first published in* Dissent. *In this essay, Young argues that we are all connected in our actions and through our institutions to the people in sweatshops who manufacture our clothes. Rather than describing us as blameworthy or liable for the conditions in sweatshops, Young argues that injustices in the clothing industry result from a range of institutions and interactions largely beyond our control, but that we all can, nonetheless, take collective responsibility for making changes in institutions and interactions. As you read Young's essay, pay particular attention to the distinctions she makes among blame, liability, and responsibility.*

✦

For nearly two years we have been living in a crisis mode, with our government suspending due process and spending our tax dollars on war and security instead of health care and environmental protection. The ongoing sense of emergency diverts political discussion and problem solving resources from the more banal harms that were on the public radar screen before we switched into crisis mode and that continue to fester—the lack of affordable housing, violence against women, declining water supplies, or the awful labor conditions in which many workers around the world sweat to produce clothes, shoes, toys, and other everyday goods.

Barely three years ago, a student protest movement swept hundreds of campuses in the United States demanding that university administrations do something about sweatshops. The students called on university administrations to take responsibility for the conditions under which clothing sold in their bookstores and worn by their athletic teams are produced, often by young women, in export processing zones in Asia and Latin America. Other labor and social justice activists leafleted at major retailers, educating consumers and criticizing executive indifference. These activities achieved significant successes in creating better monitoring organizations, for example, and forcing corporate manufacturer's to acknowledge what goes on in factories to which they have subcontracted much of their production. Public debate about sweatshops overseas led to the discovery of sweatshops closer to home-in major American cities.

While there have been some reforms, the basic problem of horrendous labor conditions in a globalized clothing industry, as well as in other industries, remains. Many stalwart activists continue to organize their fellow students and their fellow union or church members, to support union organizing among the most exploited and to mount court action to hold companies liable for labor rights violations. Since the heyday of the campus antisweatshop activity several important books have appeared. In *Behind the Label*, Edna Bonacich and Richard Appelbaum describe the structural underpinnings of sweatshops in Los Angeles and show their connection to others in Asia. Ellen Israel Rosen provides a history of the political economy of the U.S. clothing industry as it has been globalized in her book, *Making Sweatshops*.

The antisweatshop movement has been a consumer and citizens movement as well as a movement of the most affected workers and the labor organizations supporting them. Students on hunger strikes protested university administrations as well as corporate leaders. Leaflets distributed on the street not only criticize big corporate retailers, but also exhort consumers entering stores to pay attention to the conditions of workers in factories far away producing the products they buy, and to join the movement to put pressure on the powerful institutions that can put pressure on the factory owners.

What interests me about the claims these activists make on universities, city governments, and individual consumers is that they are not simply moralistic. They don't claim that these institutions and individuals, who seem so disconnected from the far-away factories, should care about their workers simply because they suffer oppression and injury. The discourse of the antisweatshop movement, as I hear it, draws attention to complex structural processes that do connect persons and institutions in very different social and geographic positions. The harm the workers suffer comes most immediately at the hands of factory owners and managers who set hunger level wages and inhumane hours and intimidate anyone who tries to change these conditions. These owners and managers themselves operate, however, in a huge global system that both encourages their practices and constrains their ability to modify those practices—because of a realistic fear of being undercut in a highly competitive environment. The antisweatshop movement argues that all the persons and institutions who participate in the structural processes that produce this constraint should take responsibility for the condition of the workers. We are connected to them; we wear clothes they make; we sell them in our stores. So the movement has done much to de-fetishize commodities, revealing market structures as complex human creations.

LIABILITY VS. POLITICAL RESPONSIBILITY

I think that this claim of responsibility, implicit in the antisweatshop movement, as well as some other contemporary labor and environmental movements, is rather novel. It involves an argument that agents are responsible for injustice by virtue of their structural connection to it, even though they are not to blame for it. My main purpose in this essay is to outline the elements of this argument and contrast it with the more familiar concept of responsibility as blame or liability.

The most common model of assigning responsibility derives from legal reasoning about guilt or fault for a harm inflicted. Under the fault model, one assigns responsibility to particular agents whose actions can be shown to be causally connected to the circumstances of the harm. This agent can be a collective entity, such as a corporation, treated as single agent for the purposes of assigning responsibility. The connected actions must be voluntary. If candidates for responsibility can demonstrate that their causal relation to the harm was not voluntary, that they were coerced or that they were in some other way not free, then their responsibility is usually mitigated if not dissolved. When the agents are causally and freely responsible, however, it is appropriate to blame them for the harmful circumstances. A concept of strict liability departs from this model in that it holds individuals liable for an action even if they did not intend the outcome, or holds them liable for a harm caused by someone under their command. While different in these respects, responsibility as fault and strict liability share two other features important for distinguishing them from political responsibility. The fault or liability model is primarily backward looking; it reviews the history of events in order to assign responsibility, usually for the sake of exacting punishment or compensation. Assigning responsibility to some agents, on this model, also has the function of absolving other agents. To find this person or group guilty of a crime usually implies that others accused of the same crime are not guilty.

Assuming that I am right so far, the antisweatshop movement must understand responsibility differently. The universities and consumers it targets are not themselves to blame for the working conditions. They are connected to those conditions only indirectly and in a highly mediated fashion through market relations and other complex structural processes. Although many people would like to say that such a mediated connection implies that they are not responsible at all, the movement argues that institutions, individual consumers, and faraway decision makers in the clothing industry, are responsible in a different sense, which I want to call political responsibility. There are four features of the idea of political responsibility that distinguish it from blame or liability.

1. Political responsibility does not mark out and isolate those who are considered to be responsible. A blame model of responsibility distinguishes those who are responsible from others who, by implication, are not responsible. Such isolation of the one liable or blameworthy person from all the others is an important aspect of legal responsibility, both in criminal and tort law. Because they argue that organizations or collectives, as well as individual persons, can be blamed for harms, most accounts of collective responsibility also aim to distinguish those who have done the harm from those who have not.

   But many harms, wrongs, and injustices have no isolatable perpetrator; they result from the participation of millions of people and institutions. Endemic large-scale homelessness in an otherwise affluent society, for example, is arguably an injustice without an identifiable perpetrator. Some people and institutions perform specific actions or enforce policies that can be shown as contributing to homelessness, but they do not intend to do that, and what they do only has this effect insofar as it is supplemented and mediated by other actions even further removed from that outcome. For other cases of injustice some specific perpetrators can be identified and blamed as immediate causes, but these too are enabled and supported by wider social structures in which millions of people participate. I have suggested already that the injustices of inhumane labor conditions should be analyzed on these two levels. In the conception of political responsibility, then, finding that some people bear responsibility for injustice does not necessarily absolve others.

2. Political responsibility questions "normal" conditions. In a blame or liability conception of responsibility, what counts as a wrong is generally conceived as a deviation from a baseline. Implicitly, we assume a normal background situation that is morally acceptable, if not ideal. A crime or an actionable harm consists in a morally and legally unacceptable deviation from this background structure. The process that brought about the harm is conceived as a discrete, bounded event that breaks away from the normal flow of events. Punishment, redress, or compensation aims to restore normality or to "make whole" in relation to the baseline condition.

   A concept of political responsibility in relation to structural injustices, on the other hand, doesn't focus on harms that deviate from the normal and acceptable, but rather brings into question the "normal" background conditions. When we judge that structural injustice exists, we are saying that at least some of the accepted background conditions of action are morally unacceptable. Most of us contribute to a greater or lesser degree to the production and reproduction of structural injustice precisely because we follow the accepted and expected rules and conventions of the communities in which we live. Usually we enact standard practices in a habitual way, without explicit reflection on what we are doing, having in the foreground of our consciousness and intention our immediate goals and the particular people we need to interact with to achieve them.

The antisweatshop movement well illustrates this challenge to normal structural background conditions. It asks consumers, universities, and other institutions that contract with retailers, brand-name clothing companies, and many other agents, to reflect on the hitherto acceptable market relationships in which they act. It challenges all the agents that are part of the economic chain between the workers who make garments and the people who buy and wear them to ask whether "business as usual" is morally acceptable.

3. Political responsibility looks forward rather than backward. Blame and praise are primarily backward looking judgments. They refer to an action or event assumed to have reached its end. The purpose of assigning responsibility as fault or liability is usually to sanction, punish, or exact compensation. Such backward looking condemnation may partly have a forward looking purpose; we may wish to deter others from similar action in the future or to identify weak points in an institutional system that allows such blameworthy actions, in order to reform the institutions. Once we take this step, however, we may begin to move toward a conception of political responsibility. For many people may be bound to undertake those reforms, even though they are not to blame for past problems.

Political responsibility doesn't reckon debts, but aims at results, and thus depends on the actions of everyone who is in a position to contribute to those results. Taking political responsibility in respect to social structures emphasizes the future more than the past. Because the causal connection of particular individuals or even organizations to the harmful structural outcomes is often impossible to trace, there is no point in seeking to exact compensation or redress from some isolatable perpetrators. If we understand that structural processes cause (some) injustices, then those of us who participate in the production and reproduction of the structures should recognize that our actions contribute to the injustice. And then we should take responsibility for changing the processes. To return to the sweatshop case, the main objective of this movement is not to compensate workers for past wrongs but to make social changes that will eliminate future harm. (Such a project cannot be undertaken, of course, without reflection on the past: we need to understand the history of processes that produce specific outcomes, and in this sense must be backward looking.)

4. Political responsibility is shared responsibility. If the injustice is a result of structural processes involving many individuals and institutions engaging in normal and accepted activities, the necessary change requires the cooperation of many of those individuals and institutions. Discharging my responsibility in this situation means joining in collective actions with others. We share responsibility for organizing changes in how the processes work. Working through state institutions is often an effective means to change structural processes, but states are not the only tools of effective action. The antisweatshop movement has begun to create information-sharing and monitoring institutions whose purpose is to connect workers in specific locales to solidarity organizations far away who try to hold manufacturers to account for working conditions. Our responsibility is political in the sense that acting on it involves joining in a public discourse where we try to persuade one another about courses of collective action that will contribute to social change.

An important corollary of this feature of political responsibility is that many of those properly thought to be victims of harm or injustice may nevertheless have political responsibilities in relation to it. In a fault model of responsibility, blaming the victims of injustice serves to absolve others of responsibility for their plight. In a conception of political responsibility, however, those who can properly be called victims of structural injustice often share the responsibility to try to change the structures. In the case of labor exploitation, the workers themselves ought to resist if they can.

Conceptualizing political responsibility as distinct from blame is important for motivating political action. When people feel that they are being blamed, they tend to react defensively. They look for other agents to blame instead, or they make excuses that mitigate their liability. Such practices of accusation and defense have an important place in morality and law. When the issue is how to mobilize collectives for the sake of social change, however, such rhetorics of blame and finger-pointing lead more to resentment and refusal to take responsibility than to useful action. If corporate executives or ordinary people buying shoes believe that antisweatshop activists are blaming them for the conditions under which the shoes are produced, they rightly become indignant, or scoff at what they perceive as the extremism of the movement. Distinguishing political responsibility from blame or liability allows us to urge one another to take responsibility together for the fact that our actions collectively contribute to the complex structural processes that produce the working conditions we deplore. Most of us have not committed individual wrongs; rather, we participate by our normal and on the face of it innocuous actions in processes that produce wrongs.

DEGREES AND KIND OF RESPONSIBILITY

In principle, all who participate by their actions in the structural processes that produce unjust outcomes share responsibility for working to alter those processes. So stated, however, this idea of responsibility may sound both overwhelming and unfair—overwhelming because most of us participate in many such processes, and unfair because some people would seem to be in a position to influence them more than others. A further step in thinking about political responsibility, then, involves distinguishing kinds and degrees. I suggest that we should think about action in relation to structural injustice along parameters of connection, power, and privilege.

10   Connection—The concept of political responsibility holds that agents have forward looking responsibilities to take action to remedy structural injustices—not just because all right thinking people should be concerned about suffering wherever it occurs, but on the more specific grounds that we are connected by our own actions to the structural processes that produce injustice. One means of deciding which responsibilities are mine, then, is by understanding particular connections between my actions and distant others. Consumer movements are often significant in this respect because, as I've said, they demystify processes of production and distribution. However mediated the connection between my life and activities and those of the people who produce the things I buy, it is difficult to deny that there is a connection. The antisweatshop movement has had some success in reducing the

anonymity of market processes by demanding that universities and other bulk consumers, as well as large retailers, identify the sites where particular items are manufactured. Such demands challenge the assumption that market exchange processes are or ought to be untraceable, and so they have had some effect in improving tracking systems and accountability.

Recognizing the power of connection in establishing responsibility, some people decide that the way to exercise this responsibility is to disconnect. They choose not to buy certain products or brands, which they have reason to think are manufactured under unjust conditions. But when such a boycott is the act of a single individual, it has no effect on those conditions. And it is nearly impossible in the contemporary world for a person to remove herself from any implication in structures that produce injustice. To the extent that this implication is a ground of political responsibility, then, the responsibility cannot be escaped by withdrawal; it has to be taken up. Organized boycotts, on the other hand, can be one effective means of exercising political responsibility.

Power—A person's position in structural processes usually carries different degrees of potential or actual influence over the processes. Organizations and institutions, moreover, vary in their ability to influence structural processes. Some of the large major clothing retailers, for example, such as Bennetton, The Gap, or Guess?, have built transnational systems not only of retail outlets, but also of small manufacturers with whom they contract. Because of the size, reach, and relative influence of such organizations, it makes sense to expect major decision makers in them to take responsibility for working conditions in factories they neither own nor directly operate. The antisweatshop movement recognizes this criterion by targeting corporate or regulatory bodies that arguably have the power to change structural processes. The power and influence parameter suggests that where individuals and organizations do not have sufficient energy and resources to respond to all the structural injustices to which they are connected, they should focus on those where they have the greatest influence. Powerful institutions, of course, often have more interest in perpetuating the status quo than in changing established structures and the outcomes they produce. For this reason individuals and organizations with relatively less power, but some ability to influence the powerful, must take responsibility to do that.

Privilege—Where there are structural injustices, these usually produce not only victims of injustice but also privileged beneficiaries. Persons who benefit from structural inequalities have a special moral responsibility to join in correcting them—not because they are to blame, but because they are able to adapt to changed circumstances without suffering serious deprivation.

It doesn't follow from this point—that privilege generates special responsibilities—that victims of injustice do not share responsibility to try to change the conditions that constrain their options. On the contrary. I pointed out earlier that one difference between a liability model and a political model of responsibility is that those who suffer injustice share political responsibility. Thus in the sweatshop case, the specific position of the workers carries with it specific responsibilities. Their conditions are likely to improve only if they organize to demand and monitor the improvements. Victims of injustice, however, can only succeed in their own efforts if others in a position to support them take responsibility to do so.

IMPLICATIONS OF THE IDEA

25   The claims of the antisweatshop movement, I have suggested, are best understood under a model of political responsibility. One of the things particularly interesting about this movement is that it raises transnational and global questions about who should act for change. The movement challenges the widely held idea that people and institutions should be held more responsible for what takes place inside their own country than for what takes place outside, that our responsibilities are necessarily greater for close-by effects of our actions than for those that are diffuse and remote. But many structural processes do not recognize national boundaries, and they often produce more widespread and long-term harms than do particular actions or policies. The basis of political responsibility lies not in membership in a political community governed by a common set of laws and regulatory institutions, but rather in social and economic connection. Laws and regulatory institutions are less a basis for political responsibility than a means of discharging it. Where it can be argued that a group shares responsibility for structural processes that produce injustice, but institutions for regulating those processes don't exist, we ought to try to create new institutions.

Stabilizing the Text

1. Summarize Young's concept of political responsibility. One way to do this might be to contrast it with her descriptions of blame and liability. How different is political responsibility from blame? How different is it from liability? Just how significant do you think these differences really are? How much do the differences really matter?

2. Young writes a great deal about structural processes. What exactly are these processes? Based on your reading of Young's essay, how do these processes mediate people's interactions? Do processes lead people to do certain things to each other? Or, do people use processes so they can do certain things to each other? In other words, where is the responsibility? In the people or in the processes?

3. Young wants to avoid blaming people for the working conditions in sweatshops. At the same time, she wants people to take some political responsibility for sweatshop conditions. Where in her essay does she make the case for taking responsibility without assigning blame? What argumentative steps does she take to make her case that the two can and should be separated? Does she persuade you that no one is directly responsible even though everyone can take some responsibility? Why or why not?

Mobilizing the Text

1. Can you think of another issue like the conditions in sweatshops, where Young's argument for political responsibility might apply? Applying her argument to another issue is a way of discovering for yourself how well it works. So, as you assign political responsibility to another issue, ask yourself whether and why this way of doing things works as it does.

2. Try using Young's concept of structural processes to argue for removing blame and liability in a problem similar to the sweatshop problem. Using Young's concept in this way, figure out for yourself whether it provides a more or less comprehensive and satisfactory account of the problem. Do you think the argument for structural processes better defines what the problem is? Does that argument enable or disable more realistic solutions?

3. One of the important points Young makes in her essay is that people do not usually work for solutions if they feel they are the problem. Just what are the relationships among public problems, collective solutions, and people's individual senses of blame, liability, and responsibility? What do the relationships among problems, solutions, and personal perceptions contribute to our citizenship?

Hate Radio

Patricia J. Williams

Patricia J. Williams is a professor of law at Columbia University. In 2000, she was awarded a MacArthur Fellowship, a "genius" award given annually by the John D. and Catherine T. MacArthur

Foundation to select individuals whose artistic or intellectual achievements and promise demonstrate extraordinary originality and dedication. A prolific writer, Williams is author of several widely read books, including The Alchemy of Race and Rights *and* Seeing a Color Blind Future: The Paradox of Race. *She is also a regular contributor to such magazines as the* Nation. *"Hate Radio" was first published in* Ms. *Magazine. In this essay, Williams describes the levels of personal discomfort and social inhospitability generated by such radio personalities as Rush Limbaugh and Howard Stern. She speculates on the power of the spoken word and argues that the use of that power by people such as Limbaugh and Stern expresses problems of tolerance that are longstanding in the United States. As you read "Hate Radio," think about the relationship between what we listen to privately and how we respond to each other publicly.*

——————— ✦ ———————

Three years ago I stood at my sink, washing the dishes and listening to the radio. I was tuned to rock and roll so I could avoid thinking about the big news from the day before—George Bush had just nominated Clarence Thomas to replace Thurgood Marshall on the Supreme Court. I was squeezing a dot of lemon Joy into each of the wineglasses when I realized that two smoothly radio-cultured voices, a man's and a woman's, had replaced the music.

"I think it's a stroke of genius on the president's part," said the female voice.

"Yeah," said the male voice. "Then those blacks, those African Americans, those Negroes—hey 'Negro' is good enough for Thurgood Marshall—whatever, they can't make up their minds [what] they want to be called. I'm gonna call them Blafricans. Black Africans. Yeah, I like it. Blafricans. Then they can get all upset because now the president appointed a Blafrican."

"Yeah, well, that's the way those liberals think. It's just crazy."

5   "And then after they turn down his nomination the president can say he tried to please 'em, and then he can appoint someone with some intelligence."

Back then, this conversation seemed so horrendously unusual, so singularly hateful, that I picked up a pencil and wrote it down. I was certain that a firestorm of protest was going to engulf the station and purge those foul radio mouths with the good clean soap of social outrage.

I am so naive. When I finally turned on the radio and rolled my dial to where everyone else had been tuned while I was busy watching Cosby reruns, it took me a while to understand that there's a firestorm all right, but not of protest. In the two and a half years since Thomas has assumed his post on the Supreme Court, the underlying assumptions of the conversation I heard as uniquely outrageous have become commonplace, popularly expressed, and louder in volume. I hear the style of that snide polemicism everywhere, among acquaintances, on the street, on television in toned-down versions. It is a crude demagoguery that makes me heartsick. I feel more and more surrounded by that point of view, the assumptions of being without intelligence, the coded epithets, the "Blafrican"-like stand-ins for "nigger," the mocking angry glee, the endless tirades filled with nonspecific, non-empirically based slurs against "these people" or "those minorities" or "feminazis" or "liberals" or "scumbags" or "pansies" or "jerks" or "sleazeballs" or "loonies" or "animals" or "foreigners."

At the same time I am not so naive as to suppose that this is something new. In clearheaded moments I realize I am not listening to the radio anymore, I am listening to a large segment of white America think aloud in even louder resurgent thoughts that have generations of historical precedent. It's as though the radio has split open like an egg, Morton Downey, Jr.'s clones and Joe McCarthy's ghost spilling out, broken yolks, a great collective of sometimes clever, sometimes small, but uniformly threatened brains—they have all come gushing out. Just as they were about to pass into oblivion, Jack Benny and his humble black sidekick Rochester get resurrected in the ungainly bodies of Howard Stern and his faithful black henchwoman, Robin Quivers. The culture of Amos and Andy has been revived and reassembled in Bob Grant's radio minstrelsy and radio newcomer Daryl Gates's sanctimonious imprecations on behalf of decent white people. And in striking imitation of Jesse Helms's nearly forgotten days as a radio host, the far Right has found its undisputed king in the personage of Rush Limbaugh—a polished demagogue with a weekly radio audience of at least twenty million, a television show that vies for ratings with the likes of Jay Leno, a newsletter with a circulation of 380,000, and two best-selling books whose combined sales are closing in on six million copies.

From Churchill to Hitler to the old Soviet Union, it's clear that radio and television have the power to change the course of history, to proselytize, and to coalesce not merely the good and the noble, but the very worst in human nature as well. Likewise, when Orson Welles made his famous radio broadcast "witnessing" the landing of a spaceship full of hostile Martians, the United States ought to have learned a lesson about the power of radio to appeal to mass instincts and incite mass hysteria. Radio remains a peculiarly powerful medium even today, its visual emptiness in a world of six trillion flashing images allowing one of the few remaining playgrounds for the aural subconscious. Perhaps its power is attributable to our need for an oral tradition after all, some conveying of stories, feelings, myths of ancestors, epics of alienation, and the need to rejoin ancestral roots, even ignorant bigoted roots. Perhaps the visual quiescence of radio is related to the popularity of E-mail or electronic networking. Only the voice is made manifest, unmasking worlds that cannot—or dare not?—be seen. Just yet. Nostalgia crystallizing into a dangerous future. The preconscious voice erupting into the expressed, the prime time.

10   What comes out of the modern radio mouth could be the *Iliad*, the *Rubaiyat*, the griot's song of our times. If indeed radio is a vessel for the American "Song of Songs," then what does it mean that a manic, adolescent Howard Stern is so popular among radio listeners, that Rush Limbaugh's wittily smooth sadism has gone the way of prime-time television, and that both vie for the number one slot on all the best-selling book lists? What to make of the stories being told by our modern radio evangelists and their tragic unloved chorus of callers? Is it really just a collapsing economy that spawns this drama of grown people sitting around scaring themselves to death with fantasies of black feminist Mexican able-bodied gay soldiers earning $100,000 a year on welfare who are so criminally depraved that Hillary Clinton or the antichrist-of-the-moment had no choice but to invite them onto the government payroll so they can run the country? The panicky exaggeration reminds me of a child's fear. . . . *And then, and then, a huge lion jumped out of the shadows and was about to gobble me up, and I can't ever sleep again for a whole week.*

As I spin the dial on my radio, I can't help thinking that this stuff must be related to that most poignant of fiber-optic phenomena, phone sex. Aural Sex. Radio Racism with a touch of S & M. High-priest hosts with the power and run-amok ego to discipline listeners, to smack with the verbal back of the hand, to smash the button that shuts you up once and for all. "Idiot!" shouts New York City radio demagogue Bob Grant and then the sound of droning telephone emptiness, the voice of dissent dumped out some trap-door in aural space.

As I listened to a range of such programs what struck me as the most unifying theme was not merely the specific intolerance on such hot topics as race and gender, but a much more general contempt for the world, a verbal stoning of anything different. It is like some unusually violent game of "Simon Says," this mockery and shouting down of callers, this roar of incantations, the insistence on agreement.

But, ah, if you *will* but only agree, what sweet and safe reward, what soft enfolding by a stern and angry radio god. And as an added bonus, the invisible shield of an AM community, a family of fans who are Exactly Like You, to whom you can express, in anonymity, all the filthy stuff you imagine "them" doing to you. The comfort and relief of being able to ejaculate, to those who understand, about the dark imagined excess overtaking, robbing, needing to be held down and taught a good lesson, needing to put it in its place before the ravenous demon enervates all that is true and good and pure in this life.

The audience for this genre of radio flagellation is mostly young, white, and male. Two thirds of Rush Limbaugh's audience is male. According to *Time* magazine, 75 percent of Howard Stern's listeners are white men. Most of the callers have spent their lives walling themselves off from any real experience with blacks, feminists, lesbians, or gays. In this regard, it is probably true, as former Secretary of Education William Bennett says, that Rush Limbaugh "tells his audience that what you believe inside, you can talk about in the marketplace." Unfortunately, what's "inside" is then mistaken for what's outside, treated as empirical and political reality. The *National Review* extols Limbaugh's conservative leadership as no less than that of Ronald Reagan, and the Republican party provides Limbaugh with books to discuss, stories, angles, and public support. "People were afraid of censure by gay activists, feminists, environmentalists—now they are not because Rush takes them on," says Bennett.

U.S. history has been marked by cycles in which brands of 15 this or that hatred come into fashion and go out, are unleashed and then restrained. If racism, homophobia, jingoism, and woman-hating have been features of national life in pretty much all of modern history, it rather begs the question to spend a lot of time wondering if right-wing radio is a symptom or a cause. For at least four hundred years, prevailing attitudes in the West have considered African Americans less intelligent. Recent statistics show that 53 percent of people in the U.S. agree that blacks and Latinos are less intelligent than whites, and a majority believe that blacks are lazy, violent, welfare-dependent, and unpatriotic.

I think that what has made life more or less tolerable for "out" groups have been those moments in history when those "inside" feelings were relatively restrained. In fact, if I could believe that right-wing radio were only about idiosyncratic, singular, rough-hewn individuals thinking those inside thoughts, I'd be much more inclined to agree with Columbia University media expert Everette Dennis, who says that Stern's and Limbaugh's popularity represents the "triumph of the individual" or with *Time* magazine's bottom line that "the fact that either is seriously considered a threat . . . is more worrisome than Stern or Limbaugh will ever be." If what I were hearing had even a tad more to do with real oppressions, with real white *and* black levels of joblessness and homelessness, or with the real problems of real white men, then I wouldn't have bothered to slog my way through hours of Howard Stern's miserable obsessions.

Yet at the heart of my anxiety is the worry that Stern, Limbaugh, Grant et al. represent the very antithesis of individualism's triumph. As the *National Review* said of Limbaugh's ascent, "It was a feat not only of the loudest voice but also of a keen political brain to round up, as Rush did, the media herd and drive them into the conservative corral." When asked about his political aspirations, Bob Grant gloated to the *Washington Post*, "I think I would make rather a good dictator."

The polemics of right-wing radio are putting nothing less than hate onto the airwaves, into the marketplace, electing it to office, teaching it in schools, and exalting it as freedom. What worries me is the increasing-to-constant commerce of retribution, control, and lashing out, fed not by fact but fantasy. What worries me is the reemergence, more powerfully than at any time since the institution of Jim Crow, of a socio-centered self that excludes "the likes of," well, me for example, from the civic circle, and that would rob me of my worth and claim and identity as a citizen. As the *Economist* rightly observes, "Mr. Limbaugh takes a mass market—white, mainly male, middle-class, ordinary America—and talks to it as an endangered minority."

"I worry about this identity whose external reference is a set of beliefs, ethics, and practices that excludes, restricts, and acts in the world on me, or mine, as the perceived if not real enemy. I am acutely aware of losing *my* mythic individualism to the surface shapes of my mythic group fearsomeness as black, as female, as left wing. "I" merge not fluidly but irretrievably into a category of "them." I become a suspect self, a moving target of loathsome properties, not merely different but dangerous. And that worries me a lot.

What happens in my life with all this translated license, this 20
permission to be uncivil? What happens to the social space that
was supposedly at the sweet mountaintop of the civil rights movement's trail? Can I get a seat on the bus without having to be reminded that I *should* be standing? Did the civil rights movement
guarantee us nothing more than to use public accommodations
while surrounded by raving lunatic bigots? "They didn't beat this
idiot [Rodney King] enough," says Howard Stern.

Not long ago I had the misfortune to hail a taxicab in which
the driver was listening to Howard Stern undress some woman.
After some blocks, I had to get out. I was, frankly, afraid to ask the
driver to turn it off—not because I was afraid of "censoring" him,
which seems to be the only thing people will talk about anymore,
but because the driver was stripping me too, as he leered through
the rearview mirror. "Something the matter?" he demanded, as I
asked him to pull over and let me out well short of my destination
(I'll spare you the full story of what happened from there—trying
to get another cab, as the cabbies stopped for all the white businessmen who so much as scratched their heads near the curb; a
nice young white man, seeing my plight, giving me his cab, having to thank him, he hero, me saved-but-humiliated, cabdriver
pissed and surly. I fight my way to my destination, finally arriving
in bad mood, militant black woman, cranky femi-nazi.)

When Yeltsin blared rock music at his opponents holed up in
the parliament building in Moscow, in imitation of the U.S.
Marines trying to torture Manuel Noriega in Panama, all I could
think of was that it must be like being trapped in a crowded subway car when all the portable stereos are tuned to Bob Grant or
Howard Stern. With Howard Stern's voice a tinny, screeching
backdrop, with all the faces growing dreamily mean as though
some soporifically evil hallucinogen were gushing into their
bloodstreams, I'd start begging to surrender.

Surrender to what? Surrender to the laissez-faire resegrega-
tion that is the metaphoric significance of the hundreds of "Rush
rooms" that have cropped up in restaurants around the country;
rooms broadcasting Limbaugh's words, rooms for your listening
pleasure, rooms where bigots can capture the purity of a Rush-
only lunch counter, rooms where all those unpleasant others just
"choose" not to eat? Surrender to the naughty luxury of a room in
which a Ku Klux Klan meeting could take place in orderly, First
Amendment fashion? Everyone's "free" to come in (and a few of
you outsiders do), but mostly the undesirable nonconformists are
gently repulsed away. It's a high-tech world of enhanced choice.

Whites choose mostly to sit in the Rush room. Feminists, blacks, lesbians, and gays "choose" to sit elsewhere. No need to buy black votes, you just pay them not to vote; no need to insist on white-only schools, you just sell the desirability of black-only schools. Just sit back and watch it work, like those invisible shock shields that keep dogs cowering in their own backyards.

How real is the driving perception behind all the Sturm and Drang of this genre of radio-harangue—the perception that white men are an oppressed minority, with no power and no opportunity in the land that they made great? While it is true that power and opportunity are shrinking for all but the very wealthy in this country (and would that Limbaugh would take that issue on), the fact remains that white men are still this country's most privileged citizens and market actors. To give just a small example, according to the *Wall Street Journal*, blacks were the only racial group to suffer a net job loss during the 1990–91 economic downturn at the companies reporting to the Equal Employment Opportunity Commission. Whites, Latinos, and Asians, meanwhile, gained thousands of jobs. While whites gained 71,144 jobs at these companies, Latinos gained 60,040, Asians gained 55,104, and blacks lost 59,479. If every black were hired in the United States tomorrow, the numbers would not be sufficient to account for white men's expanding balloon of fear that they have been specifically dispossessed by African Americans.

25   Given deep patterns of social segregation and general ignorance of history, particularly racial history, media remain the principal source of most Americans' knowledge of each other. Media can provoke violence or induce passivity. In San Francisco, for example, a radio show on KMEL called "Street Soldiers" has taken this power as a responsibility with great consequence: "Unquestionably," writes Ken Auletta in the *New Yorker*, "the show has helped avert violence. When a Samoan teenager was slain, apparently by Filipino gang members, in a drive-by shooting, the phones lit up with calls from Samoans wanting to tell [the hosts] they would not rest until they had exacted revenge. Threats filled the air for a couple of weeks. Then the dead Samoan's father called in, and, in a poignant exchange, the father said he couldn't tolerate the thought of more young men senselessly slaughtered. There would be no retaliation, he vowed. "And there was none." In contrast, we must wonder at the phenomenon of the very powerful leadership of the Republican party, from Ronald Reagan to Robert Dole to William Bennett, giving advice, counsel, and friendship to Rush Limbaugh's passionate divisiveness.

The outright denial of the material crisis at every level of U.S. society, most urgently in black inner-city neighborhoods but facing us all, is a kind of political circus, dissembling as it feeds the frustrations of the moment. We as a nation can no longer afford to deal with such crises by *imagining* an excess of bodies, of babies, of job-stealers, of welfare mothers, of overreaching immigrants, of too-powerful (Jewish, in whispers) liberal Hollywood, of lesbians and gays, of gang members ("gangsters" remain white, and no matter what the atrocity, less vilified than "gang members," who are black), of Arab terrorists, and uppity women. The reality of our social poverty far exceeds these scapegoats. This right-wing backlash resembles, in form if not substance, phenomena like anti-Semitism in Poland: there aren't but a handful of Jews left in that whole country, but the giant balloon of heated anti-Semitism flourishes apace, Jews blamed for the world's evils.

The overwhelming response to right-wing excesses in the United States has been to seek an odd sort of comfort in the fact that the First Amendment is working so well that you can't suppress this sort of thing. Look what's happened in Eastern Europe. Granted. So let's not talk about censorship or the First Amendment for the next ten minutes. But in Western Europe, where fascism is rising at an appalling rate, suppression is hardly the problem. In Eastern and Western Europe as well as the United States, we must begin to think just a little bit about the fiercely coalescing power of media to spark mistrust, to fan it into forest fires of fear and revenge. We must begin to think about the levels of national and social complacence in the face of such resolute ignorance. We must ask ourselves what the expected result is, not of censorship or suppression, but of so much encouragement, so much support, so much investment in the fashionability of hate. What future is it that we are designing with the devotion of such tremendous resources to the disgraceful propaganda of bigotry?

Stabilizing the Text

1. What are the defining features of hate radio according to Williams? Try to consider all aspects of communication as you answer this question, including what is said, what is heard, how it is said, and even where it is heard.
2. How does Williams account for the popularity of hate radio? Whose needs does hate radio satisfy and how does it satisfy them? Whose needs are not satisfied by hate radio? How are these needs made to matter less? Why do you think these needs matter less?

3. Williams rejects the view that First Amendment freedom of speech is the real issue at stake in the proliferation of hate radio. She does not deny people their freedom of expression, but she suggests there is more at stake. What is it? What does Williams consider more important in her criticism of hate radio than protecting expressions we disagree with? What reasons does she give in support of this view? And how persuasive is her view?

Mobilizing the Text

1. Williams asks in her essay, "What happens in my life with all this translated license, this permission to be uncivil? What happens to the social space that was supposedly at the sweet mountaintop of the civil rights movement's trail?" Try to answer these questions for yourself. What happens in your life because people are granted permission to be uncivil in the media? In your experience, what happens in social spaces as a result of media incivility?

2. Williams mentioned only a select few hate radio personalities throughout her essay, mostly Howard Stern and Rush Limbaugh. There are no doubt other hate radio personalities you could name. Does your experience with the things said by these others confirm or deny what Williams says about her experience? Does your experience in any way match hers? Given the similarities and differences in responses to hate radio, what would you want to say about hate radio's effects?

3. Williams provides an example of something that is the opposite of hate radio in her brief treatment of the KMEL show *Street Soldiers*. What would you characterize as the differences between the two kinds of radio? Can you think of other call-in shows you would characterize as the opposite of hate radio? What value do each of these shows have? Why does hate radio and its opposite matter to the quality of life in our communities?

Speaking for Ourselves
Makani Themba-Nixon and Nan Rubin

Makani Themba-Nixon is executive director of The Praxis Project, a nonprofit organization helping communities use media and policy advocacy to advance health equity and justice. She is coauthor of Media Advocacy and Public Health: Power for Prevention, *and her latest book is* Making Policy, Making Change, *which examines media and policy advocacy for public health through case studies and practical information. Nan Rubin provides organizational support to community media projects and coordinated the Highlander*

Media Justice Gathering. In "Speaking for Ourselves," which first appeared in the Nation, *Themba-Nixon and Rubin explain the concept of media justice and discuss grassroots projects to transform media in cities like San Francisco and Philadelphia. As you read this essay, pay attention to the range of voices that Themba-Nixon and Rubin bring into their essay and consider how this range helps to bolster the point their essay seeks to make.*

◆

Nearly forty years ago, a few determined civil rights activists at the United Church of Christ and the NAACP in Jackson, Mississippi, decided to take on the treatment of blacks by the television news. They drew a straight line from the racism they faced on the streets to the racism they faced in their living rooms when they turned on the TV. So they monitored newscasts at two local stations in Jackson. After determining that the stations were utterly failing to serve their African-American audiences, the activists filed petitions with the Federal Communications Commission. And when they didn't like what the FCC had to say, they took the commission to court, where they won. Big time.

The courts ultimately ruled that the broadcast license of station WLBT-TV ought to be taken away altogether. They said that while African-Americans were 45 percent of the audience, their concerns were totally ignored by the local television stations. It was a stunning decision, one that not only established the principle that news content must reflect in some fashion the actual diversity of local audiences but, just as important, that the public—not just corporate entities—had standing and could go directly to the FCC.

Today the landscape is radically different. With the Congressional deregulatory frenzy that started in the early 1990s, many media restrictions were loosened, and after passage of the Telecommunications Act of 1996, the floodgates were completely thrown open. The rapid acceleration of consolidation in media and telecommunications industries that quickly followed—and is still under way—has occurred with the eager complicity of the FCC. Media reform advocates were placed on the defensive, but they did their best to mount a holding action and not be flattened by the commercial steamroller.

Meanwhile, the Jackson decision, which was once called the "Magna Carta for active public participation in broadcast regulation," has all but disappeared from the annals of media policy advocacy. The lobbyists and scholars leading the current efforts at media reform are focusing on a whole different set of concerns—resistance to corporate media consolidation, the battle to preserve localism and against content that is commercial and sensationalistic—which are a far cry from the issues of racism and unfair treatment that launched the earlier movement.

5   There is an increasingly rebellious response to this Jeffersonian approach to media reform—and to the continued marginalization of people of color in the ever-more-consolidated world of mainstream media. In small towns and in church basements, in virtual communities and villages, a growing group of activists are going back to the movement's roots using a framework they call media justice. Drawing inspiration from the environmental justice movement, media justice proponents are developing race-, class- and gender-conscious visions for changing media content and structure. A first-ever Media Justice Summit is planned for late spring 2004. Says co-convener and technology expert Art McGee, "We're modeling the Media Justice Summit on the historic Environmental Justice Summit over a decade ago, in which people of color and the poor came together and made explicit their environmental issues and concerns, which had not been a part of the mainstream agendas of mostly white groups like the Sierra Club or Greenpeace. We're about to do something very similar."

Using media as an organizing tool is certainly not new. For more than fifty years, America has nurtured a vibrant, alternative, overtly political media voice. But in the past few years, in response to glaring news failures like the 2000 presidential election and the "homeland security" journalism in the wake of 9/11, a broad convergence of activists launched a coordinated drive to reform media and use it to advance their broader agendas. They held a flurry of confabs, from the big-tent Media and Democracy Congresses of 1996 and 1997 to the more reflective Kopkind Colony series, where a small group of progressive organizers and journalists spend a week in conversation and retreat.

But if the media justice movement had a coming-out party, it was at the venerable Highlander Research and Education Center in August 2002. Highlander convened a group of grassroots activists to discuss media organizing strategies, and by the time the group had worked out plans to create education materials, build constituencies and work in partnership with social justice campaigns, it had become the Highlander Media Justice Gathering. Because media's role in spreading capitalist values and neoliberal ideology was having a mortal impact on so many social and economic justice movements, the conclusion was that media could no longer be a sidebar—it had become one of the main issues.

Today's media organizers employ a few basic strategies: building and controlling our own production and distribution outlets; using, confronting and transforming corporate media; and changing the underlying regulatory structures, policies and framework. Activists are energetically pursuing all these directions, engaging dozens of groups across the country. The media justice perspective cuts across them all.

A growing network of organizations in the San Francisco Bay Area is working under the media justice banner. Third World Majority encourages women and people of color to engage in media work. "People say, 'We'll never be on the radio. We'll never be on TV.' They feel really disempowered and shut off that part of themselves," says executive director Thenmozhi Soundararajan. Through efforts like its Community Digital Storytelling Movement, TWM helps marginalized communities produce their own stories, including both personal narratives and community histories.

Also part of the network is Media Alliance—founded twenty-seven years ago by progressive Bay Area journalists—and the Youth Media Council, both of which serve with TWM as co-conveners of next year's Media Justice Summit. Serious about demanding that media be held accountable for their images of youth, YMC has produced several reports on the behavior of local media. "Speaking for Ourselves: A Youth Assessment of Local News Coverage" broke down the biased and acontextual press coverage of young people, and included a nine-point set of "recommendations to journalists for improved coverage of youth." Their most recent effort, "The Bay Area Media Map," is a step-by-step guide to youth for mapping local media ownership, working with news reporters and building strong relationships to get their own voices heard. "YMC's approach is straightforward," says director Malkia Cyril. "Youth are often negatively portrayed. Our voices are often absent in the public debate on the issues that affect us. We want access. We want power. We want to produce. We want to see changes in how we are portrayed—not because we just want to be on TV but because what's on TV or in the media is fundamentally setting the public agenda. People are choosing to send us to prison, execute us, cut funding to our schools—the list goes on—based on what they see on the news. How can we ignore that?"

On the East Coast, Philadelphia has become a hotbed for a cluster of young media justice activists. According to Inja Coates,

10

co-founder and director of Media Tank, a spinoff of the Independent Media Center (IMC) that does education and move-ment-building on media issues, the local movement was kicked off in 1997 when pirate radio station Radio Mutiny went on the air and, simultaneously, a new coalition was launched to get pub-lic-access channels (which still don't exist there) onto the city ca-ble system. "These two efforts got off the ground at the same time, and then when the Republican convention came to town, we all worked together in the trenches to make the Indy Media Center happen. Things have just grown from there," she says.

With the Kensington Welfare Rights Union (KWRU), also based in Philadelphia, Media Tank co-sponsored a gathering called "Break the Media Blackout: A Conference on Media Democracy and the Struggle to End Poverty." Part of the national Poor People's Economic Human Rights Campaign, the event was aimed at building "a critical alliance between the growing media democracy movement and the movement to end poverty led by the poor." To highlight the concept that media are making poverty invisible in America, the conference offered workshops to analyze the behavior of mainstream media and to teach hands-on techni-cal skills to empower grassroots antipoverty organizations.

"We have to break the media isolation of the poor, which has virtually disappeared large segments of the population," says Shivani Selveraj, one of the conference organizers. "KWRU took a busload of folks from North Philly across the country to see what urban and rural poverty looks like, since the media doesn't show us—only 'black welfare queens' or 'backward hillbilly white trash.' All along the way we put stories and pictures daily on our website, and you could see how people were moving through their own misconceptions. So we learned we have to do it ourselves."

At the Break the Media Blackout Conference, the Philadelphia-based Prometheus Radio Project (the creation of Dylan Wrynn, also know as Pete TriDish, who helped transform radio pirates into policy activists who lobbied the FCC and Congress to create LPFM, the legal low-power radio service) so-lidified its relationship with the Coalition of Immokalee Workers/Coalicion de Trabajadores de Immokalee. A community-based farmworker movement in the heart of the Florida agricul-tural industry, the coalition is made up of members from Mexico, Haiti, Guatemala and elsewhere who pick tomatoes, watermel-ons, cucumbers and peppers for what they describe as "slave wages," which haven't increased in more than two decades.

15   Prometheus helped them apply for a low-power radio license, and the coalition will be putting its station on the air by the end

of the year. Coalition staff member Max Perez says, "Meeting with Prometheus gave us the idea that we could have our own radio station." The coalition is currently running a campus campaign against Taco Bell in order to win what Perez says will be the first company wage increase for picking tomatoes in more than twenty years. "The boycott really got off the ground when we started to tell our own stories on a website," he says. "It's been really effective. But it's nothing without the grassroots action. We hope the radio station will bring us together, when we can hear our own voices and really reach the local community."

Finding independent ways to tell our stories was also the idea that sparked the first Independent Media Center four years ago. The first IMC was set up just to cover the protests set to occur in Seattle during the 1999 WTO meetings. But it quickly mushroomed into an international phenomenon, with local operations in more than 125 locations around the world. Soon after IMC's success at the WTO, Seattle attorney and co-founder Dan Merkle was traveling around the country helping to set up new IMCs. "It was a brilliant template, which saw tremendous exponential growth in a short time frame, with minimal resources and no top-down hierarchical governance," he says. "It was an organic evolution of media activists and technology that has played an extremely valuable role within the global justice movement. This is a major success story." However, Merkle sees room for improvement. "The IMC plays a really valuable role, but the movement now is too white—once again, it won't get us where we want to go unless more effort is put into addressing the needs in communities of color as well as in rural communities."

Sheri Herndon, also a Seattle IMC co-founder, agrees and, as a participant in the Highlander Media Justice Working Group, is attempting to build bridges between the IMC and media justice movements. "Indymedia is truly one of the most interesting international decentralized networks in existence," she says. "[But] if we are going to take this model to another level, we have to see beyond the narrow confines of our own experience and recognize how much this dynamic network needs racial diversity. At this point, it is crucial."

The issues that started it all back in Jackson, Mississippi, more than forty years ago are still plaguing Jackson's communities of color—most with a modern twist. Instead of fighting to get coverage, groups now fight to change *how* they are covered. But there has been some improvement, says Southern Echo's Leroy Johnson. The

Jackson-based Southern Echo, a leadership development organization, got its first invitation to the *Jackson Clarion-Ledger* editorial board meeting this year, an invitation considered long overdue by many community members, given the organization's pivotal work in Mississippi over the past decade. Says Johnson, "It's been difficult to get them to recognize black organizations or Latino or any organizations of color for that matter. They can cover the Red Cross as an institution, but in our communities, if the story is positive, they will focus on an individual. If it's negative, they will focus on the organization. It's a clear media bias that it's OK for an individual to have power but not OK for our communities to have organizations with power. It's inherently wrong, malicious and purposeful."

In some ways, the hostile climate of forty years ago is still there. The *Jackson Advocate*, the city's feisty, black-owned newspaper, has been the target of two firebombings and several attacks for its investigative reporting on racism and local government. One bombing in 1998 left the paper with barely a shell for an office. Thanks to fierce support locally and nationally, the paper is now up and running and still a standard-bearer for the values that made Jackson the place where media justice all began.

20   For media scholar and longtime advocate Mark Lloyd, the movement that calls itself media justice today is just getting back to these civil rights roots. "I think what is considered the media justice movement is less rooted in the consumer or public interest movement than it is properly rooted in a movement that began with the traditional issues and concerns of civil rights—a movement that is concerned with equality, with political representation, the impact of culture on institutions like media and schools." Lloyd observes that this historical context is key to understanding the need for groups to create a media justice "space" outside the media "consumer" or democracy movement. "The fact that we have institutions like the *New York Times* or foundations that are dominated by people who tend not to be people of color . . . [and] they see this 'public interest stuff' as separate or important and maybe see this 'civil rights stuff' as passé is, frankly, connected."

According to Media Justice Summit convener McGee, understanding the history also enables us to draw inspiration from the leadership role that people of color have played in media work. "Black journalists, publishers and activists have been fighting for media justice since before the birth of this country," he says. "For those who think that a people-of-color-led fight for media justice is new, just check out the history of both black people's overall struggle to have some degree of control over their portrayal as human beings, and the tireless work that countless black journalists have done to try to democratize the media landscape in this country. As Samuel Cornish and John B. Russwurm said in the premier issue of *Freedom's Journal* back in 1827: 'We wish to plead our own cause. Too long have others spoken for us.' "

Stabilizing the Text

1. What do you understand to be Themba-Nixon and Rubin's overall point? How do the various examples of media activism they discuss add to your understanding of that point?
2. Find a place in this essay where Themba-Nixon and Rubin use a quotation from an outside source that is particularly effective. Discuss what you think makes the quotation work well.
3. What view of citizenship motivates the kind of media activism Themba-Nixon and Rubin discuss? Is the citizenship they discuss self-interested, public-interested, or both? In what ways?

Mobilizing the Text

1. What reasons do Themba-Nixon and Rubin provide to explain why youth and other groups are becoming media activists? What do you think of those reasons? As a reader, how do they affect your sense of the issues being discussed?
2. In your view, what is the relationship between the media and citizenship in the United States? Does the media try to teach people how to live, what to believe, and how to understand others? What other forces shape citizenship and how?
3. What are some of the social groups that you identify with personally? How are those groups represented in the media? Give examples.

Pathfinders

Peter Medoff and Holly Sklar

Peter Medoff was a community organizing consultant, offering technical assistance in community-based organizing, planning, and development to groups in many cities, including Houston, Chicago, Atlanta, Denver, and Boston. Holly Sklar, a longtime journalist and activist, has authored and coauthored several books, the latest of which is Raise the Floor: Wages and Policies That Work for All of Us. *"Pathfinders" is excerpted from Medoff and Sklar's book* Streets of Hope: The Fall and Rise of an Urban Neighborhood, *a case study of an inner-city Boston neighborhood's resident group, the Dudley Street Neighborhood Initiative. In "Pathfinders," Medoff and Sklar describe the group's struggles to come together across race and generational boundaries, to unify behind a vision of community empowerment, and to establish a voice in determining the future of their neighborhood. As you read this essay, reflect on your own knowledge of the frustrations that face residents of neighborhoods trying to act together for the good of their communities. Ask yourself what was unique about the Dudley Street experience and why successful citizenship projects are so rare.*

---------------------- ✦ ----------------------

In April 1992, dispossessed Los Angeles burned in rage. Embers of anger and despair flared up the coast in San Francisco, Oakland and Seattle and across the country in Las Vegas and Atlanta. A few weeks earlier, the Dudley community had come together in celebration. L.A. exploded with the crushed dreams of inner city America. Dudley surged with the power and pride of dreams unfolding. As DSNI [Dudley Street Neighborhood Initiative] President Ché Madyun put it in the 1992 DSNI annual report, "Hope is the great ally of organizing."

The riots were a multiracial explosion of rage against past injustice and "a perception of a future already looted." South Central L.A. Congresswoman Maxine Waters told a Senate committee, "The verdict in the Rodney King case . . . was only the most recent injustice piled upon many other injustices . . . I have seen our community continually and systematically ravaged— ravaged by banks who would not lend to us, ravaged by governments which abandoned us or punished us for our poverty, and ravaged by big business who exported our jobs."

Waters quoted Robert Kennedy's words from 1968: "There is another kind of violence in America, slower but just as deadly, destructive as the shot or bomb in the night. . . . This is the violence of institutions; indifference and inaction and slow decay. This is the violence that afflicts the poor, that poisons relations between men and women because their skin is different colors. This is the slow destruction of a child by hunger, and schools without books and homes without heat in the winter." Waters added, "What a tragedy it is that America has still . . . not learned such an important lesson."

As in South Central Los Angeles, the residents of Dudley have suffered exploitation and exclusion. Their community has been used as a dumping ground for the waste of wealthier neighborhoods and starved of jobs and government services. They saw downtown Boston undergo an economic boom while Dudley continued to go bust. They have borne the burden of redlining while their tax dollars are used to bail out Savings and Loan spend thrifts. They have endured cops with a colonial mentality.

"Riots are the voices of the unheard," said Martin Luther King. Dudley's pathfinders found a way to be heard. The city found a way to listen.

DSNI board member Stephen Hanley remarks, "The people in this community know even when there were good times [In Boston], they were shafted. So while things are bad right now, at least they're on the right track."

On April 3, 1992, over 800 people filled the historic Strand Theatre in Uphams Corner to celebrate DSNI's accomplishments and thank the outgoing executive director, Gus Newport. Youth leader John Barros drew the portrait of Newport that graced the program booklet. Newport's old friend, actor Danny Glover, was the master of ceremonies. Hundreds of Dudley residents were joined by community activists from other neighborhoods, funders, politicians, the mayor and various city officials, businesspeople and others of many different backgrounds committed to seeing Dudley's rebirth.

There was a short video history of Dudley and DSNI—part of a longer film in progress by Leah Mahan and Mark Lipman. The video clip of Gus Newport rapping with kids from Dudley's Young Architects and Planners—Heavy G and the Young APs—brought the house down. Everyone shared a multiethnic meal prepared by Dudley residents and enjoyed performances by local dancers, actors, singers and musicians—among them Ché Madyun, who performed an original solo dance, and DSNI Director Paul Yelder in his persona of blues singer Luap Redley. Newell Flather presented Newport with a framed piece of the Riley Foundation's rug, which Newport had frequently trod. It was a symbolic bridge between Dudley's past—the disinvestment represented by the old worn rug at La Alianza Hispana—and the more constructive, contemporary relationship between Dudley and downtown.

When Boston city official Lisa Chapnick was asked if she had thought of DSNI at the time of the L.A. riots, she responded quickly, "I certainly did. I said, 'If there were more DSNIs, L.A. wouldn't have happened.' " Chapnick continues, "I think DSNI is the future of our country. I think the challenge is, how do you replicate it? . . . How do you find residents who have hope and heart when they should be bitter?" The riot, she says, "was a wake-up call that's long overdue. Of course, it looks like nothing is going to happen with it."

10   The embers of disrespect, discrimination and disinvestment still smolder in cities around the country. Rebuild L.A., launched after the riots with much fanfare and promises of inclusion and "greenlining," has not delivered in process or product. Rebuild L.A.'s first director, Peter Ueberroth—impresario of the commercialized 1984 Olympics and chairman of the California Council on Competitiveness, which advocated rolling back environmental and land use regulations—represented "corporatism dressed up in the language of cooperation," says Eric Mann, director of the Labor/Community Strategy Center in Los Angeles. Power on the Rebuild L.A. (R.L.A.) board "is firmly in the hands of representatives of Arco, I.B.M., Warner Brothers, Southern California Edison, U.S.C., Disney and the Chamber of Commerce."

In July 1992, says Mann, Ueberroth cheered when General Motors announced that it would channel $15 million in contracts from its Hughes Aircraft subsidiary to inner-city suppliers. The move, which would generate a few hundred jobs at most, was hyped by R.L.A. as corporate benevolence in action. One month later G.M. shut down the Van Nuys automobile assembly plant, its last in L.A., eliminating 3,000 workers, about two-thirds of whom are Latino and black." At a job training conference sponsored by Toyota and the Urban League in fall 1992, "Ueberroth hailed *minimum*-wage jobs as bringing 'dignity to those who labor in them.' Workers from Justice for Janitors, a campaign of the Service Employees International Union, marched on R.L.A. shortly after to tell him that for hundreds of thousands of Angelenos who already have full-time jobs, the minimum wage means living below the federal poverty line, usually without health insurance or job security."

"'Nothing, nothing at all has been learned from the riots," says María Elena Durazo, leader of the mostly Latino Hotel and Restaurant Employees Local 11. . . . Since the riots the business community has been pushing the city and the state to roll back environmental, tax, and workers' compensation regulations. What it means is that they want to squeeze even more out of a vulnerable work force.' Durazo adds, 'Don't they see they are creating more of the very same conditions that led to the riots?' "

In the words of author Mike Davis, California "Governor Wilson and the state legislature in Sacramento figuratively burned down the city a second time with billions of dollars of school and public-sector cutbacks." Legislators ignored "a report on the state's children that showed youth unemployment and homicide rates soaring in tandem."

In January 1994, on the day the nation celebrates Martin Luther King's birthday, Los Angeles shook and burned from the force of a catastrophic earthquake. Angelenos must now rebuild from riots sparked by repression and economic depression, nature's earthquake and the fires in between. Pacific News Service editor Rubén Martínez contemplated how, in the Latino immigrant *barrios*, the solidarity Angelenos showed each other in responding to the earthquake "is the survival mechanism of daily life." Martínez looked beyond one of the poignant events shown widely on television: the rescue of Salvador Peña, an immigrant from El Salvador, from "the pancaked parking lot of the Northridge Fashion Mall" where he was driving a street sweeper. "An army of hundreds of thousands of Salvador Peñas toils from dusk to dawn in L.A., cleaning office buildings, preparing meals for the white collars. They do so because without work there is no future, and without a future there is no hope."

"Yes, this rescue assured us, good will can guide us through tragedy," Martínez observes. But the economic, racial and ethnic fault lines that divide Angelenos remain. Looking to the future, the question is, will Los Angeles rebuild together—or apart and volatile? That's a question many others around the country can ask of their communities and their nation. 15

"TOGETHER, WE'LL FIND THE WAY"

While he was directing Rebuild L.A., Peter Ueberroth said that many businesses gutted in the riot were "not of any great, huge value." He said that local activists demanding a faster flow of money should "get out of the way."

In Dudley, residents successfully got "in the way" of both a city redevelopment plan that threatened to displace them and an agency/funder-driven coalition to rebuild the neighborhood. Dudley residents got in the way—and created a new way forward. As DSNI board member Paul Bothwell affirms, "Together, we'll find the way."

Bothwell offers three lessons he finds true to Dudley as it rebuilds. . . . First, "the heart is far more important than the head.

Lots of efforts are head efforts. Lots of things have money and expertise, they have this and that and everything else, but they don't have any heart. Anybody on the street can read that. If there isn't a heart to it then the head doesn't even matter."

Second, says Bothwell, "being is really more important than doing. What something *is* is more important even than what it can do. What you are or what I am—what's going on in the nature of heart, spirit, personhood and all that—that, in the end, is all we have. In the end . . . if we're crippled and broken by accident or anything else, what does that mean? That you're not worth something anymore? There's nothing here anymore? Of course not. Being is far more important than doing." Bothwell adds, "People don't trust DSNI just because it can do something. That's a big factor—because nobody else has been able to do anything. [But] I think people trust DSNI . . . because of what it is. . . . People see themselves reflected here."

Third, says Bothwell, "doing together, living together is far more important than doing alone. I think that reflects that proverb I gave earlier: 'Together, we'll find the way.' You try to do that alone—we're all so broken, we're all so crippled, we're all so fragile, we're all so partial, and I'm talking about organizations as well as people and communities. You try to do it alone, it's not going to go anywhere."

Bothwell's lessons speak directly to DSNI's essence. The heart is more important than the head: DSNI's efforts are not guided by professional "experts" or leaders with swelled heads. Rather, DSNI is guided by those at the heart of the neighborhood—the residents—who are, in turn, guided by their hearts, hopes, dreams, knowledge and experiences. Being is more important than doing: DSNI emphasizes process before product, knowing that in the long run the products will be more and better if the process is empowering. DSNI's way of being is rooted in diversity and unity, self-esteem and commu*nity* pride. Doing together is more important than doing alone: Dudley residents have shown that together they are powerful visionaries and together they can make their vision and plans for the neighborhood more real every day. . . .

BUILDING ON NEIGHBORHOOD ASSETS

Community development must begin by recognizing and reinforcing the resources *within* the community. DSNI assumes and demonstrates that people in low-income neighborhoods—like people in all neighborhoods—have solutions as well as problems. Like people of every income level, they have individual and community assets—a mix of skills, talents, knowledge, experience and resources—that are vital elements of the redevelopment process.

As John McKnight, director of the Center for Urban Affairs and Policy Research at Northwestern University, puts it, "No community is built with a focus on deficiencies and needs. Every community, forever in the past and forever in the future, will be built on the capacities and gifts of the people who live there."

Andrea Nagel, who first served DSNI as an organizer and later as Human Development director, underscores the capacity-building approach. DSNI, she says, is continually "exposing, strengthening and building upon the gifts that this neighborhood has—its people, its vacant land, its businesses. . . . The class is half full to us, you know. We make an effort to look through the positive lens—understanding, not denying the reality, not minimizing or understating what hardships and difficult realities that people face in this neighborhood. But never, ever losing sight of what is often written off and completely overlooked, and that is its people and resources."

Low-income neighborhoods are often viewed as dependent receivers of services and dollars—ignoring the vast resources they export in the form of taxes; underpaid labor; bank savings invested in communities that have not been redlined; exorbitant interest and insurance payments; work and purchases at businesses located outside the neighborhood; volunteering in and donating to nonprofit, religious and civic organizations; and so on.

Government, private foundations and human service agencies often demean low-income residents, viewing them as incapable, culpable, "at risk," dependent clients—clients they treat as second-class citizens or worse. Many policymakers, funders and human service "providers" have fostered atomized communities that no longer recognize their own assets, their own vision, their own power. They are, in McKnight's words, "dominated by systems that have institutionalized degraded visions for devalued people."

Many human service agencies felt threatened by DSNI's resident-controlled agenda. McKnight predicts that this conflict will always arise: "Service systems act on the premise that the professional has the expertise and the client has the problem. The problem solving power of the people in the neighborhoods is unimportant. That professional idea is exactly the opposite of what community organizing attempts to do. The organizer tells the people that they have problem solving abilities and they can change their communities."

DSNI has worked hard to build an Agency Collaborative to strengthen agency accountability to residents, minimize competition, maximize cooperation and improve human development resources and policies. Funders, as emphasized later, can play an important role by encouraging collaboration and respecting the priorities of a resident-driven collaborative process—priorities which may well differ from funders' preconceived ideas.

The community of residents as a whole brings invaluable assets to the redevelopment process. Residents have experienced the history of the neighborhood. They have been the ones to stay and struggle as the neighborhood was being disinvested in, or made a new stake where others would not. Only residents working together can create a self-determined vision of the neighborhood's future. Only residents can foster the political will necessary to make the vision a reality. After years of being disrespected, dismissed and discriminated against, residents may not always realize they have these capacities. Through organizing together, they reveal and reinforce their individual and collective assets.

30 In the words of DSNI activist Najwa Abdul-Tawwab, what's "key about DSNI is the word 'initiative.' It works to help people initiate."

CREATING VISION AND POLITICAL WILL

Reflecting on the period before DSNI's formation, Paul Bothwell says, "What continued to break my heart, as well as mobilize this terrific fire inside me personally and others," was that neighborhood decline "is not something that happens in communities by itself . . . it's not something that's just sheer chance. It's not because people here are stupid. . . . This is the result of city policy, of other kinds of large-scale things that systematically cripple or dismember a community. Nobody who can do anything about it really cares. Everybody who is here, who really to a great degree can't do anything about it, cares." DSNI's challenge was to translate caring into control.

Creating a vision begins by building up expectations and stoking a constructive "fire inside." As Bill Slotnik puts it, "First, the people have to care about the neighborhood in which they live, and I think that exists in most neighborhoods. Second, they've got to have a feeling that things aren't going to get better unless we get involved. Third, there has to be a sense of confidence that something can come together that will make a difference."

Most bureaucrats, whether in public or private agencies, will advise keeping expectations low. If expectations aren't fulfilled, they claim, people will become disappointed and lose interest in staying involved. This approach fosters dependency and passivity. Higher expectations enable a community to Think Big—the kind of thinking not only needed to create a comprehensive vision, but needed to make it real. By thinking big and acting powerful, a neighborhood can create the political will and attract the attention and resources it needs to translate vision into reality.

"If you want to separate yourself from the traditional, you have to do something nontraditional," city official Lisa Chapnick observes. "If you want to create that flash point, that special moment, that special relationship, you've got to have a component that's unique and big and risky." A bureaucracy doesn't respond well to risky ventures, but good leaders do. And that is why DSNI held to the motto of "going to the top." Time and again, DSNI members learned that when bureaucracy ground to a halt, political leadership could quickly get it moving again. All that was necessary was for the leader to possess the political will. And that political will is created back in the neighborhood.

A unified, visionary community can create political will where there was none before and make government a partner rather than an obstacle or adversary. Comprehensive redevelopment requires significant resources from outside the neighborhood as well as inside it—resources people rightfully deserve, but which are often distributed unfairly.   35

Government policymakers often point to resource limitations to rationalize why they cannot meet citizen demands. Nonprofit service agencies too often conform, however unhappily, to government's top-down limitations on what is possible. Yet, lack of resources does not limit the most costly policies seen as necessary by those in power—such as the Gulf War and the Savings and Loan bailout. The problem is *not*, as often stated, "having more will than wallet." Rather, lack of political will limits what is possible. Communities must build enough power to make government truly representative and hold politicians and officials accountable.

In a community-controlled planning process neighborhood residents are organized to provide the vision, define the priorities and plans, and participate in the implementation. As Andrea Nagel emphasizes, residents also have the best understanding of what has *not* worked in their neighborhood.

Professional staff and consultants must see themselves as working for the residents. The notion that creating a successful plan relies more on organizing capacity than on technical skills flies directly against traditional, elitist views of planning. DSNI's choice of a firm like DAC, committed to DSNI's view of comprehensive community revitalization and a resident-driven process, was crucial. DAC differentiated itself from traditional planners in its original proposal: "The principles of planning for lower-income people and their communities are the same as those on behalf of the rich. Technicians are to be hired to serve the goals and objectives set by their employers.... When it comes to low-income residents, however, the rules tend to be reversed. 'The experts' seem intent on confusing their community clients with complex terms and coded jargon with the principal message of 'let the professionals handle it, because only they understand the process.' "

Organizing produces the political will necessary for the vision's adoption and successful implementation. While the content of the plan that DSNI created with DAC was technically sound, many technically solid plans are not implemented because they lack the necessary support inside and outside the neighborhood. DSNI successfully built a consensus around development that no politician or government official wanted to challenge. When Mayor Flynn announced his support for the plan, few people believed he had ever read the document. What led politicians and others to support the plan was not so much the details of its contents, but rather, its political power derived from an organizing process that assured inclusion of all segments of the Dudley community.

COMPREHENSIVE COMMUNITY REVITALIZATION

40 The Dudley Street Neighborhood Initiative has fostered an alternative, holistic approach to community development. While recognizing the importance of affordable housing and other physical development, DSNI sees that development as part of a much larger, dynamic process of community renewal led by neighborhood residents. In DSNI's view, a revitalized community is neighborly at heart, healthy in body and spirit, and socially, economically and culturally vibrant.

DSNI's successful methodology was to begin with organizing, create the long-term vision for the community and then assure the vision's implementation. Over the years, DSNI's capacity for comprehensive human, economic, physical and environmental development has grown stronger. It has had different priorities at different times—variously combining planning, organizing and implementation and variously addressing immediate and long-term goals. After its formation in 1984, DSNI was restructured in 1985 to reflect resident control and elected its first board. DSNI hired its first staff in early 1986. The 1986 priority was organizing—developing and expanding the membership base and strengthening board leadership; undertaking the "Don't Dump On Us" campaign; strengthening new and existing neighborhood associations; putting on the first multicultural festival; and restoring the commuter rail stop. In 1987, while organizing continued in full force—including the successful campaign to close down the trash transfer stations—DSNI's priorities expanded to include creating the comprehensive master plan for development and having the city adopt it. In 1988, the priorities expanded further to include implementation of the plan—gaining land control through eminent domain and winning a grant for the town common. DSNI also closed two largely vacant streets where dumping was still a terrible problem.

In 1989–90, DSNI emphasized "We Build Houses and People Too," pursuing major human development and organizing efforts such as Dudley's Young Architects and Planners; focus groups; the Agency Collaborative; tenant organizing; developing the Community Land Trust; completing and financing the build-out plan for the Dudley Triangle; choosing housing developers; and cofounding the antiredlining Community Investment Coalition. DSNI's 1991 priorities were reclaiming the local park through Community Summerfest, with its extensive youth programs; forming a Youth Committee; and launching the Dudley PRIDE campaign, stressing community esteem and initiative, public health and safety, and neighborhood greening; as well as strengthening child care and starting the Dudley Housing List.

In 1992, Dudley PRIDE was a continuing priority as DSNI began home-buyer classes to ensure access to the new housing and stepped up planning around economic development—the area that had lagged. The 1993 priorities were the groundbreaking and construction of DSNI's first new homes; economic development, as highlighted by the first economic summit; completing a Human Development Framework and Declaration of Community Rights; community design of the town common; organizing in broad coalition against a hazardous asphalt plant; pursuing joint planning with other agencies around existing and future community facilities; and continuing Dudley PRIDE.

At this writing, DSNI's 1994 priorities are completing an economic development plan and pursuing short- and long-term economic development projects; completing phase one construction in the Triangle and welcoming the new homeowners as members of the Community Land Trust; completing design and starting construction of the town common; finalizing plans and financing DSNI's community center while maximizing use of existing area facilities; carrying forward Dudley PRIDE; launching a major focus on education, from preschool to adult education; and organizing a major event celebrating DSNI's tenth anniversary.

45 In addition to everything above, the annual meeting, periodic community-wide meetings, neighborhood cleanups and multicultural festivals are major regular events. DSNI staff also respond to immediate resident concerns, whether by connecting residents to the proper public or private agencies (and following up as needed) or becoming directly involved in resolving problems such as specific incidents of illegal dumping, the unwarranted arrest of neighborhood youth or dangerous conditions (e.g., lack of winter heat) in apartments owned by unscrupulous landlords.

As this brief review highlights, DSNI has strengthened its commitment to comprehensive community revitalization.

COMMUNITY

"We're learning how to be a better community together," says DSNI's Sue Beaton. "But whether we look perfect at the end is really not, to me, the issue. It's how many people have participated along the way, who gets the benefits of whatever we can accomplish together, and how do we hang together and not get co-opted in the process of doing whatever we're doing." She adds, "I would like us to be a community of integrity."

Clayton Turnbull observes, "This community, along with Black people in America [generally, have long felt] like they rent their community. They don't feel like they own it even when they own a house. . . . Subconsciously or consciously, they don't feel like they own it." Turnbull points to the L.A. riots: "People say, 'Why do all these people burn down their own communities?' It wasn't their community! They didn't own the stores! They didn't work in them! They didn't own the houses! . . . So, why do you call it 'your community'? Because you geographically, residentially live there? That's not what 'your community' means."

"DSNI has changed that attitude with the process, with the Community Land Trust and so on," says Turnbull. "People now say . . . 'I own it' [and 'We own it.'] . . . That's why I say to people, 'Urban America has to now set policies for politicians to come in and follow.' " That's what DSNI did, says Turnbull. "We set the policies."

The Dudley community has spent almost a decade renewing   50 their dreams, their lives and their neighborhood. They found a way to forge a united vision of the future and institutionalize resident control. They have had many victories over the years. Yet, they have much more work ahead. Ultimately, what distinguishes the residents of Dudley is not their ability to stop dumping or create a comprehensive redevelopment plan for the neighborhood or get eminent domain or attract millions of dollars in resources into the neighborhood. What distinguishes Dudley residents from many other communities is this: They found a way to dream together and not allow their dreams—to borrow from Langston Hughes—to be deferred, to dry up like a raisin in the sun, or explode. Together, they found a way.

As stated in the preamble to DSNI's Declaration of Community Rights: "We—the youth, adults, seniors of African, Latin American, Caribbean, Native American, Asian and European ancestry—are the Dudley community. Nine years ago, we were Boston's dumping ground and forgotten neighborhood. Today, we are on the rise! We are reclaiming our dignity, rebuilding housing and reknitting the fabric of our communities. Tomorrow, we realize our vision of a vibrant, culturally diverse neighborhood, where everyone is valued for their talents and contributions to the larger community."

Dudley residents have a long way to go, but they have come a long way, and the journey itself has been rewarding. They have learned from others' experiences, and they hope others can learn from theirs. For ultimately, we as a nation must find a way to progress together—with diversity, not divisiveness—lest our children inherit a world even more impoverished and dangerous than today's. A world of chaos, not community. DSNI's local alternative of multiracial, mutual progress and holistic community development is no less relevant nationally. It is an alternative vision in which no one is disposable. Together, we must find a way.

Stabilizing the Text

1. A key way in which the Dudley Street residents express their hopes for their neighborhood is by contrasting it with South Central Los Angeles in the period of the riots there. According to the authors, what similarities do the

Dudley Street neighborhood and South Central share? How do the authors explain the most important difference between these two neighborhoods?
2. What is involved in comprehensive community development? What forms of citizenship make it possible? Why do you think it is so difficult to achieve?
3. How do the authors attempt to convince readers that DSNI was and is successful? Are you convinced? Why or why not?

Mobilizing the Text

1. Who "speaks" in this essay? Are any voices left out? What contributions could those voices have made to the essay?
2. The DSNI thrived because of people working together. What implications does this have for understandings of citizenship? Can citizenship be exercised alone, or does it require involvement with others?
3. How do you define citizenship for your own life? What role can you see for yourself in a project like DSNI?

CREDITS

Abramsky, Sasha. "The Drug War Goes Up in Smoke," from *The Nation* (Aug. 18, 2003). Reprinted by permission of *The Nation*.

Blake, Mary Kay. "A Beautiful day in the Neighborhood," from *Mother Jones* (Nov./Dec. 1995). No part of this material may be reproduced in whole or in part without the express written permission of the author or her agent.

Bloods and Crips. "Blood/Crips Proposal for LA's Facelift." From *Why LA Happened*, edited by Haki R. Madhubuti (Third World Press). Reprinted by permission of Haki R. Madhubuti, Chicago, IL.

Burklo, Jim. "Houselessness and Homelessness," from the *Whole Earth Review* (Summer 1995), pp. 66-69. Reprinted by permission.

Carr, C. "An American Tale: A Lynching and the Legacies Left Behind" from the *Village Voice*. Copyright © 1994 Village Voice Media, Inc. Reprinted with the permission of the *Village Voice*.

Cofer, Judith Ortiz. "Silent Dancing," from *Silent Dancing: A Partial Remembrance of a Puerto Rican Childhood*. Reprinted with permission of Arte Publico Press, University of Houston.

Davis, Angela. "Masked Racism: Reflections on the Prison Industrial Complex," from "Introduction to the Prison Industrial Complex" from *Colorlines* (2000). Reprinted by permission.

Dent, David J. "The New Black Suburbs," from the *New York Times Magazine* (June 14, 1992), pp. 18-26.

Gates, Daryl. "Guns Aren't the Only Issue," from *The Police Chief* (No. 55, March 1988). Copyright held by the International Association of Chiefs of Police. Further reproduction without express written permission from IACP is strictly prohibited.

hooks, bell. "Homeplace: A Site of Resistance," from *Yearning: Race, Gender, and Culture Politics* (pp. 41-49). Reprinted by permission of South End Press.